ACQUIESCENCE AND RESISTANCE IN THE FICTION OF NADINE GORDIMER

Noor Hussain

Acquiescence and Resistance in the Fiction of Nadine Gordimer

ISBN 979-8-89519-467-6

Contents

Preface

This book is the outcome of my research carried out at Bodoland University. The book undertakes to examine the theme of acquiescence and resistance in Nadine Gordimer's fiction of the apartheid era in South Africa. The Afrikaner National Party came to power in South Africa in 1948. Since then successive white minority governments of South Africa had enacted and implemented apartheid laws to dominate and rule the majority black population. Thus, for instance, the Group Areas Act (1950) divided urban areas in a way that designated separate black and white neighbourhoods. On the other hand, cultural and social activists and different organizations like the African National Congress (ANC) started opposing the apartheid system that divided the society racially. Alongside blacks, many white liberals fought against the apartheid regime. Nadine Gordimer is one such white author and activist who has been a bitter critic of apartheid throughout her life. As an artist who is deeply committed to society, she has created a body of fiction that displays a culture of resistance to the dehumanizing apartheid laws. Her early fiction such as *The Lying Days* (1953), *A World of Strangers* (1958) and *Occasion for Loving* (1963) portrays characters of liberal whites who unsuccessfully attempt to cross the racial barriers and thereby pose a challenge to apartheid laws. But after their failure, there is a change in their attitude to life and society. After the Sharpeville massacre in 1960, the anti-apartheid movements became violent and subversive. Gordimer's novels such as *Burger's Daughter* (1979), *July's People* (1981) and *My Son's Story* (1990) are concerned with liberation struggle of the South African blacks. Gordimer's fiction reveals her concern and sympathy for the resistance movements against apartheid in South Africa.

Gordimer has not only highlighted the issue of apartheid but she has expressed her voice of dissent through her work –both fictional and non-fictional. This study argues that Gordimer has provided through her work an alternative discourse to resist apartheid. She has proposed in her fiction the alternative discourse through her treatment of space, interracial sexual relationship and life in borderline situation in the apartheid South Africa. Gordimer's major works of the apartheid period are discussed in the context of the troubled historical past of South Africa in the light of the postcolonial critics, Bhabha and Foucault.

The book is organized into five chapters preceded by a short introduction. The first chapter contextualizes the fiction of Nadine Gordimer through an introduction to the reflection of anti-apartheid movements in the South African novels in English. The second chapter examines the theme of acquiescence and resistance in Gordimer's fiction of the apartheid period. Apartheid has caused traumatic experiences to several generations of South Africans. The third chapter critically analyses three of Gordimer's novels in the light of trauma studies. The fourth chapter explores Gordimer's treatment of gender in her fiction. The fifth chapter is a conclusion of the study highlighting how Gordimer shows her resistance through her treatment of space, trans-racial sexual relationship and life in borderline situation.

Noor Hussain

Acknowledgements

This book is the result of the research project carried out under the supervision of Professor Pradip Kumar Patra in the department of English of Bodoland University, Kokrajhar, Assam. This research project would not have been possible without his encouragement and insistence on completing it in time. I owe sincere gratitude to him. I am also indebted to Dr. Z. Khiangte who guided me in the beginning of this work. I also thank all other faculty members in the department of English of Bodoland University for their suggestions. My sincere thanks also goes to the Librarian and to Dr. Prahlad Basumatary, Director of Students' Welfare of the Bodoland University. My colleagues at Bholanath College have always encouraged me to carry on the work. I offer my thanks to them. Finally, I extend my thanks to my family for their love and tolerance they have shown during the course of this study.

Abbreviations

In the body of this thesis references to the following books of Nadine Gordimer are identified by an abbreviation followed by page number. Both the abbreviation and the page number are given within parenthesis.

BD   *Burger's Daughter* (London: Bloomsbury, 2000).

CN   *The Conservationist* (London: Bloomsbury, 2005).

JP   *July's People* (London: Bloomsbury, 2000).

LBW   *The Late Bourgeois World* (London: Bloomsbury, 2000).

LD   *The Lying Days* (London: Bloomsbury, 2002).

MSS   *My Son's Story* (London: Bloomsbury, 2003).

OL   *Occasion for Loving* (London: Bloomsbury, 2013).

SN   *A Sport of Nature* (London: Bloomsbury, 2013).

SS   *Selected Stories* (London: Bloomsbury, 2000).

WS   *A World of Strangers* (London: Bloomsbury, 2002).

Introduction

This study entitled "Acquiescence and Resistance in the Fiction of Nadine Gordimer" attempts to explore the theme of acquiescence and resistance to apartheid in South Africa in the fiction of Nadine Gordimer. Apartheid had been a political programme of separate development for different races in South Africa. Though apparently there was nothing objectionable in this programme, it was actually used by the successive white governments to dominate and oppress the South African blacks. Apartheid may be said to have begun with the Land Act of 1913. However, its institutionalisation began in 1948 when the Afrikaner National Party came to power. Various laws were enacted and implemented to continue the rule of the minority whites over the majority people through racial segregation of the people into different races: white, coloured, Asian and black[1]. The Prohibition of Mixed Marriages Act (1949) and the Immorality Act (1950) made marriages and sexual relations between black and white South Africans illegal. The Group Areas Act (1950) divided urban areas in a way that designated separate black and white neighbourhoods. The Pass Laws (1952) forced the black South Africans to carry a pass-book that allowed them to work or remain in white areas. On the other hand, cultural and social activists and different organisations like the African National Congress (ANC) started opposing the apartheid ideology. Alongside blacks, many white liberals fought against the apartheid regime. Gordimer is one such liberal white. The resistance was passive in the beginning. But after the Sharpeville massacre in 1960, the resistance movements became violent. It continued till the first free general election in 1994, which elected Nelson Mandela as the President of the nation.

Nadine Gordimer (1923 – 2014) has been a significant voice of resistance in the cultural history of South Africa. Her fiction has been widely acknowledged as the imaginative records of the apartheid and post-apartheid South Africa. With her artistic mind and deep commitment to society, she has created a body of fiction that displays a culture of resistance to the dehumanising apartheid laws. Gordimer is often considered as the greatest contributor to white protest literature in South Africa and hence her unique place in the South African literature. She carries forward the tradition of Olive Schreiner, William Plomer and Alan Paton. Apartheid and the anti-apartheid movements made a great impact on the lives of the characters of Gordimer's fiction. Her early fiction such as *The Lying Days* (1953), *A World of Strangers* (1958), *Occasion for Loving* (1963) and the short story collection *The Soft Voice of the Serpent* (1953) portrays characters of liberal whites who attempt to cross the racial barriers and thereby posed a challenge to apartheid laws. They were unsuccessful but their failure brings about certain changes in their attitude to life and society. These novels capture the mood of the 1950s when the resistance movements were largely passive. Resistance was limited to mixed gatherings and relationships across the colour bar. This social structure is clearly visible in *A World of Strangers* and *Occasion for Loving*.

The Sharpeville massacre (1960) is a watershed moment in the history of South Africa. It marked a change in the anti-apartheid struggle and a change in Gordimer's approach. The government declared a state of emergency in South Africa. The ANC and its broke away faction, the Pan-Africanist Congress (PAC) were banned. They went underground and adopted violent and subversive actions. The ANC under the leadership of Mandela formed its guerrilla armed wing, Umkhonto we Sizwe (meaning 'spear of the nation') and the PAC formed its armed wing called Poqo (meaning pure or alone). Gordimer captures in her fiction the transition of the passive liberation struggle to a violent resistance movement. Her 1966 novel *The Late Bourgeois World* is fictional version of this transition. The underground liberation struggle forms the theme of *July's People* (1981) and *A Sport of Nature* (1987). These works reveal Gordimer's concern and sympathy for the resistance movements against apartheid in South Africa. She explores the physical and psychological relationships among the characters in her fiction and shows how power governs the racial and gender relations in the apartheid South Africa.

Through her writings Gordimer has fought against the injustice and oppression practised by the race she belonged to, and this makes her position very difficult. She has been sometimes criticised for being white – particularly in the 1970s, the decade of the rise of the Black Consciousness movement. The black leaders like Steve Biko wanted to fight their battle on their own and exclude the whites in their fight against the apartheid regime. *Burger's Daughter* (1979), written against the backdrop of the Soweto uprising, is Gordimer's response to the Black Consciousness movement. It has been alleged that Gordimer, being a white, cannot tell the story of a black as she lacks the direct experiences of such a life. Gordimer repudiates such accusations. She argues that the blacks know about some aspects of the life of the whites and the same is true about the whites. She has dealt with black and coloured characters, particularly in her later novels like *July's People* and *My Son's Story* (1990). With her high imaginative faculty she could slip inside a life which is different from hers. As a writer she considers it her responsibility to explore life and culture beyond borders.

Gordimer has gained a lot of critical attention over the years. Previous scholars have examined her work in one of the two ways: they have found her work as revealing a tension between the private and the public life, or as a fictional expression of the political or historical conditions of the time. In his 1974 book, *Nadine Gordimer*, Robert F. Haugh argues that Gordimer's talent lay in her short stories where she focuses on private relationships. Her interest in public issues, Haugh believes, leads her to writing novels, where she tries to integrate the personal with the political. The dichotomy of public and private themes is dealt in John Cooke's *The Novels of Nadine Gordimer: Private Lives/ Public Landscapes* (1985). He approaches Gordimer's fiction from the perspectives of landscapes on which her novels revolve. Cooke emphasizes the decisive influence of Gordimer's unusual childhood on her work and suggests that the novelist has endowed her private history with public associations.

Michael Wade, on the other hand, analyses the fiction of Gordimer in the political and historical contexts. In his book, *Nadine Gordimer* (1978), Wade examines the development of Gordimer's political ideas, mainly through her novels. However, Stephen Clingman's *The Novels of Nadine Gordimer: History from the Inside* (1986) is the most informative and valuable study on Gordimer as a novelist and thinker. Clingman traces Gordimer's developing consciousness of history through her novels. Contextualized in the political and intellectual developments of the time, the book offers a close analysis of the novels. Clingman locates the process of historical change in the lives of Gordimer's characters and presents a view of 'history from inside'. Clingman also edited a selection of Gordimer's essays titled *The Essential Gesture: Writing, Politics and Places*. His introductions to the essays usefully situate the essays in their historical context. Dominic Head's *Nadine Gordimer* (1994) offers a comprehensive study of the oeuvre of the author. Instead of considering only the political and historical dimension of Gordimer's fiction, he has focused on the textual politics and the craft of the author. He highlights Gordimer's complex relation to African culture and European literary form and politics of space. Judie Newman's *Nadine Gordimer* (1988) examines how the issue of gender complicates the themes of race and colonialism in the novels of Gordimer. She has shown how in Gordimer's fiction the interaction of private and public, the complex connection between psychological and political, draws upon an awareness of the relation between genre and gender. In addition to these major approaches to the fiction of Gordimer, some other scholars also have made significant contribution to the critical studies of Gordimer. Rowland Smith, Dorothy Driver, Abdul R. JanMohamed, Susan Gardner, Louise Yelin, Martin Trump and Karen Lazar are most notable among them.

However, none of these scholars have fully examined the theme of acquiescence and resistance in the fiction of Gordimer. The present study proposes to fill this gap. Though the study often refers to the historical contexts of Gordimer's work, it focuses mainly on her response to apartheid. She has demonstrated in her work –both fictional and non-fictional –that apartheid affects every aspects of life in South Africa. She has explored in her writings the social and psychological relationships and how they are governed by race, sex and gender. Gordimer has not only highlighted the issue of apartheid but she has opposed it as well. The present study examines how Gordimer has used her writing as a tool of resistance against the apartheid regime of South Africa. The thesis argues that Gordimer has provided through her work an alternative discourse to resist apartheid. She has proposed in her fiction the alternative discourse through her treatment of space, sexual relationship and life in borderline situation in the apartheid South Africa. A recurrent theme in her fiction is the inter-racial relationship which challenges the basic principle of apartheid. This thesis attempts to show how the concepts of space, power, and borderline function in South Africa in the context of apartheid and how Gordimer used them to develop the theme of acquiescence and resistance in her fiction.

The argument of the thesis is developed through a critical analysis of Gordimer's fiction of the apartheid period (1948-1994) in the light of postcolonial theories of Michel Foucault and Homi K Bhabha. In his path breaking book *Orientalism*, Edward Said very persuasively argues that the western scholars should reconsider the relationship between the West and the Orient. He contended that the image of the east as savage and underdeveloped was constructed by the Europe. "Europe saw the Orient as different and treated this difference as *negative*," argues Said (original italic, Nayar 161). Said's argument about the power of orientalist discourse to construct the orient is based on the Foucauldian premise of power and knowledge. The west had power to know the orient and that power constituted the oriental other as a particular subject of discourse. In his books, *Discipline and Punish: The Birth of the Prison* and *The History of Sexuality: Volume I: An Introduction*, Foucault has given a powerful account of the significant connections between power, knowledge, and the subject in his writings. He claims that power is exercised rather than possessed (*Discipline and Punish* 26). The history of different social institutions is the history of power relations. Knowledge gives rise to power. It is the power-knowledge relationship which controls and governs the society. He further argues that power is productive and that subjects are produced through cultural and institutional practices. He mainly focuses on practices of disciplinary power which lead to binary divisions such as sane/mad and which can be used as a means of social control. These divisions also involve the physical segregation of the population in a society. Such divisions of population are clearly found in the ideological practices of apartheid in South Africa. Apartheid operated through what Foucault calls classification and surveillance. Control over space is a mechanism to dominate the people. Gordimer has shown in her fiction such as *A World of Strangers* how the apartheid regime segregated whites from blacks by assigning them different geographical areas. On the other hand, Foucault suggests, where there is power, there is resistance. He admits the existence of state power but at the same time he points out the possibility of resistance to the centralised power at the micro level –power relations in the lives of individuals. Many fictional characters of Gordimer demonstrate resistance at the micro level.

In his influential book, *The Location of Culture*, Homi K. Bhabha examines issues such as 'borderline', cultural difference and colonial oppression which can be used to analyse Gordimer's fiction and resistance against apartheid. He considers postcoloniality as a continuity of the past and not as break from the past (6-7). Apartheid may also be said to be a continuity of the social structure created by the colonial powers. Bhabha argues that borderlines are locations for culture. They are transitory locations from where one thinks of moving beyond a barrier. Bhabha describes the border as beyond or liminal. As he puts it, "The 'beyond' is neither a new horizon, nor a living behind of the past . . . we find ourselves in the moment of transit where space and time cross to produce complex figures of difference and identity, past and present, inside and outside, inclusion and exclusion" (1-2). The border disturbs the conventional patterns. On the other hand, it is also the place of possible new ideas. Gordimer's characters attempt to cross the borderlines and show the possibility of a change. The characters of her fiction demonstrate transition from liberal to radical stance in their struggle against apartheid as in *The Late Bourgeois World*, and in breaking the barriers of the compartmentalised South African society as in *Burger's Daughter*. The major works of Gordimer are discussed in the context of the troubled historical past of South Africa in the light of the postcolonial critics Bhabha and Foucault.

As for the scope of this study, it discusses the novels and short stories of Gordimer written during the apartheid regime. It also draws on the essays and interviews in order to give a more comprehensive view of Gordimer's work and thought. However, the novel, *A Guest of Honour* published in 1971 has not been discussed in this study. This novel is set in an unnamed African country that has been liberated from the colonial rule. In that sense it depicts a post-apartheid society. Some important short stories of this period has also been analysed to illustrate the theme of acquiescence and resistance in the fiction of Gordimer.

The book comprises five chapters preceded by an introduction. The first chapter discusses the theme of apartheid and anti-apartheid as reflected in the South African novels in English in the second half of the twentieth century. The chapter begins with a brief introduction to apartheid in South Africa, which is followed by a discussion of the notable novelists –both blacks and whites –of the apartheid era. The novels of the black writers like Es'kia Mphehlele and Alex La Guma are concerned with the sufferings under apartheid and awakening the mind of the South African blacks. Through their works the white novelists reveal their opposition to the indignity and persecution suffered by their fellowmen. By doing so, they urge upon the reader to oppose apartheid. This chapter is intended to contextualise the fiction of Nadine Gordimer.

The second chapter examines the theme of acquiescence and resistance in Nadine Gordimer's fiction of the apartheid period. The chapter begins with a discussion of Postcolonialism as forwarded by Edward Said, Michel Foucault and Homi K. Bhabha. After discussing Gordimer's views on the writer's responsibility to her/his society as expressed in her fictional and non-fictional prose, the chapter analyses the fiction of Gordimer employing postcolonial concepts such as 'space' (Foucault) and 'borderline' (Bhabha). As an avowed critic of apartheid, Gordimer creates men and women who often reject racism. Her early novels reveal the inadequacy of the white liberals to resist the apartheid regime. As the fight against apartheid became violent in 1960s onward, her fiction also depicted the violent and subversive activities carried out to resist oppressive system. The chapter attempts to show how Gordimer has tried to suggest an alternative discourse through her treatment of space, sex and life in borderline situation.

Chapter three focuses on the trauma studies with reference to three novels of Gordimer. The history of apartheid in South Africa has been traumatic, to say the least. Apartheid has caused the collective trauma of several generations. Cyrulnik, a French psychiatrist argues that trauma is a kind of interplay between the past and the present and this interplay may open up the possibility of generating resilience or the capacity of a person to recover from trauma. Narrative can play a role in developing resilience. Following this argument, this chapter discusses Nadine Gordimer's novels such as *Occasion for Loving* and *My Son's Story*.

The fourth chapter concentrates on Nadine Gordimer's treatment of gender or sexual politics in her fiction. Gordimer is best known in the South African cultural history for her depiction of the contemporary socio-political conditions of the apartheid South Africa. Judie Newman observes that gender is a conditioning factor in Gordimer's fiction. But she never identified with the feminist thought though she was very sensitive to women's oppression. This is because, Gordimer argues, in South Africa racism is primary and sexism is secondary. However, this does not mean that she has been indifferent to the oppression of women. Throughout her fiction she has shown her concern for women's suffering and their subordinate position. In fact, she has analysed the socio-political issues in her fiction through her own brand of micropolitics or politics of the body. It is in the light of her idea of politics of the body that this chapter focuses on the fiction of Gordimer.

The fifth chapter concludes the study highlighting the theme of acquiescence and resistance. Gordimer's characters live in a world governed by apartheid laws. The anti-apartheid movement turned from passive to active. The fiction of Gordimer, particularly her novels reflects this socio-political condition of South Africa. Even the white liberal characters in her early novels question racism. They are often seen to accept blacks as their men and women. Her later fiction like *A Sport of Nature* and *My Son's Story* show characters who turned radical or took part in the subversive activities. Gordimer presents the theme of resistance in her novels and short stories through a focus on the physical and psychological barriers the characters face in their lives.

Nadine Gordimer delineates the trials and tribulations of life in South Africa under apartheid. At the same time she has shown the possibility of defeating the evils of apartheid. Themes and problems of racial discrimination and power struggle have a universal significance. This book makes innovative contribution to resistance literature by examining the culture of resistance in the fiction of Gordimer.

Note:

1. The Population Registration Act, 1950 classified the South Africans into White, Black, Indian and Coloured. In apartheid South Africa the population was often divided between 'whites' and 'non-whites'. However, the terms white, black, coloured and Indian have been in common use since then and therefore they are not italicised in the thesis.

Works Cited

Bhabha, Homi K. *The Location of Culture*. London: Routledge, 2017 (reprint).

Foucault, M. *Discipline and Punish: The Birth of the Prison*. Trans. Alan Sheridan. New York: Vintage Books, 1977.

Nayar, K. Pramod. *Cotemporary Literary and Cultural Theory*. Delhi: Pearson, 2010.

CHAPTER I

Reflection of Anti-Apartheid Movement in South African English Novels

1.1 Introduction

The evolution of the present-day multiracial South Africa has taken place under conditions of extreme pressures. It has a long history of conflict and oppression. In the beginning, the native communities of South Africa were colonised by the Dutch and then by the British in the seventeenth century. In 1652 the Dutch East India Company established a refreshment station in the Cape of Good Hope. Subsequently the Cape acquired a great significance. And this marked the beginning of a long history of colonial rule and power struggle. Commenting on the strategic significance of the Cape, Brendon Nicholls says, "The strategic usefulness of the Cape made it an object of Imperial envy and the Dutch were eventually forced to relinquish it to the British crown" (16). The increasing administrative and political influence of the British in the Cape Colony created conflicts between the English and the Boers or Afrikaners (the descendants of the Dutch, French and German settlers in South Africa). The Dutch were dissatisfied with the British rule in the Cape Colony. Consequently the Dutch colonists left the Cape and moved to the interior part of South Africa by ox wagon in 1930s and 1940s. The incident came to be known as the Great Trek. The English dominated the Dutch descendants known as the Boers or Afrikaners who settled in the interior of South Africa and established the colonies of Transvaal and Orange Free State. In the meantime, gold and diamond were discovered in these colonies in the late nineteenth century. The British Empire tried to annex these colonies, leading to two Boer wars of 1879 –80 and 1899 –1902. Years after conflict and warfare, a nation-state called the Union of South Africa was established in 1910 by the Afrikaner and the British. The British formed the South African Party while the Afrikaner founded the National Party. Both the parties shared power, though their relation was uneasy. Since the time of the British occupation both settler groups of Boer and British co-existed in an atmosphere of mutual suspicion. But this conflict became secondary to the common cause of military subjugation and economic dispossession of the original inhabitants (Parker 3). However, the Afrikaner National Party won general election in 1948 and formed the government. This white government rapidly adopted a policy of racial segregation known as 'apartheid,' which means 'apartness' in Afrikaans. Every community or group of people considered non-European by the government was governed separately and subordinated at every level to white South Africans. It may be mentioned that policies of racial segregation had existed as laws since the colonisation of South Africa by the European settlers. For example, the 1923 Natives (Urban Areas) Act proclaimed that the cities were 'whites only' residential areas. But under apartheid many more similar policies were enacted and implemented. The Prohibition of Mixed Marriages Act (1949) and the Immorality Act (1950) made marriages and sexual relations between black and white South Africans illegal. The Group Areas Act (1950) divided urban areas in a way that designated separate black and white neighbourhoods. The Pass Laws (1952) forced the South Africans to carry a pass-book that allowed them to work or remain in white areas. The so-called Promotion of Black Self-Government Act (1958) created Bantustans or 'independent homelands' for black South Africans (Nicholls 17). These homelands were, in fact, restricted rural reservations where life was very difficult. The black South Africans were citizens of these homelands only but not of South Africa. It is ironical that they lost their citizenship in their own country. Patrick Wilmot in his book *Apartheid and African Liberation: the Grief and the Hope* has enumerated the multiple significances of apartheid: a system of economic exploitation, a system of racial segregation, a political organisation of a European minority to deny the liberty, rights and dignity of the African majority (xi). In other words, apartheid has affected all aspects of contemporary life in South Africa.

Indeed, the apartheid laws were unjust and dehumanising. Eventually the apartheid regime was resisted inside South Africa by social activists and different organisations like African National Congress (ANC). And it was condemned outside the country by the international community. The African National Congress protested the apartheid policies and made efforts to establish an alliance of races with the objective of overthrowing apartheid and creating a multiracial society. In 1952, the Defiance Campaign was started as the political opposition against apartheid laws under the leadership of African National Congress. Mass rallies were organised all over the country. People came out of their home defying curfew, refused to carry passes and walked in the parks designated for whites only. The increasing levels of black resistance and mass-mobilisation led to violent acts of conflict and oppression by the apartheid government. In 1960, many protestors came out to oppose the pass laws. Many of them were shot dead in Sharpeville, a southern town of Transvaal.

South African police fired at a large crowd of people who were challenging the government's practice of apartheid and segregation. This incident that took the life of 69 black Africans showed the harshness of apartheid regime. In the same year, the African National Congress (ANC) and the Pan Africanist Congress (PAC) were banned by the government. The African National Congress felt the futility of their peaceful protest and so formed their armed wing 'Umkhonto we Sizwe' meaning 'the Spear of the Nation'. Several important leaders of the African National Congress, including Nelson Mandela, were imprisoned following the Rivonia Treason Trial in 1964. The government declared Afrikaans as medium of education in certain subjects on 16th June, 1976. When the black school children in Soweto protested against it, the police opened fire on them. As many as 600 people were killed in the ensuing uprising that spread to different parts of the country (Visser 69). In the meantime, the Black Consciousness Movement (BCM) emerged with the formation of the South African Student's Organisation (SASO) under the leadership of Steve Biko, a medical student in Durban. Subsequently Steve Biko was arrested. He died in police custody in 1977. His death sparked a fierce protest throughout the country. On the other hand, apartheid government tried to control the movement with greater force and brutality.

Robert Fatton in his book, *Black Consciousness in South Africa* has observed, "The history of South Africa can be viewed as the history of black resistance to white conquest and white domination" (1). The nature of resistance changes as the nature of white domination and social condition change. Since the 1970s, anti-apartheid campaign had intensified. With the formation of mass movements such as the United Democratic Front (UDF), civil unrest, trade boycotts, and violence became more frequent. The government declared a state of emergency. Plunged into crisis, the minority white government of South Africa realised the need for a change. It is because of the resistance movements against the apartheid regime and to end the growing violence, Frederick Willem de Klerk, the president of South Africa between 1989 and 1994 unbanned the African National Congress and Pan Africanist Congress. Thus Klerk made way for universal suffrage in the country. Nelson Mandela was released from the prison after 27 years. The first general election on the basis of adult suffrage was held in 1994 and Mandela was elected the president of South Africa. Apartheid was officially abolished.

1.2 Response of the South African Novelists

During the apartheid regime and subsequent transition to democracy, South African writers responded to the apartheid and the antiapartheid movements. Their works show the impact of apartheid on the life of people in South Africa. They saw through the evil design of the apartheid regime and explored the possibilities of resistance. Most of the writing written in South Africa during the apartheid period "sought primarily to document political oppression and stir the reader into doing something" (Cornwell, et. al. 8). The writers – both black and white –look at the society critically. The society under apartheid has either oppressed them as in the case of blacks writers, or confined them to their skin colour and cut them off from the majority of the people as in the case of whites. Thus South African writing is characterized with colour bar, which marks all aspects of social life in South Africa during the apartheid. The writers share a sense of political engagement and commitment. Of course, they responded to historical context differently because of their unequal social situation under apartheid. They exposed racist policies and practices of the government. Nadine Gordimer states that South African writers, both black and white expose the meaning of South African government's racist nature hidden in such euphemistic terms as 'separate development', 'resettlement', 'national states' and its grammar of a racist legislature with segregated chambers of whites, so-called coloureds and Indians. There was no representation whatever for the majority of South Africans who were classified as black ("The Essential Gesture," 295). It is, indeed, shocking that the majority South Africans were governed by the minority whites.

However, the voices of many South African writers who protested against the apartheid were censored. Many of their books were banned in South Africa. The works of anti-apartheid writers such as Nadine Gordimer, Andre´ Brink, Peter Abrahams and many others were banned in South Africa. Moreover, many South African writers such Alex La Guma were jailed in Robben Island for their writings and political activities. And yet many other writers of anti-apartheid movements such as Lewis Nkosi and Es'Kia Mphahlele were sent to exile or went into self-exile to escape from political oppression.

Anti-apartheid literature is multi-faceted and engages with many aspects of human experiences. But racism and political subjugation of majority by the minority white are central to them. Even before the beginning of the institutionalisation of the segregation policies in 1948, South African writers such as Olive Schreiner, Sol T. Plaatje and William Plomer dealt with issues of racial segregation and unjust economic policies. Thus, Olive Schreiner (1855 –1920), a pioneer of South African fiction in English, has criticised the ideologies of the Union of South Africa that excluded the non-white races from political representation. Her novel, *The Story of an African Farm*

(1883) is often considered to anticipate many of the themes which were dealt with by many later novelists. Plaatje (1876 –1932), one of the earliest black writers, examines in his book *Native Life in South Africa,* the effects of the 1913 Natives Land Act, which introduced a radical system of land segregation on the basis of race. The book documents the plight of black South Africans as a result of the Native Land Act. This act led to the eviction of the blacks from their inherited lands in Orange Free State. Plaatje laments that his countrymen and countrywomen had been driven from their home. Their homes were "broken up, with no hopes of redress, on the mandate of a Government to which they had loyally paid taxation without representation" (4). Using his journalistic skill, he could portray the hardships of the black South Africans, which they suffered due to the Land Act. So, the book appears to be a moving protest against the oldest and most devastating apartheid law. In this way the South African writers exposed the unjust policies of racial segregation, which had been in effect even before the National Party came to power in 1948.

However, two traditions had been evident in South African writing by 1950s: the black writing and the white liberal tradition. The latter was begun by Schreiner and continued, in varying degrees, by Alan Paton, Nadine Gordimer and others. The *Drum*, a magazine founded in the 1950s provided a significant platform for a new generation of black writers who attempted to change the way black people were represented in the society. It was an important vehicle for voicing the resistance during the 1950s.

1.2.1 The Black Novelists

Resistance or protest tradition in South Africa originated from the emerging black township such as Sophiatown in Johannesburg and District six in Cape Town. The fiction of many literary figures like Abrahams, Rive, Modisane and La Guma is set in these black townships and portrays the life in these towns. Many of these authors document the harshness of the apartheid policies through their works. The coloured and black people were forcefully removed from Sophiatown and District Six though they considered these places their sweet home. District Six was originally resided by the working class. By 1950, it turned into a slum. It was declared a white area in 1966 and within two years the non-white people were removed to the Cape Flats, a Cape Town township outside the city. Life in District Six has been the subject matter of a number of novels.

Peter Abrahams (1919-2017) was a person of mixed race but he identified himself as a black writer. He wrote some important novels dealing with injustices and complexities of racial politics. Though he left South Africa in 1939, most of his novels and short stories are based on his early life in South Africa. *Mine Boy* (1946) is a notable work of the early period of his career. This novel conveys Abrahams' vision of "a class alliance among workers of different races as offering resistance to the depredations of the exploitative mining houses and their racist white champions" (Cornwell, et. al. 16). It is considered to be the first to portray the dehumanising effect of racism in South Africa on blacks and mixed-race people. The novel tells the story of a young man thrown into the alien and oppressive culture of large industrial society in South Africa. A major theme of the novel is detribalization explored through the relationship of Xuma and Eliza. Xuma is a simple man who has just come to the city from the tribal village. Eliza is attracted to Xuma, but at the same time she is attracted to western ways. This sets the scene of conflict of interests. When they first meet, Eliza is smoking a cigarette like a white woman.

This becomes a barrier between them. Leah, Eliza's host and aunt, tells Xuma that she (Eliza) is a kind of fool. This is because, Leah explains, she likes you and at same time wants someone who can read books and dresses like the white folks and can speak the language of the whites and wear the little bit of cloth they call a tie. "Take her by force or you will be a fool" (51). The character of Leah is very significant. She is a woman who brews and sells liquor, a role traditionally assigned to man. The representation of her character is a challenge to the traditional gender roles and assumptions which consider women as weak and submissive. Leah is portrayed as strong and self-reliant, and engaged in economic and social activities.

Eliza shows a kind of tendency to transcend race in her consciousness, which she ultimately fails to do. But it remains in her and cripples her as well. Abrahams has a sympathetic attitude to the plight of Eliza. She is in an unfortunate position. She is caught between two worlds. Her educated, well-dressed young men are unable to fulfil her needs. She is happy with Xuma: "Something hard drives me . . . One minute I know what I want, the next minute I do not know" (87). She explains her situation to Xuma that something is wrong with her because she wants the things of white people. She expresses her desire to be like the white people. She wants to go where the white people go and do the things they do. But she knows she is a black and so cannot materialise her desire. She claims, "*Inside* I am not black and I do not want to be black person. . . It is no good but I cannot help it" (emphasis added, 89). The injustice of apartheid deeply affected Eliza. It is apartheid that denied the right to enjoy books or music though she appreciates them. So she rebels against the system. On the other hand, Xuma fails to understand her plea. He believes, "A white man and a black man cannot be friends.

They work together. That's all"(93). Xuma does not like things of the white man. But he gradually feels comfortable with white people. And finally, as result of his association with Paddy, Xuma starts thinking about people independently of their colour. People are people. There is no white or black people. This vision carries him along. He imagines Eliza and Paddy and his woman and himself sitting at a little table in one of those little tea place in the heart of Johannesburg –all drinking tea and laughing and talking. He envisages a world where all are happy and without colour. Xuma's struggle to rise above his colour consciousness is an attempt to invalidate the colour bar in the contemporary society. It may be noted that Xuma's struggle is a reflection of Abrahams' own struggle to conquer colour consciousness.

Among his other works, *The Path of Thunder* (1948) shows a young couple of mixed-race under the fearful shadow of segregation. The love between Lanny Swartz, the coloured school teacher, and Sarie Villier, the white Afrikaner daughter, functions as a 'protest' against a perverse racial segregation that destroys something which is natural between two people. *A Night of Their Own* (1965) depicts the plight of Indians in South Africa. In the apartheid South Africa, the Indians are discriminated against by the whites and the blacks though the Indians feel that their chances of survival rest with the ant-apartheid forces. Richard Nkosi, known as Richard Dube, is a black artist of South African origin. He returns to his native land as a messenger for underground anti-apartheid movement spearheaded by blacks. Nkosi's mission is discovered by the white security agents who tightened the net surrounding resistance movement. They could arrest Nkosi. But he manages to escapes with the help of a reactionary businessman. The incidental love affair between Nkosi and an Indian woman is intended to intensify the racial complications. In short, Abrahams' works show his impatience with racial categories. As he puts in *Mine Boy*, his vision is man without colour. He envisages a world where every man would be judged as an individual and where colour would be irrelevant. Through his political novels he shows the attempts of black men to regain their manhood and self respect, which alone can help them achieve true freedom in a world dominated by white men.

Es'kia Mphahlele (1919-2008) began his career as a short story writer with the publication of the collection of stories, *Man Must Live and Other Stories* (1946). His early career as a teacher of English and Afrikaans was terminated by the government because of his stiff opposition to the highly discriminatory Bantu Education Act. The story, "Mrs Plum" included in his third collection, *In Corner B and Other Stories* (1967) explores "the emotional relationships between black and white" (Heywood 199). It critically examines white liberalism in South Africa through a black narrator whose steady growth in knowledge and understanding allows her to lay bare the hypocrisy that runs through the white liberalism. His autobiography *Down Second Avenue* (1959) is, perhaps, his best known work. The work is an impressionistic representation of the author's life from childhood up to his departure into voluntary exile in Nigeria in 1957. Often considered as a South African classic, it tells the story of a young man's growth into adulthood with sharp criticism of the conditions forced upon the black South Africans by the apartheid government. The prevailing situation in South African urban life is vividly portrayed by Mphahlele. For their survival, the black people had to condition themselves by the socio-political forces of the day. Though the white man needed them for his work, he hated them.

People flowed to Pretoria from the north and the east. But soon they found that their life was insecure in the locations, "putting up tin shacks on the small plots allotted to the residents. Perpetual refugees seeking life and safety"(93). According to Cornwell and others, *Down Second Avenue* shows Mphahlele's growing realisation of bitterness toward the political barriers that come in the way of his personal freedom and achievement. To be stuck 'down second avenue' becomes a metaphor for the lot of the black man trapped in the township ghettoes of apartheid South Africa (18). They further argue that Mphahlele's experience of race or ethnicity as an artificially imposed and arbitrarily limiting identity helps to explain his and other South Africans' fierce opposition to essentialist African ideologies such as negritude.

Bloke Modisane (1923-1986) is another black South African author who also wrote an autobiography *Blame Me on History* (1963). The book frankly captures the life in Sophiatown of his youth and at the same time exposes the harshness of the apartheid regime. Sophiatown is a suburb of Johannesburg. In the 1950s, it was a centre of multicultural activities and home of black people. As the neighbouring areas were inhabited by the white working-class people, the National Party government planned to relocate the black population. In 1955, 2000 policemen forcefully removed the black people to Meadowlands, Diepkloof and Moroka, which are now part of Soweto. The forced removal of the black families from Sophiatown exemplifies some of the excesses of South Africa under apartheid. Modisane laments in *Blame Me on History* that Sophiatown died not because it was a social embarrassment, but because "it was a political corn inside the apartheid boot" (14). His contention is that the destruction of Sophiatown was the result of discriminatory legislation. The classification of races and the deep rooted apartheid ideology were a painful experience for the blacks in South Africa, and Sophiatown became a site of resistance to this ideology in the late 1950s.

Alex La Guma (1925-1985) is perhaps one of the most accomplished writers whose work has come to be known as "protest writing" (Cornwell et. al. 19). This is perhaps because of his politically sharp commentary and his focus on episodes of brutality and violence. He wants to raise the consciousness and indignation in the non-white people, and speaks to the international community so as to inform them about the everyday reality of the system of apartheid. The common theme of his work is the suffering of the oppressed and the revolutionary awakening of the black South Africans. La Guma's fiction continuously questions the principles and policies of apartheid. His fiction intersects with the social and political developments that characterised apartheid. This places his fiction within the perspective of historical enquiry into the dynamics of apartheid and its consequences. The history of conflict and violence pervades South Africa under the apartheid regime. *A Walk in the Night* (1962) is probably his best known work. Set in the ghetto of District Six, the novel focuses on a few fateful hours in the life of Michael Adonis who has been fired from his job because he defied a white foreman. Consequently he vents his frustration on a white old man and killed him. The police suspected an innocent bystander and shot him dead. Toward the end of the story, Adonis joined a gang of violent men and drifted into a life of crime. The novel portrays the inhabitants as little more than a feature of their dilapidated environment. Adonis moved to another street far away from the artificial Hanover. This street is surrounded by stretches of dump and battered houses with broken railings and cracked walls. By the end of the narrative, Adonis agrees to join a group of men and drifts into a life of crime. The characters of the novel lack political insight. They appear to the reader as little better that ghosts "doom'd for a certain term to walk the night" (quoted in Cornwell et. al. 19).

La Guma's second novel *And a Threefold Cord* (1964) deals with slum life. The narrative revolves around the Pauls family at the heart of a rain drenched ghetto in South Africa. The family comprises Charlie, Ronny and Johnny, their sister, Caroline, their mother and their father, aged and ailing. They have to face the harsh and relentless nature, and on the other hand, they are pitted against the brutality of the police. Nature as represented by rain and the police is portrayed as competing to submerge the ghetto and the people living in it. The following lines demonstrate how the police very rudely intrude the dreary and rain drenched life in the ghetto:

> The house was in darkness. Van Den Woud ordered one of his men to knock. The man stepped forward and banged on the door. The whole house seemed to shudder. The man banged on the door again and Van Den Woud shouted, 'Come on, open up. Open the door' (*And a Threefold* 31).

The above passage clearly reminds the reader the dark surrounding and dilapidated condition of the house. However, behind this gloomy and oppressive situation, there is a passionate desire for life and freedom. Through the depiction of the condition of the working class, the novelist seems to suggest that though the situation is unbearable, the condition is not permanent and people can reverse it. He advocates through the main character, Charlie that for personal survival and collective resistance to oppression it is essential to establishing links with other people in similar oppressive circumstances. This central message of solidarity – a threefold cord – is conveyed throughout the novel as reflected in the dialogue of Charlie: "We all got to stand by each other" (112). As Nahem Yousaf observes, the novel represents La Guma's belief that only as a united community of people the oppressed can fight against the apartheid regime. "Only when the oppressed are politically aware will they come to the realization that they are subjects rather than objects" (Yousaf 60). In short, the novel reveals that La Guma has graphically described the pathetic condition of the blacks in the apartheid South Africa and attempted to awaken the blacks to their suffering.

A member of the South African Coloured People's Organisation (SACPO) and a successful defendant in the Treason Trial (1956–61), La Guma was detained and put under house arrest several times for suspected underground activity before he went into exile to London in 1966. As a prisoner he experienced brutality, cruelty and antagonism that permeate the South African society during apartheid. This is nicely captured in his novel *The Stone Country* (1967). The novel is set in a Cape Town jail which may be said to symbolise the imprisoned state of South Africa. Guma has beautifully described the prison. It was very hot. There were over forty prisoners in it in the middle of the summer season. So the smell of sweat of the prisoners was so heavy it seemed to be the smell of death. "The heat seemed packed in between the bodies of the men, like buyers of cotton wool, like a thick sauce which moistened a human salad . . ." (80). The narrative shows how an inmate of the prison succeeds in politicising his fellow prisoners.

La Guma's fourth novel *In the Fog of the Seasons' End* (1972) centres around the plight of two resistance fighters who are on the run from the authorities. One smuggles three young men over the border for military training and the other dies at the hands of the security police. The novel is dedicated to Basil February and other resistance fighters who died in Zimbabwe in 1967. The protagonist, Beukes is a leader of the underground forces of the anti-apartheid movement. In the novel there is a combination of 'the separate seasons' from which arises the resolve to make the final political standpoint in view of the relentless and violent apartheid order. The working class, as represented by Beukes, Elias Tekwane and Isaac, have organised themselves into a movement to fight the repressive state. The police force, representing the state, reacted violently. In fact, the central theme of the novel is the destruction of apartheid and to establish a democratic and humane social order. In the delineation of the theme and characters of the novel, La Guma highlights two aspects of the liberation movement: the prominence of the working class and the necessity of violence in the struggle for liberation. He envisages the working class as the potential force of the resistance movement in South Africa. In this respect, he seems to be informed by the socio-historical realities of his time. As seen in his novels such as *A Walk in the Night*, *The Stone Country* and *And a Threefold Cord*, La Guma depicts the pain and suffering of the working class. The novel *In the Fog of the Seasons' End* gives such a picture in chapter five. Beukes saw the train stopped at the station. The next moment he found the platform was crowded with passengers moving towards the subway. As La Guma describes, "Around the police block the stream swirled against the dam of blue uniforms and the jerking flashlights, then slowly trickled through accompanied by shouts and curses" (66). La Guma has beautifully described the scene of a railway station.

However, Beukes has been given the task to unify the working class and develop their consciousness and political awareness. This was an uphill task for him as the whole "authoritarian state" was against the movement: "The movement writhed under the terror, bleeding" (48). It had been beaten down though not destroyed. The leaders and cadres were sent to the prison or they had to retreat into exile. In the opening chapter Beukes and Isaac discuss the progress of the movement. Beukes expresses his concern about the factory connections through which the organisation can operate. Later in the novel Abdullah refers to the canteen of the factory where leaflets are to be deposited so that workers can easily access them. References to the workers recur in the novel. These references and the major characters, which are from the working class, point to the fact that the working class plays a pivotal role in the struggle against apartheid. La Guma therefore focuses on the movement and attempts to show how the social and political realities of South Africa necessitate the acceptance of violence as a means of resistance. In brief, La Guma's fiction is informed by his socialist convictions. His fiction depicts the process of increasing radicalisation of the oppressed communities under apartheid.

Since its demolition in the late 1960s, District Six of Cape Town has become a symbol of what is evil about apartheid. Poets, novelists, song-writers, and journalists all recorded their anger through their work of art. They were upset with what had been done to the district. Richard Rive (1931-1989) is one such novelist. He joined the growing band of writers protesting against the evil effects of apartheid with his fictional works such as *Emergency* (1964) and *Buckingham Palace, District Six* (1986). The first novel explores the events during the state of emergency declared by the government after the Sharpeville massacre. *Buckingham Palace, District Six* is about the life in District Six before the town was declared a 'whites only' area. The story focuses on the inhabitants of a row of cottages called 'Buckingham Palace' by the locals. The novel has three parts –"Morning 1955", "Afternoon 1960", and "Night 1970". The last part of the novel documents the destruction of District Six when the first houses were bulldozed. In the first two parts of the book, Rive describes the facts of life in the town. He seems to celebrate the efforts of the community of black and coloured people, whose members stand by each other no matter what may come and no matter that they have no closer binds than living in the same place. The characters in the novel are not respectable or obedient citizens but they have been depicted as likeable men and women who love District Six as their home. As one of the characters, Milton Zoot remarks that it might appear funny but he felt safe only in the District Six. Zoot further says that District Six is an island –an island in the sea of apartheid. He believes that the whole of District Six is "one big apartheid" though it cannot be seen. He and his fellowmen can see it only when the white man comes and forces it on them. When the police come, only then they feel or see apartheid. Zoot is aware that the District is dirty, that it is only a slum. But he has no regret for it because it is a place which is their own. Unlike the whites they never put notices in this place. It is the whites only who put notices, stating "Slegs blankes" or "Whites only" (Tucker 69).

The novel opens with the novelist's own memories of his childhood and then, through different anecdotes, places the characters in their respective cottages. The most colourful and interesting are Mary and her girls at number 201. They keep the Casbah, a "House of Pleasure". Zoot and the Boys live next door, number 203. The Jungles live at 205, the narrator at 207 and Last-Knight barber at 209. This companionable little community is a microcosm of the whole District. This little community's white landlord, Katzen supports and stands by his tenants when District Six is declared as 'white only' area. What emerges is the tolerance that each household learns for the other and their capacity to rally behind each other in times of need. Rive wants the District to enter the history of South Africa as a community of heterogeneous people who have learnt to live together and who thereby challenge the central argument of the apartheid. Rive's first novel *Emergency* (1964) was banned soon after its publication perhaps because of its subject matter and the author's approach to the subject. The novel focuses on the State of Emergency following Sharpeville massacre, and it traces the process by which Andrew Dreyer, the protagonist decides to commit himself to the cause of liberation from the oppression. He is a young coloured schoolteacher in Cape Town who, as a marked man when the emergency is declared, is faced with a choice between exile and staying in the country and court arrest. And he chooses to stay. Within its socio-political context, the novel initiates a debate about the ways in which legalised oppression should be resisted. The debate is conducted through Dreyer and his friends. Abe is represented as an intellectual, a rigorous thinker but one who is unable to see his way to actions that satisfy his own theoretical position. For example, he is fiercely critical of the PAC organised campaign against the Pass Laws because he believes that the way it is conducted will perpetuate the racial awareness against which they are protesting. On the other hand, Dreyer is dependent on knowing himself through other people. Though a coloured himself, he loves a white girl. He participates in the march to Caledon Square Police Station against the white led by Philip Kgosana for being there made him feel part of it. In 1990

Rive wrote *Emergency Continued* which is obviously a sequel to his first novel *Emergency*. This novel also captures the lives of group of political activists who experience and live through the Sharpeville in 1960. Decades later, they were again caught up in the storm of protest and resistance to the apartheid regime in the 1980s.

After the Sharpeville massacre, the National Party government intensified its repression to control and curb widespread conflict and civil unrest. The government jailed, banned or exiled most of the anti-apartheid leaders. In response to this, intensified struggle against apartheid and a new set of organisations emerged to fill the vacuum created by the banning of the African National Congress and the Pan Africanist Congress. In this context, the Black Consciousness movement emerged under the leadership of Steve Biko, the leader of the South African Students Organisation. The Black Consciousness movement emphasised cultural revival and assertion of black dignity and identity. The black started believing that they must be conscious of and celebrate their blackness and that they *alone* should fight against the apartheid regime. The white liberals could not genuinely fight against the white government. However, the revolt spread countrywide and made a far reaching impact on the South African society. A manifestation of the Black Consciousness movement was the Soweto revolt that opposed the use of Afrikaans in black schools as a medium of instruction.

Miriam Tlali (1933-2017) as a novelist was heavily influenced by the Black Consciousness ideology. Her novel *Amandla* (1980) is one of a few Black Consciousness novels that make a fictional rendering of the June 1976 Soweto uprising. Based on Tlali's experience as a Soweto resident in 1976, the novel minutely depicts the uprising and its aftermath. Written from the perspectives of several young revolutionaries of the time, the novel vividly sketches the dynamics of the Black Consciousness ideology in the service of anti-apartheid activism. Through the protagonist of the novel, Pholoso, Tlali speaks to the reader from various points of view that the different communities of black South Africans have been affected by the Soweto uprising when police opened fire on the protestors. Pholoso objectively represents the Soweto events that shaped the uprising. No one in Soweto, he says, will forget the 16th June of 1976. Every household or family suffered in one way or the other. As he puts, it was a disaster that

> had left its indelible mark on everyone. The after-effects of the student demonstration and the resultant widespread riots were similar to the perils suffered during wars and epidemics (*Amandla* 272).

The above passage very effectively records the pain and suffering of the blacks resulting from the revolt. On the hand, while documenting the history of the 1976 Soweto rebellion, Tlali also throws light on the nature of the revolutionary programme in the resistance to apartheid. Pholoso masks his identity as a student leader in order to carry on the revolutionary activities. Pholoso has adopted the Christian name Moses. His survival depends on his becoming Moses. So Pholoso has to disguise himself in a Christian name. But this is not enough. His final disguise, final denial of identity awaits him. He goes into exile. He did not want to flee, he tells Felling. But he has to go because the student leaders thought it was the best thing he could do instead of rotting in the jail. Thus exile has become a necessity in the struggle against apartheid.

Tlali's *Amandla* is one of the four novels considered 'Soweto novels' that make a fictional rendering of the 1976 Soweto uprising.

The other three novels are Mongane Wally Serote's *To Every Birth its Blood* (1981), Sydney Shipo Sepamla's *A Ride on the Whirlwind* (1981) and Mbulelo Mzamane's *Children of Soweto* (1982). Poet and novelist, Mongane Wally Serote was born in Sophiatown in 1944. He was actively involved in political activism and establishing a black identity. He was arrested and imprisoned under Terrorism Act in 1969. After nine months he was released without being charged. Serote wrote *To Every Birth its Blood* at a time when resistance caught hold of a new generation and South Africa witnessed fierce attacks and bombings. The chief character of the novel, Tsi, a black journalist narrates the first part of the novel. Tsi works for a daily newspaper which is owned by a white in Johannesburg. Throughout the early part of the novel he opposes joining the anti-apartheid movement although he is aware that many of his friends have done so. His family is rather badly affected by the apartheid policies which created a fear psychosis and poisoned daily life of people. His brother, Fix is jailed without any trial in Roben Island and none has any news about him. He tries to overcome his frustration and hopelessness growing out of regular killings, brutal treatment and threats from the white police through drinking, sex and aimless roaming. The narrative then focuses on a new group of characters: John whose young wife was shot by police; two young women, Onalenna and Dekeledi; Tuki, another journalist; and Tsi's nephew, Oupa. These people slowly come together. By fits and starts, they join the movement and carry out acts of sabotage.

In this novel, Serote shows in a convincing manner the multifaceted and inexcusable horror of the apartheid regime in South Africa. The government had an overpowering control over the mundane, day to day life of people. Influenced by the events of the

Soweto uprising, Serote seems to suggest that there is no other way to change the social conditions of South Africa except putting up a brave fight against the oppressors. Similar thoughts are expressed by Dikeledi whose father is imprisoned in Roben Island. He realises that there is not any way to deal with the present way of life in "this South Africa . . . there was nothing else that could be done to save it; there was only one way left –people had to fight" (132). Hence they resort to acts of violence.

Sydney Shipo Sepamla (1932-2007) was a poet, playwright and novelist. His second novel, *A Ride on the Whirlwind* is a fictional narrative about the 1976 Soweto riots and its aftermath. The novel chronicles daily life in an atmosphere of fear, suspicion, distrust and terrorism. Dedicated to the young heroes of the day, the novel gives a rich account of the pivotal moments in the anti-apartheid movement. The action of the narrative covers a brief period in the summer of 1976 when the stability of the white rule in Soweto was shaken by the violent attacks of the black. The young Mandla and his group of saboteurs took great pride in their ability to challenge the heavily armed police. In such a time and atmosphere, the protagonist Mzi enters Soweto to join the terrorist training. Devoid of past and future, Mzi exists as a point of focus for larger movement of history. A trained guerrilla warrior, his mission is to kill the policeman Batata who in his madness and cruelty symbolises racial oppression.

Lewis Nkosi (1936 - 2010) is a multifaceted personality who tried his hand at almost every literary genre. He spent long 30 years in exile due to the restrictions placed on him and his writing. Though he began his literary career early, he entered the realm of fiction much later than his *Drum* colleagues. He published his first novel, *Mating Birds* in 1986. The novel deals with inter-racial sexual relations.

The narrative revolves around a South African black, Ndi Sibiya who tells the story from prison. While awaiting death sentence for his sexual relation with a white girl, Veronica, he narrates how he was found guilty of rape by the white South African court of justice during apartheid regime. The publication of *Mating Birds* received great critical attention. It received positive reaction outside South Africa. It was appreciated well by many reviewers in leading newspapers such as *The Washington Post* and *The New York Times*. Thus, for example, the eminent black literary critic Henry Louis Gates Jr. who in his review of the novel in *The New York Times* describes Nkosi as "a sensitive, articulate and lyrical narrator". He further observes that *Mating Birds* "confronts boldly and imaginatively the strange interplay of bondage, desire and torture inherent in interracial sexual relationships within the South African prison house of apartheid" (3). However, there was mixed reaction to novel in South Africa. Many newspapers such as *The African Communist* praised it but many others condemned it. South African author Andre Brink scathingly criticises it in his review, "An Ornithology of Sexual Politics: Lewis Nkosi's *Mating Birds*". Brink calls the novel "sexist" with "clichés of cheap soft-porn magazines" (8). He argues that Nkosi denies any voice to the white girl, Veronica and thereby revealing that he is not concerned for her. He is rather more interested to establish his own identity through Ndi Sibiya as an arrogant male.

However, as Ndi Sibiya tells the events of his life while waiting for his execution, he reveals the divided South African society. He tells how he becomes obsessed with a white girl in the racially divided Durban beach. He is lying on the non-white side and she on the border of the 'Whites only'. Though the apartheid laws prevent any interracial sexual relationship, they fall in love with each other through a mode of wordless communication ignoring the invisible barriers of apartheid. Challenging apartheid through sexual discourse also forms the theme of Gordimer's novel, *An Occasion for Loving*.

1.2.2 The White Novelists

The writers of the white liberal tradition such as Alan Paton and Nadine Gordimer passed through a peculiar situation during the apartheid regime. Born as whites into a race from which it was impossible for them to separate themselves, they were searching through their writing a suitable position. And in doing so they played a unique role in the fight against apartheid in South Africa. The characters in most of the novels of the liberal tradition are often defeated by social and political conditions. But the values the characters or the novelists assume seem to achieve symbolic vindication. They advocate individual freedom, nonviolent resolution of conflict, justice and fair play, and so on. "In this way the white authors of these novels express their outrage at and opposition to the indignity, disadvantage, and persecution suffered by their black countrymen, and they did so in the name of humanist values shared by enlightened liberals world over" (Cornwell et. al. 10). In this context the important novelists are Alan Paton, Dan Jacobson, Andre Brink, and Nadine Gordimer.

Alan Paton (1903 –1988) occupied a distinctive position in the literary history of South Africa. He attempted to draw the attention of the world to the condition of the black in South Africa. His famous novel, *Cry, the Beloved Country* had been published four months before the National Party came to power. Paton along with some of friends formed the Liberal Party of South African in 1953, which fought against the apartheid legislation introduced by the National

Party government. However, *Cry, the Beloved Country* is considered as the best known and most enduring novel in South Africa. The novel puts South Africa in the map of world by attracting western attention to the effects of racial discrimination. Throughout the novel pervades a poignant lament for the decline of rural life and social order. It warns about the "dire consequences for South African society if harmony between races –and between humankind and nature –was not established (Cornwell et. al., 152). The central character, Stephen Kumalo is a priest who travels from rural South Africa to Johannesburg in search of his son, Absalom. The father discovers his son in the prison for the son has killed a white man –a man who ironically felt deeply the plight of the native South African population. The novel captures the deep complexities in the European and African experiences, cultures and their relations. Kumalo speaks of such a relation when he says that a white man taught him a number of things. "It was he also who taught me that we do not work for men, that we work for land and the people. We do not even work for money, he said" (229). Paton seems to suggest and as the title indicates, the ordinary citizens of South Africa cry for their beloved country under the pressure of racism and brutality of apartheid. Despite its vivid portrayal of darkness and despair, the novel still offers hope for a better future. It begins a fictional discourse which sought a cordial relationship between people across colour bar. Stephen Watson observes that Paton wants to solve the sociological problems through the mouthpieces of Kumalo and Msimangu. The novelist suggests to solve through love the problems caused by detribalisation and urbanisation (quoted in Cornwell et. al. 9). It may be argued that subsequent historical events bore witness to Kumalo's, or for that matter Paton's faith in the power of love. F. W. de Klerk in 1990 unbanned African National Congress and released Nelson Mandela unconditionally. Mandela came out of the prison after twenty seven years. But he did not, surprisingly, bore any bitterness against any one. He advocated reconciliation and brotherhood. Thus the belief that love can conquer fear becomes true. Thus, the novel anticipated correctly the future much ahead.

Paton's next novel, *Too Late the Phalarope* (1953) explores the traditional theme of miscegenation through an interracial sexual relationship between a young Afrikaner and a coloured girl. The protagonist, Pieter van Vlaanderen is a police lieutenant. He falls in love and sleep with a coloured girl named Stephanie. Thus he violates the apartheid law, the Immorality Act (1949) which declares sexual relations between whites and non-whites illegal. The novel records how the police lieutenant struggles all alone against the cruel apartheid society and his family. Paton adds to the familiar theme an analysis of the psychosis of racial prejudice and highlights the plight of the young police torn between his sexual desires and the repressive rules of his society. John O. Jordan describes the novel as a "personal tragedy" and also "a prelude to larger cultural tragedy" which is a threat to the Afrikaner community unless they change their ways (682). Pieter is handsome and a devout Afrikaner. He is admired for his leadership qualities and for his talent as a rugby player. In other words, he may be said to epitomise the cultural ideals of his community. So his interracial sexual relationship is a disgrace to himself and to his community as well. Such is the view of the narrator, Sophie who is the aunt of Pieter. She considers his 'misconduct' as self-destructive and seems to promote a sympathetic attitude in contrast to the stern Puritan standpoint that condemns him.

The events of the story are not shown against any specific dates. But the text of *Too Late the Phalarope* reveals the pressure of the events of the period immediately preceding the National Party coming to power in 1948. After the Second World War, Pieter and other South African soldiers who fought for the British returned home. The United Party led by General Smuts controlled the government. The Afrikaner National Party, however, was rising. Pieter's father was a chairman of National Party at Cape Town and enjoyed considerable influence. Paton has been criticised by critics for dating the action of novel in the pre-1948 period and yet not dealing with the events directly. This criticism is untenable. The novel is concerned with period when apartheid was not yet institutionalised. In this sense the novel can be described as "a prehistory rather than a history of apartheid" (Jordan 683). However, *Too Late the Phalarope* displays forces of opposition at different level. Thus, Stephanie is a character of potential resistance. Her act of going against the interracial marriage shows her transgressive energy that gives her a freedom of movement.

Paton's last novel, *Ah, But Your Land Is Beautiful* (1981) narrates the events of the 1950s in a semi fictionalised style. There are in the novel real political events and leading figures which are recorded faithfully. At the same time, the novel contains many fictional characters who resemble real figures of the time. It is particularly an account of the Liberal Party, of which Paton himself was a key figure. The novel examines the liberals of the 1950s. The Liberal Party, the novel suggests, remained only a marginal force in the titanic struggle between the Afrikaners and the native Africans. Paton seems to argue that the party nevertheless plays an honourable role in the resistance history of the country. However, to Jean-Philppe Wade the interesting point of the novel is "its *form*, a *heteroglossia* of voices across the political spectrum" (97). Besides the third person narrator, the narrative is developed through a series of letters. This allows the novel to represent the different political perspectives of the time.

Andre´ Brink (1935 –2015) is another significant novelist and academic, who was an anti-apartheid campaigner. He was a great sympathiser of the African National Congress (ANC). He joined a group of liberal Afrikaner intellectuals who met the exiled ANC leadership. He wrote many novels characterised by their unequivocal stance towards racial injustice. His work in Afrikaans was banned. He switched to English to escape censorship and was shortlisted twice for Booker Prize. Through his fiction Brink provides an interpretation of events in the apartheid South Africa. As Brink strongly opposed the apartheid policies, his novel in Afrikaans *Kennis van die aand* (translated into English by himself as *Looking on Darkness*) was the first Afrikaans book to be banned by the South African government. His novels are mostly concerned with the historical realities in his milieu during the apartheid regime though his recent works deal with new issues faced by life in post-apartheid South Africa. His early novels such as *Looking on Darkness* (1973) and *Rumours of Rain* (1978) attract world attention and made him famous. *Looking on Darkness* was his first novel to be banned in South Africa. It narrates the tale of a coloured actor, Joseph Malan who has been tortured and sentenced to death for the murder of his white lover. He recalls the past, half-history and half-fantasy, a chronicle of subjugation through the generations. *Rumours of Rain*, like Nadine Gordimer's *The Conservationist* brings out the evil effects of apartheid through the consciousness of a white businessman. He is best known for his 1979 novel *A Dry White Season*. It tells the story how a white schoolteacher Ben du Toit gets involved in search of justice for the killing of the son of his black gardener and ends up taking the entire apartheid system. The boy, who was arrested after the Soweto uprising, mysteriously disappeared. "Du Toit's investigation begins innocuously enough –he merely seeks an official explanation for the mysterious disappearance –but his discovery of the brutality at the heart of the apartheid order draws him further and further into open rebellion" (Cornwell et al. 62). In his quest, he learns the truth of his privileged position as a white, the poverty of black society and the corrupt system that has kept them apart. Du Toit loses family, friends, his job and all he has to follow his heart and get justice.

Another important novel of Brink is *The Wall of the Plague* (1984). In this novel, Brink represents a broader depiction of the issue of apartheid. The novel takes an allegorical resonance for contemporary South Africa. With his mastery on narrative techniques, specially, allegory, Brink captures his countrymen's predicaments in terms that speak more directly to the outside world. 'The wall of the plague' as allegorically rendered in the novel, is not only an attack on the plague of apartheid but also on all that come in the way of racial harmony and peaceful human relationship. The setting of the novel is far away from South Africa. It is set in the rural Provence, France. The characters have universal significance. The protagonist, Andrea Malgas is a young coloured South African woman who runs away from Cape Town with her white lover, Paul. She spends eight long years in Europe trying to distance herself from her past until she confronts Mandla Mqayisa, a black South African militant. Andrea intends to highlight the plight of apartheid by writing on the film about Black Death in Europe and by giving indirect aid to the opposition. At this point of her life, Mandla intervenes in her life. In Europe he raises money for the anti-apartheid cause. He inspires Andrea to go back and join the anti-apartheid movement. Indeed,

The Wall of the Plague is a compelling depiction of the agonising effects of apartheid in South Africa. The gory and dehumanising situation of the South African society is vividly represented through Mandla:

> The point is, I got the impression that a country like South Africa has no place for people who simply want to carry on living, indulge in their sins, have good meal from time to time, enjoy a bit of music or a good painting or a good book. You're forced to walk right into the fire. Otherwise, the only choices you have are to go man or to die (*The Wall* 37).

Racism with its wall of apartheid is the worst plague of all. It is the source of pain, death and impossibility of relationship even among people who love each other. However, a great visionary as he is, Brink is optimistic and provides solutions for the draconian policy of apartheid. He suggests that one cannot overcome racism by treating it like the plague. The only way to cure it is to treat it the way sick people are healed with patience. It is not possible to overcome racism until people change their medieval mindset. That is the way to a civilized future.

Brink suggests that the interracial conflict and violence in apartheid South Africa can be overcome through reaching out beyond the boundaries of race for human contact. This is artistically conveyed through the metaphor of ineffective walls against the plague. Andrea's visits to Provence, the Luberon and Vaucluse are described in detail. The two-metre high, dry stone wall, built in 1721 over 26 kilometres of terrain was intended to block northbound travellers during the dreadful plague that visited Marseille. But before the wall was completed, the plague had already appeared in places beyond.

An acclaimed critic and novelist, John Maxwell Coetzee, popularly known as J. M. Coetzee was born in Johannesburg, South Africa in 1940. He taught English literature at the University of Cape Town from 1972 till his retirement. He immigrated to Australia in 2002 and won Nobel Prize in 2003. His fiction is innovative and highly self-conscious. While creating fictional landscapes, his work probes the philosophical foundation of fiction. In his first novel, *Dusklands* (1974) juxtaposes two narratives –one with the setting of contemporary Vietnam war and the other an eighteenth century South African frontier story. Both the stories expose and condemn colonial violence. Coetzee's next novel, *In the Heart of the Country* (1977) is concerned with the spinster Magda's search for a language to end her isolation in a deserted Karoo farm. The novel is an extended monologue of Magda who murders her father. She is not a reliable narrator. In fact, whole narrative becomes metafictional subverting the notion of psychological realism. The navel may also be said to be a subversion of the conventions of the plaasroman (the pastoral novel). It is clear from Magda's narration that the farm is not a quiet rural retreat where one can lead a simple life. It appears to be a disturbing world of patriarchal and racial domination. *Waiting for the Barbarians* (1980) is considered to be most widely read novel of Coetzee. It tells the story of a liberal magistrate who has been serving a remote village of an unnamed empire. He is disturbed at the arrival of the dangerous Colonel Joll who was sent to put down a rumoured rebellion. The magistrate experiences a crisis of conscience as he has to choose between loyalty to his masters and protection of their alleged barbarian enemies. The setting of the novel in terms of time and place is obscure. This is, perhaps, done deliberately to explore the mindset of colonial repression. However, *Life & Times of Michael K* (1983) is considered to be the most memorable creation of Coetzee. The novel is set in a future South Africa entangled in civil war. Through the protagonist, Michael K, the narrative shows how the troubled state has taken to confining the poor and unemployed to fenced camps with a view to controlling the movement of people in the country.

In these and subsequent narratives, Coetzee clearly refers to the situation in South Africa. He does not restrict his fiction to the realist form demanded by the discourse of history. A recurrent theme of his fiction is the failure of love, relations corrupted by the abuse of power between the coloniser and the colonised. However, day by day his work becomes increasingly metafictional.

Nadine Gordimer's fiction can be discussed in the context of the above developments in fiction in South Africa. Gordimer has responded to the impact of apartheid in a more subtle way. She begins to explore the effects of apartheid in South Africa through liberal whites in her early fiction such as *The Lying Days* and *Occasion for Loving*. Her later novels like *Burger's Daughter* capture the rigid race relations and the deepening divisions in the society of South Africa under apartheid. She has shown a strong commitment to a multiracial South Africa through the anti-apartheid nature of her fiction. This forms the subject matter of the next chapter.

Works Cited

Abrahams, Peter. *Mine Boy*. London: Heinemann Educational Books, 1969.

Brink, André. *The Wall of the Plague*. London: Faber and Faber, 1984.

_______ "An Ornithology of Sexual Politics: Lewis Nkosi's *Mating Birds*". *English in Africa* 19 (1) 1-20

Cornwell, et. al. *The Columbia Guide to South African Literature in English Since 1945*. New York: Columbia, 2010.

Fatton, Robert. *Black Consciousness in South Africa*. New York: State University of New York, 1986.

Gates, H. L. "*Mating Birds*: The Power of her Sex, The Power of Her Race". *New York Times Book Review*: 18 May, 3.

Gordimer, Nadine. *The Essential Gesture: Writing, Politics and Places*. Ed. Stephen Clingman. London: Penguin, 1989.

Heywood, Christopher. *A History of South African Literature*. Cambridge: Cambridge University, 2004.

Jordan, John O. 'Alan Paton and the Novel of South African Liberalism: "Too Late the Phalarope"'. *Modern Fiction Studies*. Vol. 42 No.4 (Winter 1996), pp. 681 -706.

La Guma, Alex. *Apartheid: A Collection of Writings of South African Racism by South Africans*. New York: International Publishers, 1978.

________ *And A Threefold Cord*. Berlin: Seven Seas, 1964.

________ *A Walk in the Night*. London: Heinemann, 1967.

________ *The Stone Country*. Berlin: Seven Seas, 1967.

________ *In the Fog of the Seasons' End*. London: Heinemann, 1982.

Nicholls, Brendon. *Nadine Gordimer's July's People*. London: Routledge, 2011.

Modisane, Bloke. *Blame Me on History*. New York: Simon & Schuster, 1990.

Mphahlele, Es'kia. *Down Second Avenue*. Garden N. Y: Anchor Books, 1971.

Parker, Kenneth ed. *The South African Novel in English*. London: Macmillan, 1978.

Paton, Alan. *Cry, the Beloved Country*. Harmondsworth: Penguin, 1958.

Plaatje, Sol. *Native Life in South Africa*. Teddington: Echo Library, 2007.

Tlali, Miriam. Amandla. Johannesburg: Raven Press, 1980.

Tucker, Andrew. *Queer Visibilities: Space, Identity and Interaction in Cape Town*. Hoboken: John Wiley & Sons, 2009.

Visser, Nicholas.'The Politics of Future Projection in South African Novels', *Bucknell Review*. Vol. 37, No. 1 (January 1993), p. 62.

Wade, Jean-Philippe. 'Radical Democracy and Literary Form: Alan Paton's "Ah, but Your Land Is Beautiful"'. *English in Africa*. Vol. 28, No. 1 (May 2001), pp. 91-103.

Wilmot, Patrick. *Apartheid and African Liberation: The Grief and the Hope*. Ile-Ife: University of Ile-Ife, 1980.

Yousaf, Nahem. *Apartheid Narratives*. Amsterdam: Rodopi, 2001.

CHAPTER II

Acquiescence and Resistance in Nadine Gordimer's Fiction

2.1 Theoretical Approaches

This chapter attempts to discuss the theme of acquiescence and resistance in the fiction of Nadine Gordimer in the light of postcolonial theory as put forwarded by Bhabha and Foucault. Postcolonial studies may be described as a complex field that covers a number of issues and ideas. While it mainly focuses on the impacts of colonialism and the relation between the coloniser and the colonised, it covers a wide range of themes and ideas. As Bill Ashcroft et. al. put it, "Postcolonial theory involves discussion about experiences of various kinds: migration, slavery, suppression, resistance, representation, difference, race, gender, place . . ." (2). The works of Edward Said may be said to have inaugurated the field of postcolonial studies. It can, however, be traced back to Frantz Fanon. Fanon examined the psychological effects of colonialism on the colonised subject in his important book, *Black Skin White Masks* (1952, English translation 1986). Fanon perceives the colonial world as 'manichean', that is, the world is divided into good and evil represented by the coloniser and the colonised respectively. From this division follows the other binary oppositions such as Self and Other, and subject and object. This division is one of the basic tenets of postcolonialism. The coloniser represents the native as evil and primitive. In course of time, the native begins to accept this racialised view as true. Consequently, in order to deal with this psychological inadequacy, the native tries to be as 'white' as possible. He puts on, to use Fanon's words, 'white masks'. But soon the colonised realises that he cannot become 'white'. His life is caught in "the lasso of existence" (Fanon 178). Out of frustration he often directs his violence against his own people – the 'wretched' turn upon each other. Fanon claims that tribal wars are instance of this violence.

In his path breaking book *Orientalism* (1978), Said very persuasively argues that the western scholars should reconsider the relationship between the West and the Orient. He saw colonisation as rooted in an epistemological enquiry and project of constructing the image of the east as savage, primitive and underdeveloped by the Europe. Through discursive practices the Europe and the Orient were represented in literature and history as binary opposites. Europe was what the Orient was not. If the Europe was developed and civilized, the Orient was underdeveloped and uncivilised. "Europe saw the Orient as different and treated this difference as *negative*" (original italics, Nayar 161). The western views of the eastern cultures is coloured with prejudices. In short, orientalism may be said to be a practice of discrimination applied to non-European societies and cultures to establish imperial rule. To justify their rule, the colonisers claim to have more knowledge about the orient.

Critics like Michel Foucault and Bhabha contend that if, as Said claims, the west produced knowledge to show the inferiority of the Orient, it might be possible to read the literary texts to find moments of resistance offered by the colonised subject. Said's argument about the power of orientalist discourse to 'construct' the orient is based on the Foucauldian premise of power and knowledge. The west had power to know the orient and that power constituted the oriental other as a particular subject of discourse. In the 'General Introduction' to the book, *The Post –Colonial Studies Reader*, Bill Ashcroft, et. al. make an important observation. Quoting Said, they point out that when Arthur James Balfour stood up in the House of Commons on 13 June, 1910 to answer challenges to British presence in Egypt, he spoke with a position derived from the two indivisible foundations of imperial authority – power and knowledge. They further say:

> The most formidable ally of economic and political control had long been the business of 'knowing' other peoples because this 'knowing' underpinned imperial dominance and became the mode by which they were increasingly persuaded to know themselves: that is, as subordinate to Europe (1).

As Balfour claims in the passage, the imperial derives authority from and governs through power and knowledge. Foucault has given a powerful account of the significant connections between power, knowledge, and the subject in his writings. He challenges the traditional concept of power. He claims that power is exercised rather than possessed (*Discipline and Punish* 26). The history of different social institutions is the history of power relations. Knowledge gives rise to power. It is the relationship between power and knowledge, which controls and governs the society. He further argues that power is productive and that subjects are produced through cultural and institutional practices. He mainly focuses on practices of disciplinary power which lead to binary divisions such as sane/mad or civilized/uncivilized. These divisions can be used as a means of social control. They also involve the physical segregation of the population in a society. Such divisions of population are clearly found in the ideological practices of apartheid in South Africa.

Discourse is the connecting thread between power, knowledge and truth. For Foucault, discourse is not just language in context; it also means disciplines and social institutions. Discourses are everywhere. His books, *Discipline and Punish: The Birth of the Prison* (1975) and *The History of Sexuality: Volume I: An Introduction* (1976) show how discourses such as discourse of sickness and discourse of religion condition people's life and thought. He demonstrates that science, human relations and other social institutions are involved in a struggle for power. This struggle is carried on through discourse and discursive practices. However, in *The History of Sexuality*, Foucault argues that discourse is a means not only of oppression but also of resistance. On the other hand, Foucault suggests, where there is power, there is resistance. He admits the existence of state power but at the same time he points out the possibility of resistance to the centralised power at the micro level –power relations in the lives of individuals. Many characters of Gordimer's fiction demonstrate or show a tendency to resistance at the micro level.

Foucault's concept of power and knowledge interrogates resistance to the dominant power structure. Spivak is concerned with the possibility of representation of the subaltern. In the colonial discourse, the subaltern is cut off from representation. South Asian scholars, particularly the Indian historian Ranajit Guha undertook the subaltern project to give voice to the subalterns who were left out in the conventional historical accounts. They went against the traditional, 'elite' history that focused on the history of kings and generals only, leaving out from their account the subaltern social group. So there can be, they argue, different versions of history as alternative. However, Gayatri Spivak has been critical of this project of the subaltern studies group. She questions the possibility of giving a voice to the voiceless. She contends that one cannot construct a category of the subaltern that has an effective voice. She concludes that for the true subaltern group whose identity is its difference, there is no subaltern subject that can "know and speak for itself" (Ashcroft, et al, 10).

Unlike Frantz Fanon, Bhabha does not see the relationship between the coloniser and the colonised simply in terms of the self and the other. He argues that the relationship is ambivalent and unstable. The coloniser wishes that the natives imitate or 'mimic' his habits and values. At the same time he wants to keep the difference between himself and the natives. On the other hand, when the native mimics the colonial master, he does so with subtle variations and nuances. Thus the colonial discourse "produces ambivalent subjects whose **mimicry** is never very far from mockery" (Bill Ashcroft, et. al., *Post-Colonial Studies: The Key Concepts* 10). So the mimicry of the native displays obedience as well as disobedience. Bhabha calls this dualism resistance. He asserts that all cultures are impure and hybrid. In his book, *The Location of Culture*, he examines issues like 'border lines', cultural difference and colonial oppression which can be used to analyse Gordimer's fiction and resistance against apartheid. Bhabha argues that living at the border or margin demands a new 'art of the present' (McLeod 217). Borders are thresholds which separate as well as connect different places. They are transitory locations from where one thinks of moving beyond a barrier. Bhabha describes the border as beyond or liminal. As he puts it, "The 'beyond is neither a new horizon, nor a leaving behind of the past . . . we find ourselves in the moment of transit where space and time cross to produce complex figures of difference and identity, past and present, inside and outside, inclusion and exclusion" (1-2). Bhabha claims that the borders between cultures are porous. Cultures moves across the supposed barriers through the porous border. Hence cultures are hybrid and fluid. The border disturbs the conventional patterns. On the other hand, it is also the place of possible new ideas.

It is obvious that two of the dominant ideas that emerge in postcolonial studies are representation and resistance. The concept of resistance is nicely illustrated by Barbara Harlow in her book *Resistance Literature* (1987). For her, resistance is an act or series of acts carried out to get rid a people of their oppressors. Literary resistance can be interpreted as "a form of contractual understanding between text and reader, one which is embedded in an experiential dimension and buttressed by a political and cultural aesthetic at work in the culture" (Slemon 104). She thinks that resistance literature is a category of literary writing which emerges as an integral part of an organized struggle of resistance for national liberation. According to Said, resistance is a two-fold activity. Of these the first one is a literally fighting against outside intrusion. The second activity is the ideological resistance which can be carried through literature. Quoting Basil Davidson, Said further observes that it comprises efforts made "to reconstitute a 'shattered community to save or restore the sense and fact of community against all pressures of the colonial system'" (252-53). Thus, resistance literature can be seen as literature which resists the imposition of the ideology of colonial discourse. Colonial discourse represents and produces the reality of the colonised in a way that they accept the constructed reality. Resistance literature often decodes this reality. Literary text is a site of cultural control and an effective instrument for the determination of the native by fixing him or her under the sign of the other. In his influential essay "The Economy of Manichean

Allegory: the Function of Racial Difference in Colonialist Literature",
Abdul R. JanMohamed contends how literary texts contain features
that can be appropriated to the oppositional and anti-colonial
purposes of contemporary postcolonial writing. JanMohamed
divides colonialist texts into two categories: 'imaginary' and
'symbolic'. He says that the writers of imaginary texts show a fixed
opposition between the self and the native. On the other hand,
symbolic texts attempt to use the native as a mediator of the
European desires. The authors of this kind of fiction are willing to
examine the specific individual and cultural differences between
Europeans and natives and to reflect on the efficacy of the European
values, assumptions, and habits in contrast to those of the indigenous
cultures. JanMohamed subdivided the symbolic texts into two types:
fiction like E M Forster's *A Passage to India* and Rudyard Kipling's
Kim explores to find syncretic solutions to the manichean opposition
of the coloniser and the colonised. The symbolic fiction of the second
type is represented by the novels of Joseph Conrad and Nadine
Gordimer. This kind of fiction argues that syncretism is impossible
within the power relations of colonial society. But it examines
rigorously "the imaginary mechanism of colonial mentality" and
thus "manages to free itself from the Manichean allegory ..." ("The
Economy", JanMohamed 20).

The colonial experience has been explored imaginatively by
writers of fiction. But the distinction between the historical and the
fictional representation is not clear cut. Critics in the postmodern
period, particularly the new historicists have often questioned the
objectivity of history and its representation of facts. The historian
has to interpret his materials or data to construct a picture of the
period he deals with. But there will always be more facts to record
than he can possibly accommodate in his work. So he has to

be selective and can only present a segment of it. In doing so, he applies his own mind and interprets his materials on inferential and speculative grounds. Thus imagination or subjective element finds its way into the narration of the facts. In his 'Translator's Introduction' to *The Writing of History*, Tom Conley has observed that students of fiction and history show us that understanding is based on effects of representation. The criteria of selection become "the object of study no less than an archive or a literary text"(x). This principle of selection and interpretation of facts is common to a historian and a writer of fiction as well. The postmodernist concept of history as narrative further problematises the treatment of history. Hayden White suggests that all historical facts come to us only in the form of narrative. The fact that history is always narrated implies that the past is available only as it is represented. History is thus understood to be the recreation of past events, through a combination of imagination, intuition and narrative discourse. This, in turn, indicates a parallel between history and fiction. In his significant book, *The Novel of Nadine Gordimer: History from the Inside*, Stephen Clingman has observed that literature represents history as it has been lived and experienced by people. In other words, history is represented in literature through living, breathing men and women. It is an effective medium for exploring the questions such as how people see the world they live in. For him, "it is in fiction that individual and social narratives are given visible and public voice" (xxxv). This is very important for South African literature, for South Africa has a unique and peculiar history. Apartheid can be seen as an extension of colonisation. It has produced a vision of history which is singular to that country. This singular history has often been delineated and interpreted by South African literature, particularly fiction. In this respect Nadine Gordimer's fiction is significant, besides its artistic merits.

2.2 Gordimer's Fiction

The socially committed writers like Nadine Gordimer in the apartheid South Africa passed through a precarious situation in the country. Very often their words were considered equivalent to the actions of the people who were "politically active and important because they might help to give a voice to those who found themselves beaten into silence but not into submission" (Yousaf viii). The writers produced work which exposed the oppression suffered by the black in the hands of the white. As a result the rulers considered the act of writing as a form of resistance. This led the apartheid government to ban and exile many writers of the time. It is in this light that the resistance novels of Nadine Gordimer will be analysed in the following pages. Her literary impulses and social commitment lead her into the heart of anti- apartheid to create a body of fiction that brought her the Nobel Prize in 1991. Sensitive as she was, she had a deep consciousness of the history of her time. She has derived inspiration from a host of international authors to pursue artistic freedom by exercising social responsibility. Some of them are Bertolt Brecht, Albert Camus, Ivan Turgenev, Antonio Gramsci and Georg Lukacs. These authors are associated with the Marxist philosophy in one or the other way. Gordimer's works also display the influence of Marxism.

However, there is a parallel between the beginnings of her career and the rise of the Afrikaner-dominated National Party that ruled South Africa for about half a century. In a 1982 "Conversation" she described herself as a natural writer and claimed that she did not write about apartheid. "I write about people who happen to live under that system" (Robert Boyers, et al. 27). It is true that she was a natural writer for she started writing quite early in her life when she did not know much about apartheid. But she admitted that she was living in a society of intense racial prejudice. It was obvious that racial politics gradually entered her work and she was perhaps aware of it. This is clearly seen in her views on the role and function of the writer in the society. In her essay "Literature and Politics in South Africa", she calls the writer as "the creative consciousness of his society" (219). It is natural that the writer influences and is influenced by his society. Apartheid permeated all spheres of South African life in the second half of twentieth century. So a writer who aimed to depict truthfully his society could not avoid the political issues influencing his mind. Gordimer rightly observes in an article, "A Writer in South Africa", that society means political situation in South Africa. "Politics is character in SA", she says (23). On the other hand, as Gordimer argues in her essay, "A Writer's Freedom," the main responsibility of the writer is "to write the truth as he sees it" (105) and his immediate goal is the "enlargement of the reader's apprehension of reality" (107). Through the fulfilment of this social responsibility, the writer offers his "unique contribution to social change" (107). His ultimate aim is the transformation of society. In the context of South Africa under apartheid, it was the goal of the writer to awaken the conscience of his readers to the evils of his society with a view to removing the evils and laying the foundations of justice and freedom in society. She has observed in her essay, "The Essential Gesture", "South African writers [were] answerable in their essential gesture . . . [to] the historical and existential situation of blacks" (293). The writers –both black and white writers –should speak against the oppression of blacks in their works. Gordimer asserts that the white writer as a cultural worker should raise the consciousness of the white people. She understands that he may lack the experience of "the life of the black ghettoes". But, she continues,

> black writers do share with white the same kind of influence on those whites who read them; and so the categories that the state would keep apart get mixed through literature –an unforeseen 'essential gesture' of writers in their social responsibility in a divided country." ("The Essential Gesture", 293-294)

Gordimer contends that the writers should speak against the oppression of the blacks in their works. That is the demand made upon the writers of the time. Every society imposes social responsibility on the writer in terms of its concept of the writer's essential gesture. At the same time the writer has also responsibility to his art. Sometimes the writer's social responsibility may conflict with his creative vision and sometimes there may be a reconciliation between social responsibility and "the writer's commitment to his artistic vision" ("The Essential Gesture" 289). In the case of a conflict between the two, the writer can resolve it exercising his fundamental freedom as a writer. As Gordimer states in "A Writer's Freedom", this freedom is the writer's "right to maintain and publish to the world a deep, intense, private view of the situation in which he finds his society" (104). The fiction of Gordimer responds to the historical situation and at the same time, she maintains her fidelity that fiction should be the servant of truth only. All her novels and short stories which are set in South Africa reflect the socio-political condition of South Africa. She has been aware of the socio-political issues. In fact, she has been a social activist herself. But she attempts to deal with them with utmost honesty at her command as an artist. She herself says that in the work of the honest writer social truth appears naturally. So she asserts that the anti-apartheid nature of his novels is not due to her personal abhorrence of apartheid. It is, she argues, because the society she lives in "is the very stuff of my work *reveals itself* ... If you write honestly about life in South Africa, apartheid damns itself" (original italics, quoted in Clingman 12). So, her fiction, focusing primarily on human lives and situations, represents a fictionalized history of apartheid. By exposing the evils of racism, she has contributed to the resistance of apartheid and thus she has discharged her social responsibility.

2.2.1 The Early Fiction

Gordimer's first novel *The Lying Days* (*LD*) was published in 1953, five years after the Afrikaner National Party government came to power. It deals with the development of racial consciousness of the protagonist, Helen Shaw. Many critics also opine that the novel is autobiographical. Helen's development reflects Gordimer's own development. Dominic Head sees the novel as Helen's search for her "social and political identity, just as this first novel has Gordimer beginning her search for her own artistic identity, and an appropriate literary form" (35). The novel captures a picture of South Africa in the late 1940s when the National Party came to power in 1948 and began enforcing the apartheid policy. The narrator, Helen Shaw lives in the white community of Atherton gold mine where her father is a secretary. Her parents and the other white people associated with the mine socialize only with one another. It is in this world of white community that Helen spends the first seventeen years of her life. One Saturday, Helen, in the absence of her parents, ventures to the concession stores that serve the black mine workers. In her first attempt to venture into the black world, she saw the "red dust path turning off the stores" somewhere she had never been. She also saw in the mine little children in pushcarts whose mothers allowed the maids to take them anywhere they liked. They went down the "filthy kaffir stores to gossip with the boys" (*LD* 8). This act of the maids exposes the little babies to dirt and disease. Her mother often condemned their negligence.

This is the beginning of Helen's awareness of the world around her. The above passage reveals her mother's racist attitude. She condemns 'the filthy kaffir' stores with their atmosphere of 'dirt and disease'. Immediately after this, Helen makes her way along the path and observes dozens of natives in their dark skin and with their dark brown faces. Helen experiences the world of the blacks. The incident shows Helen's tendency to break the ideological confinements of the whites. This is more clearly evident when she befriends a black girl in the university, Mary Seswayo. Helen wishes Mary comes to their home and stays till the latter writes the examination –not in the house exactly but in the 'cooler', a storeroom built for keeping food. This is Helen's compromise solution –the creation of a makeshift space which is neither inside the house of the whites nor outside where the blacks stay. But Helen's mother is very angry at this idea. Helen is frustrated by the white parents' racist ideology towards the blacks. She attempts to go beyond her ideological confinement by befriending Mary Seswayo, a black co-student at university. She does not succeed. In the apartheid South Africa, Mary is not only a person but a black person. She is the other. This incident also points to the issue of spatial provisions for the blacks in South Africa. Helen is surprised that there are no public toilet facilities for native men and women in the whole shopping centre of Johannesburg. In fact, her concern with space for the blacks in the township illustrates the idea of spatial provision as a political issue. Gordimer's description of the township where Mary Seswayo lives may be called a rudimentary version of Foucault's notion of space expressed in the term 'heterotopia'— a site of difference and resistance. Charles and Helen's visit to the native location Mariastad is a kind of "culture shock", which is similar to Helen's reactions at the concessions stores (Head 42). This native location was much like the other locations:

> All around the veld had been burned and spread like a black stain. And all above the crust of vague, close, low houses, smoke hung, quite still as if it had been there forever; and shouts rose, and it seemed that the shout had been there forever, too, many voices lifted at different times and for different reasons that became simply a shout, that never began and never ended (*LD* 171).

As they move along the township, Helen and Charles are so shocked that they stopped talking as people do when they feel they have lost their way. The spatial compression of the location gives the reader an illusion of permanence despite its transitory nature. The narrator expresses this paradox through some significant images. The polluting smoke has been described as something permanent, and the 'many voices' of the township forming a single shout suggests the disorder and incoherence of compression and squalor of the location. Paradoxically, the single voice also suggests "the unity of common experience of repression, and there is a clear sense here of the unity required for political action . . . an (as yet) unarticulated, but nevertheless unified, 'shout'" (Head 43). The single shout reduces Helen and Charles to silence. Their silence suggests their guilt, their awareness of the white complicity in the material manifestation of repression. There is a possibility that the shout represents an emerging black political voice which may silence the whites. The politics of space gives the scene an extra dimension. This is an early version of the heterotopia. Heterotopias are sites of differences and resistance. They are different from and yet have links with other social spaces. A better example of heterotopia is the township description in *Burger's Daughter*. Foucault uses the term to refer to the way through which spaces surrounding the subject in social existence can reduce his autonomy and even his sense of identity. According to Foucault, heterotopias are almost invisible and perceived as natural by members of a society though they are measures of disciplining and controlling. Space is a device that helps the colonizer to control and regulate the movement of people in a colonised country. This is quite evident in the apartheid South Africa. Different acts such as Population Registration Act (1950), Group Areas Act (1950), etc. were enacted to classify the natives and regulate their movements. But while the regulation of space within apartheid South Africa is enforced to keep the whites and non-whites apart, characters in Gordimer's novels frequently cross the spatial divide. Thereby they resist the division.

Gordimer has also touched upon the issue of space through the character of Joel Aaron. He receives training to be an architect. Earlier the reader is informed that Joel's future plans include the possibility of building houses –cottages –for blacks (*LD* 155). It is appropriate that he is studying the provision and organization of social space. It has a bearing on the political vision of the novel. In the final chapter of the novel, Joel sails for Israel in the hope of realizing, says Helen, "a concrete expression of his creative urge, in doing his work in a society which in itself was in the live process of emergence, instead of decay" (*LD* 375). Helen makes this remark when she identifies herself as the writer. Joel's "creative urge" may suggest his intended participation in the construction of a new society. Gordimer, perhaps, implies that the novelist should have such an objective, particularly in South Africa. Gordimer's concern with spatial politics points to her intention to build a just society.

When Helen lives in the city of Johannesburg, she shares a flat with a married couple. Here she meets Paul Clark, an Afrikaner and a Welfare Officer in the Native Affairs Department. In course of time she starts living with him. In the beginning her parents favour Paul because he belongs to Natal which is known for its close ties with England. However, through the Paul-Helen episode, Gordimer explores an important issue. Before the Afrikaner Nationalist government came to power, 'trusteeship' had been the official ideology of the government (Clingman 35). This ideology allowed the whites to act as guardians of the blacks and to act for the welfare of the blacks. Under the nationalists this was replaced by *baasskaap* (literally meaning 'boss-ship'). This was done to assert the white supremacy. In the novel, Paul's job is to deal with the housing problems of poor blacks. Paul feels that it (his job) gives him access to the world of the blacks. On the other hand, it allows him to undermine the oppressive system by using its resources or, at least, to reduce the sufferings of the blacks. This demands that Paul lives a double life –working for a government that enforces apartheid and collaborating with his friends in African National Congress. Soon he realises that his position inherits some contradictions. Under the Nationalist government in 1948, the state policy of apartheid becomes more prominent. On the other hand, his friends in African National Congress adopt a militant attitude. This situation tears him apart. As Helen puts it, "He cannot lose, and he cannot win. He scarcely knows anymore what to hope for" (*LD* 300). In depicting the replacement of the ideology of trusteeship the novel has addressed a central aspect of the history of its times and, more importantly, it has "dramatized the implications of this change for individual life" (Clingman 38). Paul's relationship with Helen also begins to fail when his political anxiety increases. She thinks of a private life with her lover Paul and she has it at least for a short time. She seems to be happy to meet the demands of an inner life with her lover. But it does not take her a long time to understand that their life is in a "state of suspension" (*LD* 295). The tensions of their life reflect "the tensions of the external divisions in public life" under the nationalist regime (Green 82). After witnessing the May Day Strike in which Paul's friend Sipho becomes a victim, she decides to go to Britain. She seems to understand that she has no place in the country of her birth, South Africa. It dawns upon her that she belongs neither to the black nor to the white. This is a kind of withering "into the truth" as the epigraph of the novel from the poem of Yeats suggests.

Though political events have not been given any prominence in the novel, Gordimer nevertheless refers to certain crucial measures of apartheid such as the Mixed Marriages Act and the Suppression of Communism Bill. Sexual relations between whites and non-whites were prohibited through the Immorality Act (1950). This is conveyed by the novelist through a very short incident when the headlights of the police van shine into the bedroom of Helen and Paul Clark. This is to remind the reader that they are enforcing the Mixed Marriages prohibition. The apartheid government's intrusion into the private life of individuals points to Foucault's concept of surveillance. This surveillance leads to self-surveillance as seen in Helen's reaction that night. As Paul recalls the incident of the police van shining on the mixed couple in the bed, Helen recoils instinctively from him. These are some of the instruments of oppression of the apartheid regime. The whites are still living a life of comfort and leisure, Helen realises. So there develops a feeling of guilt in her mind. She attempts to overcome them by mixing with some blacks and visiting the locations. The May Day riot that Helen and her friend Laurie confront in the black township is an eye opener for Helen. She is horrified to see how the police shoot and kill a black rioter. The traumatic death of the rioter affects her deeply. She realizes the realities of South Africa of 1948. She thinks that in South Africa she can be only an observer and never be a participant in the struggle of the blacks. Hence, perhaps, she decides to leave South Africa. Though Helen decides to leave the country, she is hopeful that she will return. This is conveyed through the image of "the phoenix illusion that makes life always possible" (*LD* 376). The illusion of the phoenix suggests a realistic understanding of the limits to the contribution of a creative writer in building an alternative political future.

Published in 1958, Gordimer's second novel *A World of Strangers* (*WS*) was set against the background of the movements opposed to apartheid in the 1950s. The philosophy of these movements spearheaded by the Congress Alliance was multi-racialism. In fact, multi-racialism was a social way of life of the time, at least some part of the country. The magazine, *Drum* provided a platform to the writers, reporters, critics and photographers who attempted to change the way black people were represented in the society. Sophiatown, a suburb of Johannesburg, became a hub of multiracial culture. In this context Clingman observes that Sophiatown itself became a vital symbol of the 1950s. It was an ethnically mixed and vibrant black township on the borders of Johannesburg. In fact, it was virtually part of Johannesburg. In a number of ways this social world reflects the broader political movement of South Africa. Gordimer herself was involved with different aspects of Johannesburg life of this time. She developed friendship with the members of the *Drum* such as Henry Nxumalo ('Mr Drum'), Can Themba, Bloke Modisane and others. More importantly, it is at this time she began her lasting friendship with a banned Afrikaner trade unionist, Bettie du Toit.

In *A World of Strangers* Gordimer explores the life in South Africa from the point of view of an outsider, Toby Hood. *The Lying Days* almost ignores the black world and focuses mainly upon the development of consciousness of the white protagonist, Helen. In *A World of Strangers*, however, the narrator often visits the townships, particularly Sophia town. Toby Hood, an Oxford graduate, comes from England to South Africa to look into the affairs of the publishing agency of the family. But he does not have any inclination to the family's interest in anti-colonial causes. He tries to remain neutral to South African politics and leads a life oscillating between the white high society and the black townships. He tries to understand the nature of these unbridgeable 'world of strangers' through his personal relationships. His black bachelor friend Steven Sitole, who is apolitical likes him, takes him to the townships. On the other hand, his prejudiced lover Cecil Rowe epitomises the traits he finds in privileged white society (Head 48). He gains his first significant experience of South African white society when he visits the High House. It is a huge mansion of the wealthy mining magnate Hamish Alexander who has been a friend of his mother. It is at this place he meets the three important people of his life. He meets Cecil Rowe, a divorcee, who becomes his mistress. Another important person is Anna Louw, the Afrikaner lawyer and activist, who married a South African Indian and then divorced. Anna introduces him to different people who were engaged in the struggle of the black for liberation. Most significantly, Anna takes him to a party of mixed races, where people get together and makes friends across racial divide. In such meetings, Toby meets Steven Sitole who has returned from England, and Sam, a struggling musician. Steven makes a profound effect upon Toby's life. From his visit to the parties and other places, Toby realizes that colour and social barriers keep the white and the black far away from knowing each other. He discovers that there exists a void between the worlds of the blacks and the whites: "I passed from one world to another –but neither was real to me. For in each, what sign was there that the other existed" (*WS* 197)? Gordimer effectively depicts the contrasting worlds of the whites and the blacks. Against the hard, poverty stricken world of the blacks, she represents the lavish world of the whites. In the parties at the High House, Toby meets the rich white businessmen and industrialists. On the other hand, there is a careless attitude to life in the black township. Food, survival and reproduction are the primary concern of life in this township. In fact, Gordimer has pitted the blacks against the whites throughout the novel to make the differences prominent. Toby finds that there is a deep divide between the rich white life and the poor blacks. In such a situation he just carried along his daily life though it exerted an enormous stress and strain, "where one set of loyalties and interests made claims in direct conflict with another set, equally strong" (*WS* 258). He had to keep his friends physically apart. He could not even speak to one group about the others either.

Though he plans to remain neutral to South African politics, he moves between the white society and the poor world of the blacks. He is upset that the white society makes no room for relationships with blacks like Sam and Steven. He wonders what he will write in his letters to his family and friends back in England:

> Could I tell them how pleasant it was to be lulled and indulged at the High House? Could I explain the freedom I felt where I had no legal right to be in that place of segregation, a location? I suppose that to have a 'life out there', a real life in Johannesburg, you'd have to belong in one or the other, for keeps (*WS*, 203).

Toby finds that the divide between the whites and the blacks is deep and that it is irreconcilable. Toby finds himself in an 'in-between' reality, a borderline existence (Bhabha, 19). The binary divisions develop in him a sense of despondency and alienation. "I had not been to Alexander's for weeks. I couldn't go there any more, that was all" (*WS*, 257). His failure, though temporary, to continue his contact with the privileged whites and his friendship with Steven and Anna makes him understand the success of separateness of apartheid in South Africa: "You couldn't really reconcile one with the other, the way people were, the way laws were and make a whole" (*WS* 203). Thus he expresses his anxieties and experiences of both the worlds of South Africa.

But Gordimer does not represent the character of Toby as one who is disappointed at the prevailing racial prejudices in South Africa. His complicity with the apartheid does not escape the critical lens of Gordimer. Like Steven, he is indifferent to the politics of South African life. But his lack of commitment to the fight against apartheid does not give him the freedom of a private life. His mistress Cecil Rowe has a different attitude to life and to the blacks. She wishes she had enough money and lived in Europe. So she ultimately marries Guy Patterson in her greed and fear of life. She is out and out acquiescent to the apartheid ideology. She has a strong racial prejudice. So much so that she shudders at the thought of touching a black skin: "Her hand came out in the imaginary experiment and hesitated, wavered back" (*WS* 263). She cannot take it easily that Toby socializes with the blacks or treat a black person as an equal. Though Toby befriends Steven, he makes it sure that the latter never meets Cecil. He conceals his friendship with Steven from Cecil because he fears that if he does so he will lose her. Thus, though he intends to remain indifferent to the politics of the land, he himself contributes to the segregation of the races.

Steven's death in a car accident provides him a check, a pause to think about the kind of life he has been living. He quickly realizes that even when black and white people live together in South Africa, they are strangers in each other's world. He says, "What I had known of Steven, a stranger, living and dying a life I could at best only observe; my brother" (*WS* 252). His acquaintances with white and black worlds and his failure in personal relationships across colour bar make him feel the necessity of a commitment to the resistance against apartheid. According to Clingman, Toby suddenly realises that the kind of "self-centred indifference" attitude he has adopted contributed to the "social divide of the 'world of strangers'" in South Africa (55). In this sense he cannot deny his complicity in the death of his black friend Steven. So, he must commit himself to a different kind of social commitment for his moral rehabilitation. His experiences of the black and the white worlds move him to "a new social commitment" against the apartheid structure (Clingman 55). And this time he makes his commitment through a friendship with another black, Sam Mofokenzazi.

This friendship between Toby and the black Sam is very significant. It marks a change in Toby, at least in his attitude and intention. Just before leaving the Johannesburg railway station for Cape Town in business trip, Toby promises Sam to be the godfather of Sam's baby when it is born. However, Sam is not sure of Toby's decision: "May be you won't come back at all" (*WS* 266). Gordimer seems to suggest that their friendship transcends all ideologies and signals the beginning of a cultural synthesis against the apartheid. Through the epigraph of the novel, which is taken from Federico Garcia Lorca, she seems to anticipate the emergence of a revolutionary spirit against the apartheid:

> I want the strong air of the most profound night
>
> to remove flowers and letters from the arch where you sleep,
>
> and a black boy to announce to the gold minded whites
>
> the arrival of the reign of the ear of corn.

The action of the novel revolves around Toby's oscillation – both physical and mental – between Johannesburg and the black townships. The mixed gatherings are borderland spaces that have the possibility of bridging the racial divide. These parities of mixed people may be described as what Bhabha called borderlands. They are the meeting points, thresholds of two worlds. Clingman describes the novel a "frontier" text, suggesting a transition from one world to another (71). Toby moves to the borderlands or frontier places to find a world of friendships across racial divide. In addition to the cross racial friendship, there is Steven who has "the network of contacts" within which he operates. Toby notices that Steven "seems to know 'a fellow somewhere'" (Head 59). This 'network' helps him avoid the restrictions imposed by adverse legislation: "The more restrictions grew up around him and his kind –and there seemed to be fresh ones every month –the quicker he found a way round him" (*WS*, 204).

By avoiding the legislations and thereby opposing them, Steven offers a site of individual resistance that links with a broader movement which can generate practical resistance.

If *A World of Strangers* explores the possibility of a multi-racial society, *Occasion for Loving* (1963) shows its failure as the dominant ideology to oppose segregation. Multi-racialism had been challenged since long. The African nationalists seceded from the African National Congress and founded the Pan Africanist Congress (1959) and questioned the idea of multi-racialism. On the other hand, the apartheid regime was implementing its policies more strictly. It banned organisations like African National Congress and also resorted to violent action against the anti-apartheid activists. Gordimer was aware of this socio-political condition of the time. *Occasion for Loving* (OL) acknowledges this challenge and historical realities of the time. The novel explores this issue through the theme of love and sex across colour bar, which runs through South African fiction from Plomer to Paton and beyond.

The action of the novel moves around a love affair between the black artist, Gideon Shibalo and a white woman, Ann Davis, who visits South Africa with her husband, Boaz. They stay with Tom and Jessie Stilwell in Johannesburg. Tom Stilwell is a university teacher who participated in the campaign against the Extension of University Education Bill. The Bill was introduced to bar the blacks from the universities. As Thompson says, this apartheid legislation was passed in 1959 to prevent the black students from enrolling in the established universities unless a cabinet minister granted them special permission (197). In a protest meeting, an acquaintance of Tom tells him: "Fight them over this business if you want to, man, but don't think that anything you do really matters. Some of you make laws, and some of you try to change them. And you don't ask us" (*OL* 69). This shows, on the one hand, the exclusion of the blacks from the mainstream politics and, on the other, the growing suspicion of the liberal whites of their complicity in the oppressive system.

Foucault argues that power is exercised in public as well as in private spheres (Ransom, 28). The family is an important private sphere for the operation of power in society. In the first part of the novel, Jessie evaluates her past, her relation with her unhappily married mother. She painfully realized that she lost her youth because of her mother's confining love. Jessie's mother withdrew her from school on the pretext of a non-existent heart complaint. It left a deep scar on her mind. While watering the garden, a feeling comes to her mind that she has never left her mother's house. This is a sign of the inner struggle of Jessie to find the meaning of her past in the present situation. Both Tom and Jessie strongly believe in the sanctity of personal relationship but they ironically involve themselves in the inter-racial relationship between Ann and Gideon. However, Jessie may be said to represent Foucault's contention that public or state institutions continue the process of producing 'docile' subjects through family or individuals. Danaher et. al. explain in the context of Britain that mothers were entrusted with the responsibility to perpetuate the values and attitudes of the state (Danaher 76). In South Africa, the racial differences or apartheid governed the institutions of the white family. Jessie believes that "the race business" had been settled long ago (*OL* 290). But when she comes in close touch with Ann and Gideon, she realizes how the race factor lies at the core of their life and identity. When they suddenly turn up at her family beach cottage, she discovers the effects of apartheid on her psyche. As she converses with Gideon, she gradually feels her childhood fear growing in her. She was often told that she must not be left alone with a black man in the house. Nobody explained to her the reason. But it had an adverse impact on her mind: "I used to feel, at night, when I turned my back to the dark passage and bent to wash my face in the bathroom, that someone was coming up behind me" (*OL* 290). Jessie now recognizes the racist taboos that have been inculcated in her mind by her mother. Thus the institution of family plays an important role in the racial politics of apartheid.

The affair between Ann and Gideon breaks down because of racial and psychological barriers. There cannot be any occasion of loving between the black and the white in the context of South Africa under apartheid. Gideon is disappointed at the racial politics in his country. He cannot go to Italy on a scholarship because the government denied him passport because of his involvement in African National Congress. So his friend Sol reacts: "Most of the whites don't want to talk to you … *They* are the ones who decide what's going to happen to us" (original italic, *OL* 144-145). In the beginning of their relationship, Ann does not show any inhibition about race or colour. She enjoys visiting the townships and making acquaintance with the blacks. Her frank nature attracts many people to her as well. But as the narrative moves forward, she shows that she is not committed to the blacks. She does not remain faithful in her love for Gideon either. Despite her fascination for Gideon, she understands the inadequacy of their love when she runs away with him. A sense of alienation and a strange feeling comes over her during their journey to his native place. In a scene when Ann is sleeping by road, she is warned by a white African farmer of "drunk boys around on Sunday" (*OL* 268). When the man leaves, she feels a growing sense of fear in her. Ann's fear suggests that in a black majority country there is no space beyond the control of white race. And the control over space is a disciplinary practice to maintain power. The colour-blind Ann gradually becomes conscious of Gideon's colour. She tells Jessie:

> "You know when the man in the garage looked at Gid, and I stood next to him seeing Gid at the same time, it wasn't the same person we saw…" (*OL* 308).

She realizes that blackness count even in their intimate relationship. When they stay in the African village, Ann experiences the laws that prevent the whites and the blacks from mixing in social and public meetings in South Africa. The teacher, who provides them lodging in the African village, finally tells them to leave because of fear of persecution by the apartheid regime. Realizing the realities of racial politics in South Africa, Ann decides to leave South Africa with her husband, Boaz. This is an effect of what Foucault calls disciplinary practices which produce 'docile' subjects who are afraid to transgress the social binary oppositions. In the present instance it is inter-racial sexual relationship. The end of the affair is painful for not only Gideon but Jessie as well. She feels that there is no occasion for loving between a black and a white in the racially divided society of South Africa. Apartheid pervades through every aspects of South African life, even through the most intimate relationship of man and woman. In other words, apartheid has been internalized. The love affair between Ann and Gideon fails due to external as well as internal pressure. The Immorality Act, 1950 partially accounts for the failure of their relationship. It is the effect of disciplinary practices that silently internalized the apartheid. As Clingman says, the repressions of apartheid have become "psychologically inscribed" (82). This failure makes Jessie see the futility of any attempt to love across the racial divide. She ultimately realises that blackness counts even in the matter of love between a white and a black. This shows how the personal relation inevitably turns out be social, or the private affairs becomes political. So, Jessie believes, as long as the law like the Immorality Act remained unchanged, "nothing could bring integrity to personal relationships" (*OL* 321). Jessie painfully realizes that Ann has not been committed to her relationship with Gideon. "She did not love him *across the colour-bar...*" (original italics, *OL* 309). Ann who once claimed to be passionately in love with Gideon leaves South Africa without even bidding good bye to him. It is this attitude of arrogance of the white people to the South African blacks that Gordimer seems to criticize. Ann finally surrenders to the barriers of apartheid. The white liberal, Ann acquiescently accepts apartheid. On the other hand, her irresponsible behaviour exasperates Jessie. She cannot come to terms with the situation. She wonders how a person (Ann) falls in love with a man (Gideon) and at the same time destroys him. She reveals her feelings of annoyance and anger in a long conversation with Tom. He tries to calm her down and tells her that what else Ann could do if she didn't want him. She asks him not to make her suggest it. They do not distinguish between black and white; they behave decently to both the colours. She asks her husband

> But how can that ever be, so long as there's the possibility that you can escape back into your filthy damn whiteness? How do you know you'll always be fair?" . . .

> First he couldn't get out on his scholarship because he's black, now he can't he stay because she's white. What's the good of us to him? What's the good our friendship or her love?" (*OL* 312 -13)

The above conversation reveals Jessie's painful realization of discriminatory race relations between the white and the non-white. People like Gideon refuse to live according to a particular set of circumstances governing their life and another set governing the life of the whites. Gideon expresses his true feelings when he tells Jessie "White bitch –get away" (*OL* 331). This is a moment of confrontation and realization for Jessie. She cannot forget the words of Gideon. They open her eyes to another reality –the pain and torture of voiceless millions like Gideon Shibalo. This understanding on the part of Jessie keeps her meeting him "in a friendly fashion sometimes in the Lucky Star, occasionally at the houses of friends" though she could not his words (*OL* 332). These (places like Lucky Star) were the places where coloured and white people mixed opposing the apartheid ideology that segregated people into different spaces. And these borderlands are the locations of culture where new dimensions of existence emerge.

The interracial relationship between Ann and Gideon is also an example of the idea of resistance to the racial hegemony in the apartheid South Africa. Gordimer has often shown the inter-racial relationship between white women and black men. She has been criticized for the depiction of this relationship because, as Ian Glen points out, liaisons between white men and black women were prevalent in South Africa (cited in Waxman 139). Gordimer has reversed the relationship to use it as subversive force against the traditional imbalance of power. She suggests an alternative discourse to the generally prevalent social discourse exploring the connection between sex and power. Foucault argues that the existence of state power cannot be denied but the power relations in the lives of individuals can act as resistance to power. He believes, "Power comes from the below" (*The History* 103). And he considers sexuality as a "transfer point of power". Gordimer explores the complexity of power relations among the racial groups of South Africa through her characters' personal and sexual relations. She searches for new alliances and forms and provides an alternative discourse which may act as a resistance to the apartheid regime.

The first three novels of Gordimer show how her characters get the opportunity to come close to each other and build a society of mixed races. But they lose the opportunity largely because they are marginalized in the society they live in. They accept or submit to the barriers of apartheid. Helen in *The Lying Days* leaves Joel, Mary and Paul, and Toby in *A World of Strangers* moves away from Anna and Steven. In *Occasion for Loving* Jessie loses her friend, Gideon though they continue to meet in friendly fashion occasionally. Gordimer's protagonists in the early fiction attempt to live a non-racial life and thereby resist the segregation as the liberal whites did in the fabulous fifties. But they fail because of the harsh reality that prevailed in South Africa.

Gordimer tries to show the liberal whites and their actions that offer some inspiration as an alternative despite their limitations. This is reflected in her early novels and short stories as well. Thus, the story "The Smell of Death and Flowers" from *Six Feet of the Country* (1956) presents a young white woman Joyce McCoy who involves herself in a multi-racial demonstration and finally ends in jail. She goes to a party attended by members from different races. This kind of party of mixed races is unusual in apartheid South Africa. Such parties are also found Gordimer's *The World of Strangers*. However, McCoy dances with a black man, Eddie in the party and catches the attention of Jessica, a white anti-apartheid activist. Out of her impulse, McCoy asks for permission from Jessica to join an anti-apartheid march to be organised by a group of people of different races. The story depicts the psychological changes in the young woman Joyce McCoy as she decides and involves closely with struggle for equal rights of the black South Africans. Gordimer describes the period in Joyce's life from the time of her decision to join an anti-apartheid movement up to her act of resistance itself and her arrest by the police. The author has recorded the changes in Joyce in a very short time and this makes her a little unconvincing. Nevertheless, the significant fact is that by the end of the story there is "a marked change and developing sense of commitment in the young woman" (Trump 351). The story also reveals the nobility of the young woman –a twenty five-year old girl. In the Introduction to *Some Monday for Sure*, Gordimer describes the girl as "experiencing her generation's equivalent of religious ecstasy in the comradeship of passive resistance action in the company of blacks" (n p). The moment of her arrest is the climax of the experience and perhaps at this moment she also feels the helplessness of the black. When the policeman comes to her, she looked at the helpless faces of the black African onlookers who stood near her. As the policeman came to her, she saw the faces of the blacks –two men, a small boy and a woman who were dressed in "ill-matched cast-offs of European clothing." They meet her gaze as she looked back at them.

> And she felt, suddenly, not nothing but what they were feeling, at the sight of her, a white girl, taken –incomprehensively, as they themselves were used to being taken –under the force of white men's wills, which dispensed and withdrew life, imprisoned and set free, fed or starved, like God himself ("The Smell of Death and Flowers", *Selected Stories* 134).

This passage from final paragraph of the story shows the young woman McCoy's involvement in the world around her and her sympathy for the black onlookers and the repressive condition of their life. Gordimer has outlined in the story McCoy's journey to political commitment and the inner struggle she has faced. Her politeness inherited from her family tradition and suggested by the smell of incense (death and flowers) moves her to join the anti-apartheid protest. The same smell or kindness returns to consciousness when she suffers inner struggle and decides to take part in the anti-apartheid demonstration. Gordimer seems to suggest the smell of death and flowers also suggests the possibility of a new life (flower).

In the pair of stories entitled "Town and Country Lovers" from the collection *A Soldier's Embrace* (*SE*), Gordimer examines the inter-racial relationship under the apartheid South Africa. The stories depict a white man having a sexual relationship with a black woman and show the failure of the relationship due to the intervention of the apartheid state. The first story introduces Dr. Franz-Josef von Leinsdorf, an Austrian geologist working for South African mining company. Like Toby Hood, he has no interest in politics of South Africa. One day he meets a coloured girl in the supermarket next to his apartment, who unexpectedly offers to help him by bringing razor-blades. As she goes to his apartment to deliver the blades, she, who lives in a township, experiences a new feeling: "She didn't wait for the lift marked GOODS but took the one meant for whites" (*SE* 76). After this initial meeting, an intimate relationship develops between them. They start living together almost like husband and wife though they are not seen together in public. He even begins to educate her with a view to promoting the coloured girl to "the white-collar category", considering her not-so-black skin (*SE* 76).

She dreams about a future with the white man –she would type notes for him, take him inside her body without saying anything and sit beside him in his car, like a wife. But their happy life comes to a halt abruptly as the police knock at the door one summer night. She immediately realises the danger and hides herself in the bedroom closet to save her. As Dr von Leinsdorf opens the door, the police inform him about the presence of the coloured girl, which is illegal under the apartheid laws (the Immorality Act, to be specific). The police ransack his room and eventually find out the girl. They took both of them to the police station and the girl is sent for medical examination to ascertain whether they have had sexual relation. A court-case has been filed by the authorities. The story ends in stylistic rupture as the court-case is narrated in the style of newspaper reporting. The couple is finally acquitted of the charges as the state failed to prove sexual relation had taken place.

Throughout the story the girl is not named. It suggests that she represents a vast majority of non-white people affected by the apartheid policies. In her attempt to move upward in life, she becomes a victim of the apartheid government. As Trinh T. Minh-Ha points out, the policy of separate development demands "you keep to your way of life and ethnic values *within the borders of your homelands* (italics original 247). The moment one steps out one's limits, they have to suffer.

2.2.2 The post-Sharpeville Fiction

The early fiction of Gordimer depicts the rise of liberal ideology or a liberal world. The characters make attempts to cross over the barriers of race. At the same time, the early fiction shows how the people are moving from a peaceful, non-violent struggle against apartheid to a radical solution to the oppression and injustice they face. The Sharpeville massacre is considered to be the turning point of this passive resistance. Kalu E. Ume has given a precise account of the historical incident and its consequences. The Pan Africanist Congress (PAC), which broke away from the African National Congress in 1959, launched a campaign of positive action against pass laws. On 21 March, 1960 all men left their passes at home and marched to the police station. They courted arrest and decided against bail and fines. Sharpeville, a township in the south of Johannesburg participated enthusiastically in this protest. About ten thousand people from this town marched to the police station. The police became nervous and

> opened fire on the weaponless Africans killing 67 and wounding 186 critically. This bloody and merciless repression was designated as the Sharpeville Massacre, a nadir of an unprecedented ruthlessness against peaceful demonstration. In Cape Town there was another shooting which left two Africans dead and 49 injured (quoted in Uledi- kamanga, 33-34).

The government declared a state of emergency on 30 March, 1961 and continued with mass arrests. This was followed by the banning of the ANC and the PAC. As a result of this measure, these two organizations went underground. On the other hand, the Africans were not cowed down by the police atrocities. On 16 December, they formed *Umkhonto We Sizwe* (Spear of the Nation) and urged the activists to indulge in the destruction of state property. The Africans intensified their resistance, at least sporadically. The government, on the other hand used the police forces to carry out unlawful arrest against the native South Africans.

Clingman calls this transition from passive to violent resistance "the first stage of the double movement of the 1960s" (93). He further elaborates that the second stage of the movement consists of the way in which the movement was crushed by force and brutality of the South African government. The government used the police as a tool of brutal force and repression. By 1963, most of the underground *Umkhonto* rebels including its leader, Nelson Mandela were arrested and then sentenced to life imprisonment in the famous Rivonia Trial in 1964.

Gordimer's fiction written after 1960 shows the fall or inadequacy of the liberal world to meet the historical realities of South Africa. The liberal ideology could not match with the apartheid policies. Hence the blacks and many liberal whites felt the necessity of revolutionary tactics such as sabotage. This new radical stance towards apartheid finds expression in the novels, *The Late Bourgeois World* (1966), *Burger's Daughter* (1979), and *July's People* (1981). *In Occasion for Loving*, Jessie hints at the possibility of helping someone blow up a power station. In *The Late Bourgeois World*, Max, a liberal white, blows up a post office. He is arrested and tried. Consequently he is sentenced to imprisonment for five years. But he turns a state witness after fifteen months and comes out of the prison. He commits suicide afterwards. The novel unfolds the events of a single day in the lives of the protagonist –Max's ex-wife Elisabeth. One morning Elisabeth is having her breakfast with her lawyer boy friend, Graham. Suddenly she receives a telegram informing her that Max drove his car into the sea and drowned himself along with his secret writings on "methodology of African Socialism" (*LBW* 67). Without wasting time Elisabeth visits her son Bobo in his school to break the news. She spends the day alone till the afternoon when she visits her grandmother. In the evening she is busy cooking for the black activist who visits her late night. In successive flashbacks, Elisabeth touches upon the key issues –her views about Max's politics, her affair with Graham and its implications for her son and the nature of her own emerging commitment. She remembers her being pregnant during the Defiance Campaign in 1952. The Sharpeville tragedy flashes through her mind. She remembers the declaration of the Communist Party as illegal, the formation of the Pan Africanist Congress and the confidence and prestige that African nationalism has gained in "the eyes of the world through the passive resistance campaigns" (Head 54). Her reflections capture her social marginalization and political alienation in the contemporary South Africa.

The novel is set against the backdrop of the sabotage campaign of a young group of white men connected with an organization called the National Committee for Liberation. Later it changed into the African Resistance Movement (ARM) and began an extended campaign of sabotage. Recalling her objective in writing the novel, Gordimer says: "My short novel *The Late Bourgeois World* was an attempt to look into the specific character of the social climate that produced the wave of young white saboteurs in 1963-64" (quoted in Clingman 96). Max may be said to be a representative of the African Resistance Movement and the movement itself represents the mood of the revolutionary moment – the failure of the liberal ideology and the desperation for a change. There was a growing distances between the blacks and the liberals for they (the blacks) thought that any African movement seeking mass support for liberation struggle cannot afford to have white members. It is in this context that Elisabeth says that there was a move among politically active Africans to keep out of the white houses and "to reject friendship and even intimacy with whites as a part of white privilege" (*LBW* 77). Gordimer herself experiences the historical reality of the period and therefore the African Resistance

Movement provided a logical point of focus for her in relation to her own historical and ideological development. However, Max defies the colour bar and becomes a member of a "Communist cell" (*LBW* 30) because of his unconventional and different attitude to life and society. He spends time with African and Indian students who take him to the locations and ghettoes. By the time his association with the black activists is disrupted, he associated himself with the people who wanted to organize a new underground white revolutionary group. That is, Max establishes contact with whites after his loss of contact with the blacks. This may be seen as an anticipation of the Black Consciousness Movement that rejects the participation of the whites in the African struggle because of their complicity in the white supremacy. Gordimer seems to comment on the ineffectiveness of the liberalism against the apartheid policies of the government. The protests and petitions of the liberal-minded whites have achieved nothing but they remarked on the inefficiency of the terrorists and senselessness of their attempts. They (the whites) cannot "unseat the great alabaster backside with a tin-pot bomb" (*LBW* 79). The police arrest some of the revolutionaries. Some others flee the country. Max finally commits suicide. His death may be said to signal the failure of the white radicals in the struggle against the apartheid. Gordimer questions Max's bourgeois attitude to life. She does not completely idealize his deviation from his parents' way of life. He dies perhaps because he has been over ambitious. As Elisabeth says he has the desire to win approval in all what he does. As he fails to become the centre of attention in his family, he revolts. And he revolts against his parents and the system represented by them. He appears to take upon the role of a saviour. This indicates his bourgeois egoism. He seems to inherit from his ancestors a rage to succeed and the necessity of a revengeful need to be acknowledged.

However, Gordimer seems to suggest, through Elisabeth, beyond this aspect (selfishness) of the character of Max. His revolutionary ideas cannot be totally ignored. Elisabeth appreciates what Max has been doing. Perhaps she understands, "The madness of the brave is the wisdom of life" (*LBW* 79). Even after their divorce, she supports him in his fight to overthrow the white regime. She feels that perhaps he didn't die for the anti-apartheid activists but perhaps he did more than that. On an earlier occasion when Elisabeth meets her son Bobo, she tells him that he (Max) went after the right things, even if perhaps it was in the wrong way. He has at least attempted to set the wrong right. The only thing is that in his attempt to love, he lost even his self respect. "If he failed, well, that's better than making no attempt" (*LBW* 19). Elisabeth is well aware of his limitations. She understands that Max was in a mess and that he could not deal with what had happened to him. This is because, she thinks, " he wasn't equal to the demands he took upon himself" (*LBW* 19). She further observes that he was stubborn to play in the first team but he was good enough to play for the third team only. His speech on the moral sclerosis in the wedding of his sister nicely captures his thought. He rejects the life and values of a white bourgeois world and has to lead a life of alienation and loneliness in the white society. He could have become a lawyer but all such professions are part of the white club and he had already torn up its life membership ticket. Elisabeth further contemplates that he would have been a good revolutionary if he had little more time to hone his political discipline. He takes one job after another. He leaves his first job because he would not be given three days' leave to attend a Trade Union Conference. It is a time when so many other things were happening all around South Africa. There were discussions, open-air meetings, demonstrations and study groups in the rooms of liberal whites like Elisabeth and in the black townships. Elisabeth further informs the reader that their group comprises Indian, African Coloured and white. Thus their rooms as well as the black townships are what Bhabha calls 'beyond' – transitory location from where one thinks of moving beyond a barrier. It is also the place of possible new ideas and new beginnings (McLeod 217). Elisabeth seems to suggests this when she says, "The future was already there; it was a matter of having the courage to announce it" (*LBW* 54). Defying the colour bar, Max goes to an African area prohibited to whites. He also visits Durban to camp with Africans and Indians on a public square in protest against segregation. Unfortunately, he experiences isolation not only from the whites but the blacks as well. Unlike other whites, says Elisabeth, he wanted to come close to the people and in South Africa the majority people are black. "Set aside with whites, even his own chosen kind, he was still left out, he experienced the isolation of his childhood become the isolation of his colour" (*LBW* 69). That is to say, he suffers alienation even in the midst of his own community.

As he shuns the path of the so-called white supremacy and joins the Defiance Campaign, Max is considered dead by his parents because their white identity is at stake and for them it is a question of prestige. His father who has been a prominent Member of Parliament comes from an English family which immigrated to South Africa when works in the gold mines began. His mother is a descendent of a Dutch family who has intermarriages with English speaking white people. The marriage between the Afrikaner and the man of English origin reflects the historical reality of South Africa – the union between two white classes. Max's mother is always conscious of her being a 'Boer girl'. when Mrs Van Den Sandt spoke of 'we South Africans' she meant the Afrikaans and English-speaking white people, and when his father, Theo Van Den Sandt called for a united South Africa, going forward to an era of progress and prosperity for all, he meant the unity of the same two white groups. The whites maintain their white supremacy through power and control over economic production. They, like Max's parents, behave with the African blacks in an act of "essentialising blackness" (Bhabha 4). Elisabeth has rightly pointed out,

> For the rest – the ten or eleven million 'natives' – their labour was directed in various Acts of no interest outside Parliament, and their lives were incidental to their labour, since until the white man came they knew nothing better than a mud hut in the veld (*LBW* 31).

So the life of the natives is valuable only because of their labour. That is the way they are recognized in South Africa. Before the arrival of the whites in South Africa, the natives "knew nothing better than a mud hut". This is, in Fanon's terminology, the 'othering', the process through which the blacks are seen in relation to the whites. The blacks are the 'other' in relation to the whites and they are valuable as long as they can serve the interest of the colonisers. Gordimer wonders at the Europeans' obsession with their racial superiority. In her interview with Alan Ross, she says that her struggle against the apartheid was her war: "the colour bar is wrong and utterly indefensible" (34) and therefore it must be opposed.

Elisabeth observes how Max's mother spoke Xhosa with her black servants and Afrikaans with her Coloured cook. Max's parents show their racism in more ways than one. Elisabeth refers to the fact how her father and she herself were complicit in the apartheid history of South Africa. She narrates how she met Max in the summer when she was helping her father at his shop. She was at the counter of fancy goods such as painted coasters for glasses, clocks and watches. She knew that the black men who bought the watches, paying from their small savings would return to the shop within a week because those watches did not work properly. She knows the sickening secret –the inferior quality of the stuff and

> that this quality of life was apparently what our fathers and grandfathers had fought two wars abroad and killed black men in 'native' wars of conquest here at home, to secure for us. (*LBW* 88-89).

The above passage shows Elisabeth's father's complicity with and even her own personal involvement in the economic exploitation of the blacks through 'shoddy materials' at her father's store. Dominic Head calls this "youthful political awakening" which is "associated with a sexual awakening" (84). Like the father-daughter duo, many South African whites explore every possible way for racial oppression.

Elisabeth has so far reflected upon Max as her ex-husband and as a revolutionary. This has been her past. Her present centres on her son, her grandmother and her boyfriend Graham Mill. She has an affair with Graham who is an advocate and older than herself. If Max takes the path of revolution and loses everything, Graham remains within system and works for possible change. He provides legal help in the court to people who are repressed by the state for anti-apartheid activities. He is one of those few lawyers who work in this line. However, Elisabeth's relationship with Graham is partial and incomplete. Elisabeth describes their affair as "not classified, labelled" (*LBW* 45). She does not want them to be regarded as a couple either. In fact, she even doubts if Graham is trying to form a lasting friendship by paying special attention to her son Bobo. She thinks that Graham tries to take the responsibility of the child as a means of creating some sort of surety for his relationship with her. So, she argues that it is not for nothing that he has a lawyer's mind. "If Bobo starts looking upon any man I'm friendly with as a father, it could be awkward if the friendship were to wane" (*LBW* 3). Elisabeth's personal relationship is ambivalent. She cannot clearly describe her relation with Graham: "A sexual connection. But there is more to it than that. A love affair? Less than that"(*LBW* 50). She has not been sure even about the nature of love between Max and herself. He wanted to please and make love with her. In fact, he demanded her approval and admiration for his every action. She also wanted to make love to Max. So, she tried to give him the approval he demanded because she wanted to please him. "What I wanted was for him to do the right things so that I could love him. Was that love" (*LBW* 70)?

In fact, relationships in the novel, particularly Elisabeth's affair with Graham, show their failure to establish any contact – personal or social. This is even more clearly seen when Graham asks her how she would describe the things as they are with them. She is caught off guard and she does not know how to respond. There is what she "can only describe as a power failure" between them (*LBW* 99). Graham's question is not only about their personal relationship but also about the contemporary age. Elisabeth becomes aware of the vacuum that exists in their relationship and the lack of social contact as well.

In his discussion of this novel, Dominic Head refers to Ernst Fischer's *The Necessity of Art* from which Gordimer borrows the title *The Late Bourgeois World*. In his book, Fischer examines the relationship between art and social reality, especially the relationship between content and form. He points out that 'truthful' art, in a decaying society, must reflect the social decay, and yet must also indicate the means of social improvement. Like all other novels of Gordimer *The Late Bourgeois World* examines the possibilities of social change in South Africa. But this is her first novel "in which the social decay is overtly reflected in the form . . ." (Head 79). Head further says that socialist art should present a hopeful and broad historical vision of the future and this is not found in the artists whom Fischer associates with the late bourgeois world. Gordimer writes and designs *The Late Bourgeois World* to represents a particular situation in South Africa. This is a situation of political uncertainty and failure of personal and social contact. And this is conveyed through the content and form of the novel. The narrative reproduces a situation of political uncertainty which makes the path of progressive action very difficult. Seen apparently the novel appears to be negative in its vision of the future. But it has a deeper significance. To overcome the complex situation, Elisabeth has to face manifestations of the nuclear age, "the apocalyptic view which Fischer requires art to get beyond in offering an alternative vision of the future" (Head, 85). Elisabeth has been in a complex situation. She is trying to come to terms with it and at the same time find a way beyond it. The novelist conveys this through the Luke – Elisabeth episode. On insistence of Luke to provide him a bank account which he can use to transfer funds from abroad, the bank account of her grandmother comes to her mind. She does not tell Luke about it at that moment. But she begins to think about it. Perhaps she discovers the possibility of using it and thereby participating in the underground black politics. The use of her dying grandmother's bank account to transfer money for the underground blacks is a crucial act of subversion of the bourgeois institutions – here the bank. This hints at Elisabeth's acceptance of the black leaders' radical movement. She recalls her grandmother asking her repeatedly "what happened" and she says "well that's what's happened" (*LBW*, 141). She, perhaps, realizes that there are possibilities for her but she does not know under what stone (*LBW* 79). No doubt, this is an act of minimum personal commitment on her part. But, as she admits, a white woman who is sympathetic to blacks does not have anything to offer except the connection she has to the good old white Reserve bank. She also knows that it was quite possible he would make love to her next time he visits her. She thought she should accept his proposal gratefully because in that case "we shan't owe each other anything, each will have given what he has, and neither is to blame if one has more to give than the other" (*LBW* 142). With this idea she keeps awake a long time at night as her heart beats 'afraid, alive, and afraid, alive'. The passage also points to the cross racial sexual relationships between Elisabeth and blacks. She confesses that she has had a black lover some years ago. Max also had sexual relationships with several women, such as Eve King and Roberta Weininger. As in *Occasion for Loving*, Gordimer has often used the cross-racial relationship to resist the racial segregation.

The uncertain or reluctant commitment of Elisabeth reflects the social conditions of South Africa in the early 1970s. The position of the liberals was made politically untenable. Gordimer's short fiction of this period also reveals that liberalism can no longer be effective against apartheid and that cross racial relationship is impossible. Her stories, "Open House" and "Africa Emergent" depict this social reality of South Africa. The story, "Open House" opens with Frances Taver, a liberal white woman who is an activist for black rights. She belongs with a group of people who wanted to discover the "truth about South Africa" (*SS* 375). Most of her political friends are in jail. She organizes a meeting between a visiting American journalist and three black men of the town. The journalist wants to prepare a report on the country's political situation from the perspective of the blacks. Hence wants to interact with the blacks. But the few blacks he meets are deceptive and opportunistic. The blacks he should have met have been in jail or have gone underground. The few blacks available for interaction are corrupted by the system, the white woman tells the journalist. She warns him not to be "taken in" by them because corruption is real. She further explains "Being phoney is being corrupted by the situation . . . and that's real enough" (SS 386). Frances as a host of the lunch meeting is in a good position to reflect upon the social and political situation of South Africa in the 1970s. Thus, she observes the changes in the social climate and narrates that a few years before it had been "fun and easy" to arrange meeting for visitors which would turn into a party. The visitor would enjoy "learning to dance the kwela with black girls . . . he couldn't remember finding where there were *no* laws against the mixing of races" (SS 376). Then two paragraphs later in the story she points out that people did not want to talk any more. Even if they did something, it would not be talked about. The people whom the visitor or any journalist wanted to see were "shut away" (SS 378).

The story, "Africa Emergent" portrays the betrayal of trust as well as the uncertainty in the society. This story about the apartheid state is distinguished by the fact that the story is told by a liberal white man. The narrator talks about his friendship with two men who are black. One of his friends commits suicide in the USA and the other ends up in detention in South Africa. Early on the story the narrator talks about friendship between whites and blacks. They hardly knew what they could do and what could not. They were, perhaps, passing through a condition of interregnum. Later in the story, the liberal white man observes that 'trust' became a commodity on sale to the police. He regrets that they had reached a stage where if a literate black man had "'political" friends and white friends *and* a passport, he must be considered a police spy' (*SS* 434). People believed in the integrity of a black man only when he ended up in jail. The narrator ironically comments that the white friends could purge themselves of the shame of rumours. They were satisfied that the black man was in 'prison'. "He's proved himself, hasn't he" (*SS* 434)? Gordimer has directed bitter irony at the whites in these last sentences of the story. Martin Trump observes that Gordimer has depicted a picture of "a fractured society" through the stories "Open House" and "Africa Emergent". However, one more important thing that these stories imply is that blacks and whites continue to mix even at the time of uncertainty. Against the apartheid practice of keeping the races separate, Gordimer's fiction often shows the mixed gathering and thus suggests the possibility of resistance.

Gordimer's sixth novel *The Conservationist* (1974) responds to the contemporary historical situation in South Africa through its rich texture. It proves to be prophetic in its prediction of the political change –the transfer of power from the white to the black South Africans. Clingman describes the novel as having a "strong sense of history" (140). In this novel, Gordimer engages with the restlessness and alienation of the contemporary white South Africans through the central character, Mehring who belongs with the minority group that continues their dominance of the land and thereby maintain the white supremacy. Mehring is rich and has all the privileges that white South Africa can offer. He purchases a farm in the rural South Africa and enforces the apartheid laws. He represents the white European settlers for whom the whole world is theirs. Intelligent as he is, he uses the farm as a means to connect to the African land and gain tax benefit. Another motive behind his purchase of the farm is to secure a place to bring women. Through this Gordimer seems to suggest a "parallel between geographical and sexual acquisition and power" (Head 100). He spends Sundays on the farm to get a break from his busy city life. This also provides him a space to think upon his sensual attitude to the women in his life, his prejudices against the South African blacks and his moral distance from his son. But when he leaves the farm, he takes away "the empty space that was clear in him this afternoon" (*CN* 61). He only pretends to be conservationist.

In contrast to Mehring, the black Africans have a natural attachment to the land. Mehring understands that Jacobus honestly manages the farm and that he (Jacobus) does have a sense of attachment to the place. This is evident in Jacobus's effective management of the farm in the absence of Mehring. He acknowledges that blacks will continue to live on the farm long after he is dead. He knows well that they were here when he came. He wonders, "they were squatting God knows how long before he bought the place and they'll expect to have their grand children squatting long after he's gone" (*CN* 243). On the other hand, Gordimer portrays Mehring's son, Terry, as homosexual. This may be seen as suggesting a sense of discontinuity for Mehring, or for that matter, sterility of the white settlers in South Africa. He wishes to plant European trees on the farm to make sure his connection with and continuity in South Africa. But his wishes prove futile. He himself tells, though sarcastically, his mistress Antonia that he is planting European chestnuts for the blacks to use as firewood when they take over the farm. Earlier Antonia reminds him that the four hundred acres is not going to be handed down to his children's children, not even to his children. She tells him,

"That bit of paper you bought yourself from the deed office isn't going to be valid for as long as another generation. . . The blacks will tear up your bit of paper. No one'll remember where you're buried" (*CN* 210).

Antonia predicts the future of South Africa. Gordimer weaves the texture of the novel that reveals not only the 'inside' of Mehring but also the future of South Africa. In fact, Gordimer's novels from *The Conservationist* onward are concerned with the future of South Africa.

Gordimer's characterization of Antonia has often attracted attention of the critics. Antonia has taunted Mehring for his self interested engagement in capitalist life and style. But at the end she escapes from South Africa with the help of Mehring and takes shelter in the U.K. Gordimer seems to ask why Antonia, the liberal does not find any place for herself in South Africa. In her interview with Grey, Gordimer says that life in South Africa under apartheid is covered with "incredible layers of concealment" (Grey 265). She has frequently criticized the white liberals to unmask the pretences of white liberal attitudes. In her characterization of Antonia, she has unmasked the latter's liberal attitudes. Clingman remarks that liberalism as shown in *The Conservationist* is created within and by capitalist society (145). Antonia who is Mehring's mistress is symbolic in this regard. When Antonia is detained, she turns to Mehring to obtain the service of his company lawyer for defence, and this shows ultimately her own collusion with the oppressive regime.

As in many modernist novels, in this novel Gordimer employs the stream of consciousness to capture the internal drama of Mehring. Gordimer represents him as psychologically alienated from the white South African community. He has no relationship with other people and no one to talk to. Hence he often takes recourse to interior monologues. He is conditioned by a lack of contact with South African people –both white and black. Apartheid has even isolated the white from the land and the people as well. The fluidity of the narrative method captures his psychic confusion and alienation. Thus, for example, Mehring's final interior monologue that captures issues, growing around his characters:

> He's going to run, run and leave them to rape her or rob her. She'll be all right. They survive everything. Coloured or poor white, whichever she is, their brothers or fathers take their virginity good and early. . . . no no no. No no, what nonsense, what is there to fear. . . No, no, no. RUN.

> --Come. Come and look, they're all saying. What is it? What's it? It's Mehring. It's Mehring, down there (*CN* 320).

The focus in this passage is on the psychic confusion and disintegration of Mehring. It portrays Mehring's habits of sexual and geographical exploitation, and his underlying fear of being discovered by the police and his subsequent arrest for violating the Immorality Act. This instantly produces in him a feeling to give the farm –'the whole four hundred acres' –as compensation.

Mehring's feeling of fear and guilt is intensified by the presence of the black man's corpse discovered in his farm. If Mehring represents the whites, the body stands for the blacks. It is symbol of everyman who is a victim of apartheid abuses. Its emergence may be said to indicate eventual transfer of South Africa's rule to the blacks. Hence Mehring's desire to conserve the land over which he has no right and his mental deterioration following the discovery of the black body collapse by the end of the novel. Dominic Head points out that the body assumes symbolic significance as Mehring's 'Other', and eventually it resurfaces after a storm displacing Mehring. In Gordimer's politics of the body, this is her most extravagant extrapolation. A single body or a corpse is "'disinterred' in a development which symbolizes the end of black African dispossession" (Head 100). In this sense, the body may be said to decolonize the farm.

However, the presence of the body disturbs and keeps Mehring haunting throughout the narrative. Finally, by the end of the novel, a storm blows in and the body resurfaces out of mud in the third pasture of the farm. This threatens Mehring's psychological condition and ultimately breaks him down. On the other hand, the blacks on the farm claim the body and give it a burial with proper rituals. This final ceremonial and respectful burial of the body symbolises Africans claim over the land. The Africans claim the body as one of their own. The body which the farm received bears no name and he had no family. But the women of the farm wept a little for him. "They had put him away to rest, at last; he had come back. He took possession of this earth, theirs; one of them" (*CN* 323). Though the body had no child but the children of the black would come to live there after him.

In this context it will be relevant to refer to Gordimer's short story, "Six Feet of the Country". In this story, a black worker from Rhodesia dies and the authorities disposed off the body, assuming it to be unknown in the area. But the local farm workers wish to bury the body according to their custom. They could get back the body with the help of the farm owner. But the wrong body is returned. They discover the deception only when the father of dead worker, who travelled from the distant Rhodesia for the funeral, complains that the body is too heavy to be that of his son. The story mainly implies that even six feet of South Africa is not available to the blacks in their death. But in the 1974 novel, the body returns to receive a proper burial according to customs of the land and this time the body claims more than six feet of the country. Thus, Gordimer challenges the apartheid by envisioning a reversal of role of the white and the black in South Africa through the figure of the body. So Clingman observes that the novel is prophetic; its vision is one of historical transfer of land or power to the blacks. The action of the novel suggests a point where the white history comes to an end and black history marks a beginning.

> Referring to the return of the body, almost the very last words of novel, 'he had come back' . . . are a direct paraphrase of the great rallying cry of the African National Congress in the 1950s: 'Afrika Mayibuye!' ('Africa! May it come back!') (Clingman 141)

Thus, Gordimer imaginatively represents historical records through her fiction. Though imaginative or fictional representation has often been questioned, her fiction affirms the assumptions of the new historicism that history and literature or culture are interdependent and that literary texts call into question existing vision and power relations of society.

Land has been a vital tool of power and authority. It has been a means of constructing identity in colonial history. In the South African context, it is very significant as separate areas were allotted for the South African blacks to continue with the political programme of racial segregation. The farm is an important site of origin because farms capture the essence of the settler aspect of a white colonial expansion. In a conversation with Robert Boyers, Gordimer herself admits that the landscape is an important character in *The*

Conservationist (13). Land or for that matter nature is a powerful force. Nature, if hostile and rebellious, can resist colonisation. As Fanon points out in *The Wretched of the Earth*, colonisation becomes successful when the docile nature has finally been tamed (cited in Nasr, 7-8). The storm that blows over Mehring's farm and raises the body stands for the struggling force of nature. It is also an important symbol of the African culture.

Mehring's exploitative nature is seen in his sexual behaviour as well. In his imaginary conversation with his mistress, Antonia, he admits that there is "special pleasure in having woman you've paid" (*CN* 83). Antonia describes this as his 'sexual fascism'. Mehring's impulses of sexual exploitation are seen in his frequent erotic imaginings about young girls and women –such as his desire for the young daughter of a dinner hostess or his desire for seduction of his colleague's daughter whom he meets in a coffee bar. A most significant and relevant scene of this kind is the one which occurs in one of Mehring's business flights when he molests a young girl seating next to him in the plane. The scene may be interpreted as Mehring's sexual colonialism. Dominic Head argues that here in this scene landscape merges in Mehring's mind with the body of the young girl as object of sexual desire. It is significant that the girl does not speak throughout the journey while Mehring keeps 'fingering' or probing her body beneath her blanket. The body of the girl becomes the land as he explores it. Throughout the night "he encountered the soundless O of the little mouth that made no refusal" (*CN* 151). The girl's 'soundlessness' confirms that this is Mehring's narrative, that the power of speech belongs to him. But a sudden fear takes hold of him when he checks out at the immigration centre, fearing that the girl might denounce him finding her voice. This episode on the plane is a kind of vacuum because it is "happening nowhere" (*CN* 150) and that this is suggestive of "Mehring's own vacuous nature, socially and politically" (Head, 103). This is the result of his alienation from the white minority society in South Africa.

Along with this narrative – the story of Mehring, Gordimer employs a subtext that subverts the apparently main text. The narrative is interspersed with ten excerpts from Henry Callaway's book, *The Religious System of the Amazulu*. In her brilliant analysis of the quotations, Judie Newman shows that the quotations are the "organizing points for a subtext which slowly comes into the foreground. The story appears to be that of Mehring and of the white in South Africa, but reveals itself as that of the blacks" (56). Each quotation either initiates or complements an event in the novel. The quotations begin with prayers for corn and for children and continuation of life, which is expected in the fourth or fifth year of drought. Another series of excerpts is taken from a dream by one of Callaway's informants who dreams that he is awoken and asked to go down to the river along with his brother to fight with a spirit ancestor. This may be linked to the event in the novel in which Solomon is awakened in the night and attacked. Solomon is attacked because of his debt. This may be seen as suggestive of his failure to pay the debt to his African culture. Two later quotations introduce the image of the 'Amatongo', the ancestors who are beneath the earth. This can be linked to the dead man buried in the firm. The final quotation suggests the occupation of the land by the blacks.

According to Newman, the function of the quotations is to suggest that "there is a buried logic of fictional events, which may be expressed in the rhetoric of myth" (56). Newman further summarizes the main events in the novel: the drought, the discovery of body in the third pasture, the attack on Solomon, the spirit of Phineas's wife, the flood, and the reburial of the dead man. This subtext is buried like the black man and rises to the surface of the novel, displacing Mehring and his story. The farm worker discovers the dead man in a reed bed. His body is not "actually on the earth at all, but held slightly above it on a nest of reeds it has flattened..." (*CN* 9). Newman finds parallel between this situation and the myth of origins in *The Religious System of the Amazulu*. Callaway mentions that the cult of ancestors is connected with a bed of reeds. A father stands for 'Uthlanga' or ancestor of his children, and 'Uthlanga' is a reed. The nest of reeds, suggests the guinea, which Mehring tries to conserve. The novel opens with the image of guinea fowl eggs set out before a half circle of children. Thus, in the beginning itself the fundamental question of the novel –'Who shall inherit Africa?' –is set out in terms of Zulu myth. Continuing her discussion, Newman further says that the improper burial of the dead man conditions the later events: Solomon's attack, the fire and images of the rain bird, which are organized into a coherent pattern of Zulu belief. In the dead black's funeral in the end of the novel, female members of the sect of Zion are seen in the background. They are a breakaway sect from the orthodox Christianity –a sect in which Christian tenets have been adapted to indigenous patterns of thought. In other words Gordimer provides a formal shape to the novel through Zulu myth. The novelist conveys a message different from the public rhetoric of South Africa. "One meaning of the title has thus been indicated: the blacks conserve their beliefs, and their beliefs conserve and regenerate the land and its people" (Newman, 59). By integrating the Zulu myth into text, Gordimer problematises the stream of consciousness of Mehring's story and repossesses South Africa. This new historical method may be called a cross fertilization of European form and African culture.

It is ironical that in his concern for the extinction of African life, Mehring overlooks the fact that the blacks' existence inside and around the farm is an integral part of South African landscape. The blacks have been displaced from their land and subjected to live a life in unnatural conditions in the nearby Location. This has been possible because, as Fanon argues in his book *The Wretched of the Earth*, centuries of subjection have caused irreparable psychological damage. This is seen in the character of Jacobus. On knowing the arrival of Mehring, Jacobus runs to him but stops at a distance "as if there were a line drawn there, ten feet away from the farmer goes through the formalities of greeting, which include a hand-movement as if he had a hat to remove" (*CN* 4). This shows the social as well as psychological barriers penetrating into the heart of the blacks and the whites.

Gordimer has assessed and often put to test the liberals against the resistance movements in South Africa. Some have failed to live up to the expectations such as Ann in *Occasion for Loving* while some others show commitment in their fight against apartheid. In *The late Bourgeois World*, Max fails as a white revolutionary but Elisabeth commits to the cause of anti-apartheid. In *Burger's Daughter*, Gordimer examines Rosa, the daughter of a resistance hero. In delineating the past and present of Rosa, Gordimer narrates the history of South Africa. Rosa is a product of and is situated in a complex historical situation in which the personal cannot be separated from the public – the realities of the South African police state and the black African struggle. *Burger's Daughter* shows, through the life of Rosa, how the destiny of a nation plays a crucial role in private lives.

According to Judie Newman, Gordimer's novel *Burger's Daughter* is a historical and cultural document in its content and in its own history of censorship (10). The novel is written against the backdrop of the anti-apartheid struggle. There are references to actual events and people including Nelson Mandela and Soweto Revolt. Lionel was born in 1905, the year of the revolt against the Czar; he married Cathy Burger during the 1946 African mineworkers strike; and their daughter Rosa was born in May 1948, the very month the Afrikaner National Party assumed power. Rosa grows during the apartheid South Africa. The stages in her life are marked by the 1956 Treason trial and the 1960 Sharpeville massacre. Gordimer has employed postmodernist strategies and blurred the boundaries between fiction and reality. Many perspectives are presented, along with inserting texts from real documents. The mixing of the real with the imaginary creates parallels to actual events and lives. Alongside the dominant white world, Gordimer constructs a world in the novel that envisions a multicultural society of South Africa. Thus, says Bruce King, the novel acquires a 'baroque structure' in which, despite the focus on Rosa Burger's story, other stories, perspectives, voices and historical events intrude to disrupt and impinge on the narrative (7). King further says that in *Burger's Daughter* fragmentation replaces unity of narrative, as the social order is itself in disarray and moral imperatives require its destruction.

The novel is set in South Africa between 1948, the year the Afrikaner dominated Nationalist Party came to power, and 1976, the year of the Soweto Revolt. The history of South Africa covering this period is unfolded through the lives of Rosa Burger and her father Lionel Burger, a great communist leader. Rosa tells about her past, her childhood through her present in a quest for self-definition. In this process she first distances herself from the tradition or commitment of her family but finally comes back to it and ultimately goes to jail. The personal and the public get twinned. Thus, when the story opens, Rosa is seen outside the gate of a prison waiting to visit her mother who had been imprisoned before her father for their anti-apartheid activities. In this public scene Rosa also conveys a private message. She is experiencing menstrual cramps for the first time. 'Standing "in that public place on that public occasion," Rosa makes a small gesture to express her private self' (Cooke, 85). However, after her mother, her father was also arrested and imprisoned and he died in the jail. Both her parents were members of the Communist Party of South Africa which had been resisting the apartheid regime. Throughout the novel Rosa has been assessed and measured in relation to her father who has a significant personal history. In a sense her father 'betrayed' his people because he was an Afrikaner. He went against his own people and became a member of the Communist Party of South Africa (later South African Communist Party) which was the only party to admit blacks into its membership as equals and resist the apartheid regime. Burger had been a member of its Central Committee throughout 1940s and 50s when the party dissolved itself in the face of the Suppression of Communism Act (1950). He was captured in the mid-1960s and sentenced to imprisonment for life and he died in the 1970s. Thus the fictional career of Lionel coincided with most of the major developments in the struggle against the apartheid regime in South Africa in the second half of the twentieth century. In fact, Lionel represents the "best heritage" in the white revolutionary tradition (Clingman 172). Gordimer reflects upon the resistance movements through the novel: censorship, ban, arrest and jail of the resistance leaders. The following lines concisely capture the historical situation:

> . . . the camps, concentration, labour, resettlement, the Siberias
> of snow or sun, the lives of Mandela, Sisulu, Mbeki, Kathrada,
> Kgosana, gull-picked on the Island, Lionel propped wasting to
> his skull between warders, the deaths by questioning, bodies
> fallen from the height of John Vorster Square . . . (*BD* 211)

In fact, in *Burger's Daughter* the correspondences between fiction and history are close. The character of Lionel Burger is largely based on Bram Fischer, a leader of the South African Communist Party, about whom Gordimer had written two articles at the time of his arrest and trial. She unequivocally admired his heroism, which is quite evident in the essay, "Why did Bram Fischer Choose Jail?" Fischer was the defence lawyer of Nelson Mandela. However, as Clingman has pointed out, Gordimer has been more concerned with capturing "the *spirit* of a man like Fischer represented" (172). Lionel in the novel is a doctor. But the political careers of both Fischer and Lionel are quite similar. A traditional Marxist, he saw the solution to human problems in social terms, and he was personally warm and sociable, maintaining an open house around the swimming pool, just as Lionel does. Lionel's house which is open to both whites and blacks is a symbol of resistance to the apartheid regime which keeps people separate through what Foucault calls classification and surveillance. Like Fischer, before being sentenced, Lionel made a moving speech describing how he, as a medical student, had been saddened and brought to defy the law by the evils of South African society. As a medical student, he is not tormented by the suffering he saw in hospitals. He is pained at the humiliation of human beings they face in their daily life. He points out the contradictions of his people, the Afrikaners and the whites who, on one hand, "worship the God of Justice" and, on the other hand, "practise discrimination on grounds of the colour of skin" (*BD* 19). He laments that this contradiction has split the very foundation of his life. He continues further

> Black men, women and children living in the miseries of insecurity, poverty and degradation on the farms where I grew up, and in the "dark Satanic mills" of the industry that brought their labour cheap and disqualified them by colour from organizing themselves or taking part in the successive governments that decreed their lot as eternal inferiors, if not slaves . . . (*BD* 20).

Lionel has been fighting a crucial battle against the apartheid. His speech vividly shows the racism, hypocrisy and double standard of the white government. His defence speech from the dock contains passages from Bram Fischer's defence speech. There are in the novel extracts from Marx, Lenin and Steve Biko. Most often these passages are quoted without any textual markers or acknowledgement. Thus, says Clingman, Marx's statement – world history would be very easy to make if the struggle were take up only on condition of infallibly favourable chances – is given in a footnote in Joe Slovo's essay, "South Africa –no middle road". But it is quoted without attributing it to Marx. This statement expresses the "central sentiment" of Lionel Burger's speech from the dock (187). Gordimer incorporates words or texts from other sources in this way. In her article, "What I say will not be understood: Intertextuality as a subversive force in Nadine Gordimer's *Burger's Daughter*", Susan Barrett argues that Gordimer uses intertexuality as a force of subversion (116). It helps her make political statement to disseminate ideas, to encourage people to think and thereby to lead them to question the status quo.

However, the novel is not about Lionel Burger only, it is also about Burger's daughter, Rosa. The novelist is more concerned with the predicament faced by the inheritor of a revolutionary tradition in the context of South Africa in the 1970s. "Precisely because Lionel Burger is a recognizable type of historical figure, this is what enables Gordimer to explore most imaginatively through Rosa" (Clingman 174). In his fight against the apartheid, Lionel has inculcated the revolutionary attitude in his daughter Rosa. In fact, the very house of Lionel is a symbol of resistance. People across colour line are allowed and accepted in the house. Rosa helps her father in this fight, at least until his death. As the novel opens, we see the fourteen year old Rosa waiting outside a prison to deliver goods to her mother. The novelist reminds the reader that she had already taken in her mother's role in the household. And the household Rosa takes over is better described as a political institution than a family.

In the process of her parents' opposition to apartheid, Rosa has to sacrifice her desires and her freedom. Her parents' preoccupation with the struggle of the communists makes them forget their daughter's choices and desires. Their concern for others is as important as for Rosa. As Jan Mohammed points out, this is brilliantly epitomized in the Rosa and Noel de Witt episode. Noel de Witt is a young communist who has been imprisoned. He has no family. So Rosa's parents encourage her to visit him as his fiancée to pass communication between Noel and the network of the Communist Party. But Rosa is actually in love with Noel though she does not admit this to her parents or to Noel because she does not want to harm the anti-apartheid cause. She continues to visit him for years concealing her real desire within herself. She recollects this episode with regret and irony. She even accuses of "having prostituted herself to political necessity." However, she soon realizes that in the Burger house prostitutes are not despised as they are products of economic necessity. So, her "father's ethos even deprives her of self contempt" (JanMohamed, "The Degeneration" 121). She lost her freedom and identity. So after her father's death she feels, "Now you are free" (*BD* 35). She embarks on a quest for identity after her father's death and attempts to renounce her heritage to assert her identity. Rosa's self analysis is encouraged by her lover, Conrad. She lives with him after her father's death in the garden cottage. The time she spent with Conrad in the cottage provides her the space and time to think about herself rather than about the revolution that her father and his comrades hope for. Conrad's bourgeois values and experiences cause her look into herself and examine her heritage which privileges the public interests over her personal desires. He tells her that she has "grown up entirely through other people. What they told you was appropriate to feel and do. How did you begin to know yourself" (*BD* 41)? Conrad makes her understand personal relationship in a perspective. But this does not indicate her rejection of the Burger way – her heritage. With hindsight Rosa defends the Burgers' conception of the personal. She says that the 'creed' of her father's house that discounted the kind of individualism advocated by Conrad. They (Burger and his comrades) made a communism for 'local conditions'. The white people in that house had a connection with blacks that was completely personal. And thus, Rosa argues,

> their Communism was the antithesis of anti-individualism. The connection was something no other whites ever had in quite the same way. *A connection without reservations on the part of blacks or whites.* The political activities and attitudes of that house came from the inside outwards (emphasis added, *BD* 170-71).

Head comments that the above passage anticipates the conclusion that the novels seems to arrive at: "a genuine and politically motivated ethos of personal interaction is the securest foundation of an anti-racist opposition" (115). A motivated personal commitment for public responsibility can resist the apartheid in South Africa.

When Rosa along with Orde Greer has been going to Orlando, she comes across a black township which can be described, to use Foucault's term, as 'heterotopia'. Heterotopias are sites of differences and resistance. They are different from and yet have links with other social spaces. As Foucault points out, they have "the curious property of being in relation with all other sites, but in such a way as to suspect, neutralize, or invert the set of relations that they happen to designate, mirror, or reflect" ("Of Other Spaces", 24). These spaces are linked with other spaces and yet contradict all other sites. Thus heterotopias are the sites of social difference as well as social struggle. Dominic Head observes that the black urban experience in South Africa, especially the black township life, demonstrates dispossession as well as repression. "Yet it also contains a seed of something more positive, as . . . an implicit challenge to governmental control of urbanization" (29). In his 'Introduction' to the book (a collection of essays), *The Apartheid City and Beyond*, David Smith quotes a passage describing a township and discuss the nature of heterotopias. The narrator says whenever she had crossed the line separating the whites form the blacks, she found "a black leaves a white and goes to his 'place'". And she saw the physical divide of clean streets become rutted roads and city centres become the veld dumped with twisted metal and a perpetual autumn of blowing paper. The description continues as follows

> These restless broken streets where definitions fail –the houses the out houses of white suburbs, two-windows-one-door, multiplied in institutional rows . . . first thrown out by the white man and then picked over by the black – is this conglomerate urban or rural? . . . The enormous backyard of the whole white city, where categories and functions lose their ordination and logic . . . (*BD* 147-48)

Smith appreciates Gordimer's description that presents the geopolitical issues and "captures something of both the life and the landscape of apartheid" (1). Gordimer raises the questions how this 'place' can be defined –a rural or an urban area. She seems to understand the possibility of going beyond the deprivation or limitation imposed on the inhabitants: "a 'place'; a position whose contradictions those who impose them don't see, and from which will come a resolution they haven't provided for" (*BD* 149). Urbanization in South Africa, despite its deprivation, is a challenge to the policies of the apartheid regime. The expansion of urban settlement leads to their failure of spatial control. On the other hand, presence of blacks in the area adjoining the city is required for necessary workforce. There is a self-defeating element in this contradiction.

After her father's death, Rosa wants to use her newfound freedom to become herself, that is, to fulfil her most private desires. But to do so she would have to discard her past, her parents, and her values. That is, she would have to reject herself as she is at the moment. Although Rosa is critical of her parents' legacy, she does not rush to the apparent freedom of bourgeois society which she believes to have its own ideological imprisonment. She finds little to choose between Communism and capitalism. So she hesitantly decides to leave South Africa. Her hesitation is overcome by an incident, "an epiphanic experience of cruelty, a merciless beating of a donkey" by a black peasant (JanMohamed, "The degeneration" 123). This scene recalls some earlier texts. Louise Yelin in her book *From the Margins of Empire* provides a parallel reading with *Crime and Punishment* and Olive Schreiner's *The Story of an African farm* (Yelin 121-25). Elaborating further the incident, JanMohamed says that Rosa is aware that she could easily stop this violence but she refuses to do so because she feels that this specific instance of pain is a product of whole chain of torture. The man's cruelty is the result of his own suffering and frustration produced by the apartheid system of South Africa. Rosa sees her own complicity with the system. So Rosa says: "If somebody's going to be brought to account, I am accountable for him, to him, as he is for the donkey. Yet the suffering – while I saw it it was the sum of suffering to me" (*BD* 212). The scene is symbolic of a broader political situation and thus the personal is linked with the public. South Africa becomes the embodiment of human grief, and Rosa cannot tolerate this. She decides to leaves: "After the donkey I couldn't stop myself. I don't know how to live in Lionel's country" (*BD* 213). So, she leaves South Africa, and by extension, the world of moral responsibility. She secures a passport with the help of Brandt Vermeulen and leaves for France.

Rosa's stay in Europe forms the second part of the novel. She stays with her father's first wife Katya in Nice, France. Released from the responsibility and the harsh reality of South Africa, she is changed. She is happier and carefree whose only imperatives are pleasure and loyalty to friends. Rosa thinks that the major merit of this life is tolerance: no one expects her to be more than what she is or seems to be, whereas her comrades in South Africa expected her to be 'equal to everything'. Her involvement in the Communist Party and her heritage are replaced by a life of all pleasures and her passionate love for a married man, Bernard Chabalier. Dominic Head argues that Rosa's attention to the self "facilitates a growth that is preliminary to a successful return to the social world" (118). She takes pleasure in becoming Bernard's mistress, not wife. This is perhaps because mistress, unlike the position of the wife, has no obligations. This is quite opposite to her father's other -oriented ethos.

History is a dialogue between the past and the present. So far Gordimer has dealt with the past. In the first part of the novel Rosa re-evaluates her past –her heritage and her need of self-expression. Her present comprises her life in France in an effort to 'defect' from her father and finally her active involvement in the resistance to apartheid in South Africa. Clingman observes that the present to which *Burger's Daughter* responded is the movement of Black Consciousness and its culmination in the Soweto Revolt. On 16 June 1976, thousands of schoolchildren gathered at Orlando West Junior Secondary School in Soweto to protest against the enforced use of Afrikaans as a medium of instruction in black schools. The protest began peacefully but by the time it ended two children were killed by the police. Many more deaths followed. Soon the uprising spread over other parts of the country. The underground activists resorted to violence and destruction. It turned out to be one of the most "climactic periods of modern South African history, as an unexpected phase of resistance burst with extraordinary intensity" (Clingman 180). Clingman further suggests that it was not only a sustained episode of cultural but also political resistance. The immediate cause of the revolt was the issue of the use of Afrikaans in schools and it gave impetus to the Black Consciousness movement, with its emphasis on cultural revival and assertion of black dignity and identity. The black started believing that they must be conscious of and celebrate their blackness and that they alone should fight against the apartheid regime. The white liberals could not genuinely fight against the white government, the blacks thought. However, the revolt made a far reaching impact in the South African society. Many, young and adult, died violently during the revolt. Among them was the Black Consciousness leader Steve Biko. Indeed, the Soweto Revolt occupied a central place in the history of resistance to the apartheid South Africa.

Towards the end of her stay in France, Rosa visits London to attend a party given in honour of the resistance activists. In the party she comes across Baasie, the black boy who had been like her brother and with whom she spent her childhood. She wants to talk to him but he refuses to recognize her. Later at night he phones her and expresses his anger and vengeance. He is angry at the way she is honoured. He resents that her father, Lionel is praised as a resistance hero while hundreds of black men like his father are neglected and forgotten. When Rosa tries to interrupt and addresses him as 'Baasie', he becomes furious at her use of his name 'Bassie' (meaning 'little boss'), given by the Burgers. He retorts that his real name is Zwelinzima Vulindlela (meaning 'suffering land') as if he is the embodiment of the suffering of his race and of his community. Rosa repeatedly tires to re-establish their personal relationship but in vain. Baasie insists upon her to see the racial difference. He tells satirically that everybody in the world should be told that her father was hero and that how much he suffered for the blacks. On the other hand, there are dozens of black men suffered and died like dogs but nobody noticed them. So, he reminds Rosa:

> Listen, there are dozens of our fathers sick and dying like dogs, kicked out of the locations when they can't work any more. Getting old and dying in prison. Killed in prison. It's nothing. I know plenty blacks like Burger. It's nothing, it's us, we must be used to it … (*BD* 328)

The confrontation between Rosa and Baasie is short like the one between Gideon and Jessie in *Occasion for Loving* at the end of the novel. But this is a more significant scene in the fiction of Gordimer when considered in the context of resistance movements in South Africa in the 1970s. It epitomises the oppression of the blacks and their rejection of the whites' collaboration in the struggle for liberation. The accusation of Baasie reflects the accusations of the Black Consciousness. Gordimer allows Baasie or, for that matter, the blacks speak in their own voice. Thereby she shows the emerging resistance voice that will dominate or, at least, will be heard in the South Africa of near future. This voice is also echoed early in the novel. At Fats Mxange's party some young blacks reject the class analysis of South Africa offered by Orde Greer who is communist. Duma Dhladhla angrily refutes him.

> *This* and *this* should happen and can't happen because of *that* and *that*. These theories don't fit us … When he goes for fruit, the kaffir gets the half-rotten stuff the white won't buy. That is black (original italics, *BD* 161-62).

Gordimer has been critical of the practice of communism in South Africa. She seems to suggest that the blacks have began speaking and their voices will not go unheard for a long time.

Another subversive force in the novel is intertexuality, as mentioned in the beginning of the discussion on *Burger's Daughter*.

The most obvious and significant example of it is the pamphlet distributed by the Soweto Students Representative Council (SSRC). This pamphlet describes what happened on 16 June 1976 and calls upon the blacks to continue their fight against injustices done to them. It has been reproduced in the text without any correction of the spelling and grammatical mistakes. Though the Censorship Board claimed, when they unbanned the novel, that they were unsure of the authenticity of the incorporated text, Gordimer clarifies several times that it was genuine: "I reproduced the document because my stylistic integrity as a writer demanded it: it is a necessary part of the book as a whole" ("What the Book", 162). She further said that she reproduced it as documentary evidence in contrast to the fuller, fictive versions of events and that it expresses more eloquently and honestly the spirit of the young people who wrote it. This technique of intertexuality becomes politically very significant when it is seen the context of Black Consciousness. The young black activists often criticized the white writers for speaking on behalf of the blacks. As Susan Barrett points out, Gordimer solves this problem in a unique way. By incorporating the pamphlet completely she withdraws herself and allows the blacks speak in their own voice (116). And thus she imparts a kind of objectivity to her story.

Rosa's confrontation with Baasie makes her realize that she must return to South Africa. Perhaps she has come to believe like her father that if the whites do not support the blacks' political demand of majority rule, the blacks would become exclusively racist. As she recalls the devastating telephone conversation with Baasie she feels an overwhelming awareness of commitment to the cause of the blacks. However, Rosa does not succumb to any ideology or politics. Her sole concern is suffering. Her understanding and acceptance of the universality of suffering give her courage to bear the wretchedness of South Africa.:

> I don't know the ideology:
>
> It's about suffering.
>
> How to end suffering (*BD* 343-44).

More importantly, there is another reason for her return which she does not recognize consciously. Her confrontation with Baasie makes her see that in a single night they had negotiated the position "their history books back home [South Africa] have ready for us – him bitter; me guilty. What other meeting place could there have been for us" (*BD* 341)? The last sentence reminds the reader of Gordimer's short story titled "Is There No Where Else Where We Can Meet?" This early short story of Gordimer expresses her search for a 'meeting place' in apartheid South Africa where the whites and the blacks can meet. The story is about the fearful experience of a white woman as a consequence of her encounter with a black man. They meet on an empty veld, which may be described as a borderland between a white suburb and a black location. The man struggles to rob the woman of her handbag and parcel. After her initial efforts, the white woman relinquishes them out of fear. When she reaches safely the white world, she regrets fighting the man and decides not to report the matter to the police. This is perhaps because she recognizes the black man's economic inequality due to his race. This understanding on the part of the woman signifies that there is hope for a meaningful relationship between the white and the black. Rosa does not show any fear like that of the unnamed heroine of the story. But both of them search for a location where blacks can live with dignity and control their destiny, and where the two races can meet as equals. Of course, ideologically and politically Rosa is more committed than the heroine of the story. The search for a place or location where blacks and whites can live together has been the purpose of Gordimer's fiction. Her style and technique changed or refined but her objective remains same throughout her career. It is in order to continue her search for such a location that Rosa returns to South Africa. Rosa and therefore Gordimer know that it is located in the future, on the other side of a revolution that will overthrow apartheid.

Rosa does not, however, re-engage herself politically like her father. She realizes that the role of the whites in the changing circumstances cannot be the same as it was in the past. But she is ready to do what she can. The past is evaluated only to get inspiration for the present. The change in Rosa coincides with the change in South African political situation. The Soweto Revolt is a protest by black children against the whites. The blacks who so far avoided to act politically have began to see themselves as their children see them. They have been radicalized by their children. So they are now being arrested and detained. As Rosa puts it,

> "The real Rosa [she means Rosa Luxemburg] believed the real revolutionary initiative was to come from the people . . . This time it's coming from the children of the people, teaching the fathers –the ANC, BPC, PAC, all of them . . ." (*BD* 361).

It is against this background Rosa takes up her work as a physiotherapist at Baragwanath Hospital instead of leading the struggle from the front like her father. She teaches the black children, who have been deeply wounded by the police, to walk again and helps them put one foot before the other. She renews her contact with Marisa Kgosana and other black activists at Soweto. But she is soon arrested. Now Rosa resides with Clare Terblanche and Marisa in the same prison. The symbolic contact of black and white is established again (Heinemann 145). Gordimer depicts Rosa and other rebels as being lovelier and younger as if they have reconciled to their destiny. Rosa in her new haircut looks fourteen – the age at which she is seen at the beginning of the novel, waiting outside the prison to meet her mother.

Burger's Daughter is not only a radical work of fiction but it constitutes a political act. Instead of acquiescently accepting apartheid, Rosa fights against it and faces the consequences. So does Gordimer. By publishing this novel she "shows her willingness to accept, in addition to the certain banning of her novel, her own banning, house arrest, or even imprisonment" (JanMohmed, "The Degeneration" 129). The novel is Gordimer's response to the Black Consciousness as well as an examination of white South African psyche. In the given racial privilege, the way forward for the white lies in their radical self-examination and their relation to the blacks under the changing conditions.

Burger's Daughter captures the South African life before and immediately after the Soweto revolt. Gordimer's next novel, *July's People* (1981) focuses on the "full-scale revolution" in South Africa (Green 93). The 1980s was an era of massive political actions and counter-actions. The United Democratic Front was established in 1983. Strikes, boycotts and civil unrests destroying shopping malls and white suburbs became the order of the day. Rowland Smith argues that *July's People* depicts a South Africa where "the white power is tottering, if not already fallen" (141). Gordimer explores this by reversing the social relationship between the whites and the blacks. Gordimer reverses the order of master and servant pattern.

She has shown July, the black servant having power and control over the white family. Previously the black servants were less significant or less visible. Nevertheless, this does not reduce the centrality of the inner struggle she ascribes to her white protagonists. The middle class white family of Bamford Smale, Maureen Smale and their three children has fled from their Johannesburg home and take shelter in the native village of their servant, July. The novel highlights their life they spend in the hut of July's mother. The servant plays host to his master. Every day they anxiously listen to their radio to know the result of the revolution, which remains uncertain even at the end of the novel, for the new world is not yet born, as the epigraph of the novel from Antonio Gramsci indicates. Gordimer envisions the revolutionary process that has begun in the 1980s and may bring about changes in South Africa in the near future. *July's People* may be said to be a preparation for that future.

In the face of riots, arson and bombs, the Smales cannot but migrate from the white urban world to the poor village of their black servant, July. This implies their loss of geographical control. This is an important sign of any revolutionary transition. Foucault sees space in terms of power. He argues that space is created in terms of social relations and it is "a site of contesting social forces" (cited in Shabanirad, 117). Gordimer's fiction all along shows the importance of the politics of space. Bam not only loses the urban space but fails to adjust to the new African rural environment. Once he wrote a paper on "Needs and Means in Rural African Architecture" (*JP* 132). He can argue about the pragmatic use of African social space but he himself is unable to adapt to that environment. This exposes the "false credentials" of Bam, the representative of white bourgeois (Head 133). Gordimer's treatment of issue of space is best exemplified in the passage of the novel where Bam Smales move around in a small space behind Maureen. She could hear him hitting his fist against his palm as he used to do in the town when he would talk about some building project to be commissioned to him:

> Impossible to imagine what was happening in those suburban malls now, where white families ate ice-cream together . . . bought T-shirts . . . and looked, learning about foreign parts, at photographic exhibitions whose favoured subject was black township life. (*JP* 153)

The passage reveals several issues and themes. When Bam lingers on the 'small space' of the hut of July's mother, Maureen reflects upon the different and opposite spaces such as shopping malls. As an architect Bam has been involved in building these projects. These spaces epitomise the bourgeois identities and values. But they conceal the fact that the creation of these urban shopping spaces is dependent upon the spaces of social deprivation. This suppression is exposed alongside another reversal, that is, Bam's transposition – "from the designer of capitalist urban space to a lingerer in someone else's mud hut" (Head 134).

With their loss of control over space, comes the change in Bam and Maureen's relationship –personal, political and sexual. Maureen's words capture the central concern of *July's People* when she tells the Chief: "an explosion of roles, that's what the blowing up of the Union Buildings and the burning of master bedrooms is" (*JP* 142). The 'explosion' involves mainly the relations between the Smales couple and also between July and the Smales, the white people. There is a reversal of familiar roles in the changed circumstances. Bam and Maureen are surprised to discover that July has taken the bakkie, their means to escape and a symbol of bourgeois status. An argument follows between Maureen and July. July tells her that she does not want him to keep the keys of bakkie though he has been her 'boy' for fifteen years. He uses the term of subservience ('boy') to point out that she should have trusted him. Maureen is shocked at his use of the word 'boy' and tells him that their old master-servant relationship is not possible in the changed situation. To this July asks whether she will pay for the month. The novelist suggests that the relationship is based more on the economic reasons than what Maureen believes to be personal understanding. To July, their relationship is only a means to support his family. Maureen even attempts to blackmail July into submission by reminding him of town mistress, Ellen. But she fails and realises that her behaviour as a former employer is unforgivable. However, When Bam and Maureen express their concern that July's use of the vehicle will provide clue to their whereabouts, July assures them he will tell people that bakkie belongs to him. "The bakkie it's mine" (*JP* 73). This makes them aware of their helplessness and that they are dependent upon him in the present situation. Their material dispossession even leads to the deterioration of their personal intimacy. As time passes, they behave as if they know a little about each other and finally appear in the manner of divorced people trying to give the appearance of normal family life.

The incident of Bam's killing two warthog piglets shows the connection between power and sexuality. Gordimer describes the warthogs as having "heavy bodies bounded like corseted women" (*JP* 90). She perhaps suggests that the act of shooting through the bodies of these animals is an act of sexual violation. As Bam shoots through the head of one of the piglets, blood is dropping from its face. The pig with its shattered face is taken to the huts "where his function as a provider of meat settled upon him as a status" (*JP* 94).

Bam's gun is a symbol of his power and status, especially when it's used for survival. By extension it also suggests the masculinity of Bam, the provider of the family. Brendon Nicholls sees that gun as a "link between masculinity and phallic violence" which is reinforced when Bam and Maureen make love after eating the piglet (25). This is the first time Bam and Maureen make love since they have left home. In the following morning Bam sees blood of the pigs on his penis in a moment of hallucination. Soon he realises that "it was hers [Maureen's]" for she was menstruating (*JP* 97). Now the killing of the pig is linked with Bam's sexuality and his status in the hegemony. This connection suggests a latent violence in the bourgeois male sexuality, which is one aspect of the male's socially encoded power.

The Smales are robed of their material possessions – first the bakkie and then the gun. They (the materials) are now used by the blacks. This signals the shift of power under the prevailing situation. More importantly, the second most argument between Maureen and July highlights the reversal of power relations. After coming from the Chief's place, they discover that the gun is stolen. Maureen insists that July must get back the gun from Daniel. July tells her angrily that she has always held him responsible for the stolen things of the family. She is therefore "too much trouble" for him, and now "in my [July's] home too" (*JP* 184-85). At this Maureen retaliates that she has seen him stealing small things of the family such as her "scissors like a bird" (*JP* 185). July responds to this accusation angrily and powerfully in his own language so much so that Maureen understood everything although she did not knew the word. July, on the other hand, understood her "idea of him":

> But for himself – to be intelligent, honest, dignified for *her* was nothing; his measure as a man was taken elsewhere and

by others. She was not his mother, his wife, his sister, his friend, his people. (italic original *JP* 186)

This outburst shows that July can now assert himself. Through this Gordimer seems to puncture Maureen's liberal belief that she has some privileged understanding of July and that she has a respectful relation with him. Now she becomes conscious of the fact that his dignity is different from what she thought. Commenting on this, Brendon Nicholls observes that Gordimer "turns the most obnoxious consequences of Apartheid's policy of separate development into the deepest basis for respect" (31). Maureen tries to belittle him for his newfound independence. She tells him he may imagine to be a gangster driving around in their bakkie but soon he will run out of money to buy petrol for the vehicle and then it will lie there to rust. Maureen then tries to seduce July in response to her new consciousness of his dignity. When the tenderness of the evening envelopes them "mistaking them for lovers", Maureen "lurched over and posed herself" against the hood of the vehicle and her "sweat-coarsened forehead touched by the moonlight". She made of herself "death's harpy image" but it was meaningless to July who had never gone to "a motor show complete with provocative girls" (*JP* 187). Maureen resorts to sexuality, which can be considered as the "last strategy of political containment – a final sign of her political bad faith" (Nicholls 32). She hopes that she will remain his madam by seducing him and thereby becoming his mistress. But she fails. Finally she understands that their dependency on July for survival "matched" with his former dependency on them (*JP* 189).

Gordimer has narrated the near fall of the so-called white nation that has excluded from its history the majority section of South Africa. At the same time she has not failed to hint at the new culture in the making. "In *July's People* Gordimer turns to the *details* of culture and shows a new world in the making" (original italic, Clingman 196). Gordimer has seen the new culture in the children. In *Burger's Daughter*, she has noted the contribution of the black children to the anti-apartheid movement through the Soweto Revolt. In *July's People*, the white children are negotiating with the African culture. Bam and Maureen are very old for any transformation although Bam engages himself in some communal activities like building the tank for harvesting rain water. The children, particularly Gina, display a potential for future change. Gina makes friendship with the black child Nyiko. She tries to learn her (Nyiko's) language and imitate her beviour. Together they enjoy a mutual world of childlike sisterhood and as true friends at a time of social turbulence they become part of the same cultural heritage. In fact, Gina's friendship with Nyiko is an advance on the childhood friendship between Maureen and Lydia. The photos of Maureen and Lydia appearing together in a magazine, *Life* recast their "friendship in terms of Apartheid ideologies of white baasmanskap" (Nicholls 24). Gina and Nyiko's friendship is not based on racial consciousness and their friendship has absorbed African language and African cultural values. Victor seems to cling to the bourgeois ideals of ownership of property, even of nature. To his complaint that the blacks carry water from the tank, his father says that it is theirs. To his mother's question "Who owns the rain?" he replies – "It's hours, it's hours" (*JP* 77). But later he is shown adapting to the new surroundings. When July gives him a length of fishing line, he repeats the typical black obeisance. He is seen bobbing at knees and "receiving the gift with cupped palms" (*JP* 191). Thus the children are undergoing a kind of socialization. These little changes in culture will occur in the everyday life as South Africa undergoes the transformation. Bhabha considers nation as hybrid and site of differences. He argues that both nation and culture are narrative constructions resulting from the cross-fertilization of national and cultural constituents: "It is in the emergence of the interstices – the overlap and displacement of domains of difference – that the intersubjective and collective experiences of *nationness*, community interest or cultural value are negotiated" (original italic, Bhabha 2).

Gordimer has exposed the values of the white liberals through Maureen and Bam. She has also offered a critique of the black world. At the time of revolution, the blacks have failed to put up a united fight against the apartheid regime. This is evident in the behaviour of July's chief. The chief asks Bam to teach him shooting so that he can protect himself against the 'Russias' and 'Cubas' or any other black revolutionaries of South Africa. That is to say, the chief sides with the white forces and is ready to fight against his own people because "he has succumbed to Apartheid propaganda that black majority rule dispossess him of meagre traditional lands" (Nicholls 29). Bam is surprised to learn that the imagined liberation struggle is less a race war than "an intertribal conflict" (Newman 89). The Chief's behaviour can also be seen as what Fanon calls tribal wars when the 'wretched' (native) turns against each other. July is hopeful, though. He suggests the chief was ever against white taxation and he will not oppose the black fighters either when they arrive.

However, when Maureen asks Bam what he will do if the chief comes to him to learn shooting, he replies in the "old vocabulary" that cannot express their unexpected experience. He tried "hopelessly for words that were not phrases from back there, words that would make the truth that must be forming here, out of the blacks, of themselves" (*JP* 155). Gordimer seems to suggest that Bam's old language of political analysis fails because his language has been effective only within apartheid ideology. He cannot imagine anything outside that ideology. In his new place and situation, he fails to communicate. In fact, as Jennifer Gordon observes, the novel's vision of the future is limited by the "little hope of a common language" it offers (108). Even there is a near breakdown of communication between Bam and Maureen as they gradually estranged from each other in their new role and new place. So he addresses his wife as "Her. Not 'Maureen'. Not 'his wife'" (*JP* 128). As the action progresses it is seen that Maureen talks more than Bam with the blacks. She even understands July's outburst in his own language in their final argument, though not the words. Gordon argues that this is "symbolic bilingualism" a common language but it cannot sustain between blacks and whites in South Africa because of "years of conditioning" (105). Nevertheless Gordon argues that there is at least a cause of optimism as the children of the Smales are trying to learn the language spoken in the African village.

The ending of the novel has given rise to several interpretations as to future of South Africa as a nation that the novel seems to suggest. Thus, according to Clingman, the last scene of the novel – Maureen running to the helicopter – suggests that she is running from "old structures and relationships" towards a revolutionary future (203). On the other hand, Ali Erritouni argues that the last scene of the novel "prefigures a South Africa whose out lines are undefined" (76). He says that Gordimer refuses to predict the direction of the blacks' liberation struggle because the future of South Africa belongs to blacks. So, it is the blacks, not the whites, who should decide its content and nature. Nicholas Visser draws attention to the language used in describing the scene. The helicopter with its landing gear like spread legs is represented as a sexual force or imagined as a rapist.

Gordimer describes Maureen's "rib-cage is thudded with deafening vibration, invaded by a force pumping, jigging in its monstrous orgasm" (*JP*, 192). Thus Maureen is imagined here as being raped by the monstrous helicopter which is a symbolic continuation of her attempt to seduce July. Visser further finds intertextual correspondences with Yeats' poem, "Leda and the Swan" that gives the symbolic rape a cultural significance. In the poem, Zeus descends upon Leda in the form of a swan and rapes in an act of annunciation that founds the Greek civilization. Similarly the helicopter may be imagined as a godlike force that descends from the sky to found the new nation after the apartheid.

Gordimer's fiction from *The Conservationist* onwards is concerned with the future and uncertain phase of South African history. Thus, both *Burger's Daughter* and *July's People* deal with the imminent revolutions in South Africa which culminated in the 1994 General Election. While focusing on the issues of future of South Africa, Gordimer engages with more radicalized political themes. *Burger's Daughter* examines, among other things, the history of South African Communist Party. The novelist seems to advocate its need to adapt Marxist theory to local realities, and its resistance to white exploitation of blacks. The novel shows the influence the Communist Party had within the ANC leadership until the rise of the Black Consciousness movement. Since the banning of the Communist Party and the uprisings of the 1970s, the anti-apartheid forces went underground. The political leaders changed their strategies of resistance and became more violent and subversive. The political climate of anti-apartheid struggle in the 1980s pervades Gordimer's novels *A Sport of Nature* and *My Son's Story*. Gordimer deals with a coloured family in *My Son's Story* and it shows her preoccupation with the politics of race, gender and sexuality as played out in the private and public life as well. The novel demonstrates the possibilities of hybridity and fluidity of the socio-political conditions of the coloured people. Their 'in-betweenness' or 'ambivalence' colours them with a kind of transforming possibility which Bhabha points out in *The Location of Culture*. The 'in-between' spaces between identifications suggests the possibility of a cultural hybridity which may accommodate differences without imposing any hierarchy. Bhabha continues

> 'Beyond' signifies spatial distance, marks progress, promises the future; but our intimations of exceeding the barrier or boundary –the very act of going *beyond* –are unknowable, unrepresentable, without a return to the 'present' which, in the process of repetition, becomes disjunct and displaced. (4)

Sonny's coloured family marks such a progress and promise which Bhabha speaks about in the above passage. Sonny moves to a 'grey area' (*MSS* 14) in the white city of Johannesburg from 'coloured' location in their hometown. This is a symbolic move of crossing the border. This move of the coloured family into the grey area signifies the whole notion of 'coloured' identity as hybrid, in-between and transgressive. Symbolically speaking, their movement beyond the barriers of colour signals their crossing of the socio-cultural boundaries in their attempt to resist the racial segregation. On the other hand, Aila who earlier in the novel appears in the traditional gender identity as a caring mother and dependent wife emerges with a new identity in the later part of narrative when she secretly joins the underground revolutionary activities. This aspect of the novel is further discussed in the fourth chapter.

Gordimer has been an unwavering critic of apartheid. The fiction of Gordimer demonstrates a texture that allows one to analyse the theme of acquiescence and resistance. In her early fiction, she depicts mainly liberal white characters who reject or attempts to reject apartheid. As an activist and a committed artist, she has created characters and built plots that often defy the strict categorization of the population into white, black or coloured. This creates space for the characters to see beyond their particular identity and discover a perspective upon themselves and the South African life. They often fail in their efforts. But they demonstrate certain change in their attitude. The friendship between Toby and the black Sam in *A World of Strangers* marks a change in Toby, at least in his attitude and intention. Just before leaving the Johannesburg railway station for Cape Town for a business trip, Toby promises Sam to be the godfather of Sam's baby when it is born. Gordimer seems to suggest that their friendship transcends all ideologies and signals the beginning of a cultural synthesis against the apartheid.

Gordimer's delineation of cross-racial sexual relationship is a challenge to the basic principle of apartheid. Like Foucault, Gordimer seems to consider sexuality as a site of power relations governed by the dominant socio-cultural conventions. She has attempted to produce an alternative discourse about sexuality. The prevailing cross-racial sexual relationship in the colonial South Africa had been between white men and black women (Thompson 45). But Gordimer has depicted the trans-racial relationship between black men and white women in her fiction such as *Occasion for Loving*. By reversing the traditional pattern, she has suggested the possibility of resisting the apartheid ideology. The Ann-Gideon affair is an act of resistance though it failed finally. But this may be said to prepare the ground for emergence of resistance in future. This is clearly visible in Gordimer's later fiction such as *A Sport of Nature* and *My Son's Story.*

In most of Gordimer's work discussed above, the characters often find themselves at the border or at the margin where past and present, inside and outside are not separated as binary opposites but they commingle and conflict. And from this emerge new and complex forms of representation that defy binary division. Through the imaginative border-crossings in her fiction, Gordimer suggests the possibility of psychological and physical crossing of borders. After returning to South Africa, Rosa renews her contact with Marisa Kgosana and other black activists at Soweto. She is imprisoned with other women revolutionaries. She lives in the prison with Marisa, Clare and the Indian woman, establishing a kind of sisterhood. Gordimer seems to convey the establishment of the symbolic contact of blacks and whites suggesting the creation of a community out of differences –the many into one (Bhabha 204). Through Rosa's subordinate position in the revolt, Gordimer suggests that the white must take such a position to overthrow apartheid.

Works Cited

Ashcroft, Bill, Gareth Griffiths, and Helen Tiffin, eds. *The Post-Colonial Studies Reader*. London: Routledge, 2006.

_______ *Post-Colonial Studies: The Key Concepts.* 2nd ed. London: Routledge, 2007.

Barrett, Susan. "'What I say will not be understood': Intertextuality as a subversive force in Nadine Gordimer's *Burger's Daughter*." EREA 2.1(printemps):115-21 www.e-rea.org>

Bhabha, Homi K. *The Location of Culture*. London: Routledge, 2017 (reprint).

Boyers, Robert, et al. "A Conversation with Nadine Gordimer." *Salmagundi* 62 (Winter 1984): pp 3 -31.

Clingman, Stephen. *The Novels of Nadine Gordimer: History from Inside*. Amherst: University of Massachusetts Press, 1992.

Conley, Tom. Translator's Introduction. *The Writing of History*. By Michel de Certeau. Trans. Conley. New York: Columbia University Press, 1988.

Cooke, John. "Leaving Mother's House." *Nadine Gordimer's Burger's Daughter*. Ed. Judie Newman. Oxford: Oxford University, 2003.

Danaher, G., et al. *Understanding Foucault*. Sydney: Allen & Unwin, 2000.

Erritouni, Ali. "Apartheid Inequality and Post-Apartheid Utopia." *Research in African Literatures* 37 (4), Winter, 2006.

Fanon, Frantz. *Black Skin White Masks*. Trans. Charles Lam Markmann. New York: Grove Press, 1967.

Foucault, M. *Discipline and Punish: The Birth of the Prison*. Trans. Alan Sheridan. New York: Vintage Books, 1977.

______"Of Other Spaces". Trans. Jay Miskowiec. *Diacritics*: The John Hopkins University Press, Vol. 16 (1), 22 –27.

______*The History of Sexuality: Volume I: An Introduction*. Trans. R. Hurley. New York: Pantheon Books, 1978.

Gordimer, Nadine. *A Soldier's Embrace*. London: Penguin, 1982.

______*A Sport of Nature*. London: Bloomsbury, 2013.

______"A Writer's Freedom." *The Essential Gesture: Writing, Politics and Places*. Ed. Stephen Clingman. London: Penguin, 1989.

______"A Writer in South Africa." *London Magazine*, May 1965.

______*A World of Strangers*. London: Bloomsbury, 2002.

______*Burger's Daughter*. London: Bloomsbury, 2000.

______*July's People*. London: Bloomsbury, 2005.

______ *My Son's Story*. London: Bloomsbury, 2003.

______ "Literature and Politics in South Africa." *Southern Review* VII. 3 (November 1974).

______*Occasion for Loving*. London: Bloomsbury, 2013.

______ *Selected Stories*. London: Bloomsbury, 2000.

______*Six Feet of the Country*. New York: Simon and Schuster, 1956.

______*Some Monday for Sure*. London: Heinemann, 1976.

______ *The Conservationist*. London: Bloomsbury, 2005.

______ "The Essential Gesture." *The Essential Gesture: Writing, Politics and Places*. Ed. Stephen Clingman. London: Penguin, 1989.

______ *The Lying Days*. London: Bloomsbury, 2002.

______ *The Late Bourgeois World*. London: Bloomsbury, 2013

______ "What the Book Is About." *Nadine Gordimer's Burger's Daughter*. Ed. Judie Newman. Oxford: Oxford University, 2003.

Gordon, Jennifer. "Dreams of a Common Language: Nadine Gordimer's *July's People*." *Women in African Literature Today: A Review*, 15, 1987.

Green, Robert. "From *The Lying Days* to *July's People*: The Novels of Nadine Gordimer". *Nadine Gordimer's July's People*. Ed. Brendon Nicholls. London: Routledge.

Grey, Stephen. An Interview with Nadine Gordimer. *Contemporary Literature*, Vol. 22, No. 3 (Summer,1981), pp 263 –271.

Head, Dominic. *Nadine Gordimer*. Cambridge: CUP, 1994.

Heinemann, Margot. "The Synthesis of Revolution." *Nadine Gordimer's Burger's Daughter*. Ed. Judie Newman. Oxford: Oxford University, 2003.

JanMohmed, Abdul R. "The Degeneration of the Great South African Lie." *Nadine Gordimer's Burger's Daughter*. Ed. Judie Newman.

______"The Economy of Manichean Allegory". *The Post-Colonial Studies Reader*. Ed. Bill Ashcroft, Gareth Griffiths, and Helen Tiffin.

King, Bruce, ed. *The Later Fiction of Nadine Gordimer*. New York: Palgrave, 1993.

McLeod, John. *Beginning Postcolonialism*. New Delhi: Viva Books, 2010.

Minh-ha, Trinh. T. "Writing Postcoloniality and Feminism". *The Post-Colonial Studies Reader*. Ed. Bill Ashcroft, Gareth Griffiths, and Helen Tiffin.

Nasr, Rania Reda. "Land and Nature as Forms of Power and Resistance in Nadine Gordimer's *The Conservationist* and S. Yizhar's *Preliminaries*". https://www.researchgate.net/publication/314343272 (accessed on 5 June, 2019).

Nayar, Pramod K. *Cotemporary Literary and Cultural Theory*. Delhi: Pearson, 2010.

Newman, Judie. *Nadine Gordimer*. New York: Routledge, 1988.

Newman, Judie, ed. *Nadine Gordimer's Burger' Daughter*. Oxford: Oxford University, 2003.

Nicholls, Brendon, ed. *Nadine Gordimer's July's People*. London: Routledge.

Ransom, J. S. *Foucault's Discipline: The Politics of Subjectivity*. London: Duke UP, 1977.

Ross, Alan. "An Interview with Nadine Gordimer." *Conversation with Nadine Gordimer*. Ed. Nancy Topping Bazin,et al. Jackson: University Press of Mississipi,1990,34-41.

Said, Edward W. *Culture and Imperialism*. London: Vintage, 1994.

Shabanirad, Ensieh, et al. "A Foucauldian Study of Space and Power in Two Novels by Nadine Gordimer". *Journal of Language Studies*. Vol. 17(4), November, 2017. http://doi.org/gema-2017-1704-08.

Slemon, Stephen. "Unsettling the Empire: Resistance Theory for the Second World". *The Post-Colonial Studies Reader*. Ed. Bill Ashcroft, Gareth Griffiths, and Helen Tiffin. London: Routledge, 2006.

Smith, David M. ed. Introduction. *The Apartheid City and Beyond: Urbanization and Social Changes in South Africa*. London: Routledge, 1992.

Smith, Rowland. *Critical Essays on Nadine Gordimer*. Boston, MA: G. K. Hall, 1990.

Thomson, Leonard. *A History of South Africa*. New Haven: Yale University Press, 1990.

Trump, Martin. "The Short Fiction of Nadine Gordimer". *Research in African Literature*. 17 .3 Autumn, 1986. pp. 341-369.

Uledi-Kamanga, Brighton J. *Cracks in the Wall: Nadine Gordimer's Fiction and the Irony of Apartheid*. P.O. Box 1892, Trenton: Africa World Press.

Visser, Nicholas. "Beyond the Interregnum: A Note on the Ending of *July's People*." *Rendering Things Visible: Essays on South African Literary Culture*. Ed. Martin Trump. Athens, OH: Ohio University Press, 1990.

Waxman, B. F. *Multicultural Literatures through Feminist/ Poststructural Lenses*. Knoxville: University of Tennesse Press, 1993.

Yelin, Louise. *From the Margins of Empire: Stead, Lessing, Gordimer*. Cornell University Press, 1998.

Yousaf, Nahem, ed. *Apartheid Narratives*. New York: Rodopi, 2001.

CHAPTER III

Reading Trauma in Nadine Gordimer's Novels

3.1 Theoretical Approaches

The term 'trauma' may be said to mean a painful or distressing experience that leaves indelible marks on the psyche of an individual and affects his or her perception of the external world. Trauma studies generally deals with psychological trauma and the role it plays in shaping individual and cultural identities. It is also concerned with the possibility of representation of trauma through language. Recently scholars of trauma studies have often combined psychoanalytic theories with poststructural and postcolonial theories. As a literary approach, trauma theory examines the impact and representation of trauma in literature through an analysis of psychological and cultural significance of trauma.

Trauma studies in literary criticism emerged in the 1990s as a multidisciplinary field largely drawing on the Freudian theory of trauma. Scholars like Cathy Caruth, Shoshana Felman and Geoffrey Hartman critically examined the concept of trauma and its role in literature and society. They popularised the concept of trauma as an event that cannot be represented precisely. In her scholarly book, *Unclaimed Experience: Trauma, Narrative and History* (1996), Caruth views trauma through the lens of Freud and treats trauma as a delayed return of the repressed. According to Caruth, it is difficult to fully represent a traumatic experience because of its latency. Both individual and historical traumatic events are known only through an interrupted referentiality that points to the meaning of the past only as a kind of reproduction (Caruth, 11). The unspeakable nature of trauma remains a dominant concept in literary studies for "imagining trauma's function in literature" (Balaev 1). This traditional model of trauma also claims that language is unable to locate the truth of the past.

The classical model developed by Caruth and others was followed by alternative models and approaches over the last two decades, which suggest a wide range of representational possibilities. The different approaches to trauma studies have been described as the pluralistic model of trauma because of the plurality of theories and approaches employed. Critics such as Michael Rothberg and Greg Forter explore the way traumatic experience is represented in literature by a combination of psychoanalytic theory and postcolonial theory or cultural studies. On the other hand, Luckhurst, Mandel and Visser focus on the social and political implications of trauma within a variety of frameworks. The pluralistic model of trauma moves beyond the structural dimensions of trauma and concentrate on the cultural significance of trauma and the diversity of narrative expression. The early theory of trauma "centralizes pathological fragmentation" and suggests the possibility that traumatic experience "uncovers new relationship between experience, language, and knowledge" (Mambrol 9). Further, the traditional model of trauma assumes memory as a fixed process but the postcolonial trauma studies views memory as a fluid process of reconstruction which allows the traumatic past to be created and recreated in the moments of recollection. Thus socio-cultural factors influence the meaning of the traumatic event because the recollection process in the present moment is influenced by cultural and historical contexts. Craps argues that trauma studies must take into account the social and historic relations for ethical effectiveness (53). Mengel and Borzaga found Caruth's formulation inadequate to analyse the trauma in South Africa because trauma in this case is involved with the history of apartheid. It (apartheid) has caused the collective traumatization of several generations and therefore it is neither an unclaimed nor 'unclaimable' experience. Nevertheless, Caruth's notion of the inexpressible nature of traumatic wound cannot be ignored completely. Literature has to "present, represent, and dramatize trauma in its many manifestations" without claiming precision or exact nature of trauma (Visser 6).

Trauma is multi-dimensional and complex in nature. One thing is obvious that trauma is a kind of interplay between the past and the present, and that traumatic experiences may have a firm hold on the present in one's life in a way that they may fail to overcome trauma. However, Boris Cyrulnik, a French psychiatrist, argues that this interplay may open up the possibility of generating resilience or the capacity of a person to recover from trauma. Supporting Cyrulnik's arguments, Isabel Fraile Murlanch says that one of the factors behind the development of resilience is the way in which present and past combine in the narratives, the wounded person builds up to make sense of the past event he has suffered. In other words, narrative can play a role in developing resilience. Murlanch contends that facing an event that would traumatise other people, those who are truly resilient may feel wounded, but not traumatised. Resilience depends largely on the victim's ability to, what Cyrulnik calls, "organise one's own history", so that representation turns out to be healing and traumatic as well (quoted in Murlanch 117). Murlanch further agrees with Cyrulnik who asserts that trauma may not be reversible but it can be repaired. The traumatic experience can leave an indelible mark on the life of the victim forever without necessarily leading her/him to neurosis.

3. 2 Gordimer's Novels

Nadine Gordimer has written most of her fiction against the background of the apartheid South Africa. The trauma of apartheid has had a damaging impact on the life of the characters she created. Most of them either experienced apartheid or became victims of apartheid. As such their personal life is intricately related with the politics or the public world. In *Occasion for Loving*, according to Judie Newman, Gordimer draws upon her own childhood experience to "transform a personal trauma into a political metaphor" (26). Like Gordimer herself, Jessie Stilwell was withdrawn from school when she was about ten years old on the pretext of a heart ailment which she never suffered from. Prevented from physical activity and kept close to her mother, Jessie became too dependent on her mother who was unhappily married to Bruno Fuecht. This had a lasting impact on the personality of Jessie. She led a life of silence and quietude. And she carries in her mind the illusion of silence and motionlessness of her mother's house even after her marriage. However, before the birth of her son Morgan she visits a doctor and discovers the terrible lie around which her mother brought her up. She had visited a heart specialist to confirm whether her old ailment would be a cause of worry for the normal birth of a child. The doctor told her

> with emphatic quiet that not only her heart perfectly normal,
> in fact it was not possible that a heart ailment serious enough

to keep a child out of school for years could leave no sign of damage. (*OL* 83)

Jessie's mother has "brain-washed her" in such a way that she (Jessie) loses herself as woman. Due to her mother's over interest in her, Jessie could not enjoy a normal childhood. In fact, she has lost the vitality of her life. She has been leading a lonely life, which is reflective of the life of the white bourgeois –the minority –in South Africa of the time. Jessie leaves her mother's house to her husband's but still feels in her subconscious that she has not left her mother's house. After the death of her first husband in his youth, Jessie realised that "a large part of her life was missing", that she was handed from mother to husband to become a mother without ever enjoying the joy and freedom of youthful life. She felt "cheated" and therefore even the Christmas became an occasion of "revulsion and resentment" (*OL* 45).

As a woman pushed to silence and loneliness and a mother who has an awkward relationship with her son Morgan from her first marriage, Jessie "undertakes a retrospective reconstruction of her past" (Newman 27). This reconstruction runs parallel to her present husband, Tom's attempt to write an impartial history of Africa. Gordimer uses the technique of flashback of some scenes to make Jessie rebuild her past. In one such scene from her past, Jessie remembers how she awakens in the middle of the night and confronts her mother outside the bathroom door. She shames her mother with her unspoken awareness that her mother has been making love with Fuecht. This scene has the connotation of a Fruedian 'primal scene' and suggests Jessies's ambivalent attitude to her mother. Jessie was trembling with pity and shame. But it was not clear if she was angry at her mother's outrage or she wanted to "shame her mother"

(*OL* 24). Subsequently, another scene resurfaces in her mind in which she sees the "shape of cold terror" on the back of her neck as she turned her back to the dark passage behind the bathroom door at night. For twenty years she tried to find out "who it was that threatened to come up behind her" (*OL* 75). Jessie's fear is identified in Oedipal terms, which is strengthened by the juxtaposition of the bathroom scenes and by her remembered terror of brown electrical plugs, associated Fuecht because of his expertise in electrical works.

However, the arrival of Ann and Boaz Davis at the Stilwells' house rouses Jessie's desire to pursue "the life dreamt and not lived" (*OL* 74). A brilliant dancer and an open minded girl, Ann becomes a source of life in a short time with her cheerful nature and tendency to break the conventions. She rejuvenates in Jessie an intense desire for privacy. Jessie had, at last, time to ask herself why she lived though she did not search for the possible answers. As she has been exploring her past, she suddenly discovers that Ann Davis has begun an affair with Gideon Shibalo, a black painter. With her flamboyant and unreflective life style, Ann provides an alter ego to Jessie, the lost image of her youth. She tolerates the interracial love affair because, she thinks, she settled "the race business" long ago (*OL* 290). But by the end of the narrative she comes to understand that this is not the case. Ann begins her journey in the novel in an apparent colour-blindness by developing her affair across the colour bar. She gradually becomes aware of Gideon as black first, and then as a man. Their affair finally fails under its own pressure, not because of state intervention through such acts as the Immorality Act of 1950. Their relationship fails because of the repressions of apartheid which have become psychologically inscribed in them. Jessie recognizes the same "prestructuring effects of apartheid upon her psyche" when Ann and

Gideon visit her in the beach house (Newman 30). While talking to Gideon, she suddenly discovers her childhood fear as emanating from "the black man" that she must never be left alone with in their house. Jessie continues her conversation with Gideon. In her early life she used to feel at night that someone was following her from behind. She would ask,

> Who was it, do you think? And how many more little white girls are there for whom the very first man was a black man? … Gideon, I'd forgotten … It's only when something like you and Ann happens *one suddenly needs to feel one's way back."* (emphasis added, *OL* 290).

Now, as Newman points out, Jessie's memories obscure a culturally inscribed fear. In the end of the novel she discovers that the source of her repressions is not her European father Bruno Fuecht, but the black African. She has been "constructed by an African past" and by admitting it she "historicizes trauma" (Newman 31). Gordimer here links a personal trauma to the historical conditions of South Africa. Secondly, she combines the past and the present of Jessie in the narrative in such a way that she develops resilience which helps her recover from trauma. The techniques of flash back and interior monologue help the author probe into the mind of characters, particularly Jessie. Another literary technique, sudden shift in the point of view gives the text a fluidity to connect the personal and the political themes.

After the departure of Ann, Jessie comes across the abandoned black lover Gideon just as Rosa unexpectedly meets her childhood brother Baasie. Drunk and forlorn, Gideon initially fails to recognize Jessie but finally he seems to recognize her. And when he recognizes her, his reaction is characterized with colour and gender. "White bitch –get away" (*OL* 331). Subsequently he forgets the episode. But Jessie knows that what Gideon revealed has not gone away. Jessie's specific moments of critical challenge to her consciousness connect with that of Rosa and Baasie or Zwelinzima. The midnight phone call that Rosa Burger receives from Baasie has had a traumatic effect on her. She wants to defect from the resistance heritage of her father in order to assert her identity. So she leaves South Africa and joins her step mother Katya in Nice, France to lead a personal life of luxury. Away from the racially divided society of South Africa, Rosa leads in France a happy and carefree life among people whose sole objectives are pleasure and loyalty to friends. But her uncompromised individual life of pleasure is suddenly shattered by her chance meeting with Baasie, her childhood 'black brother' at a conference in London attended by South African exiles, British journalists and others. Baasie's real name is Zwelinzima, meaning "suffering land". In other words, he embodies the sorrows and sufferings of his race and country. In the meeting Rosa can recognize him and wants to talk to him but his response has been cold and talked little. He is, in fact, offended when one of the exiles delivers a speech in memory of her father, Lionel Burger. He also takes offence at the fact that even Rosa attracts much attention as the daughter of the dead resistance hero. So, after returning from the conference, he telephones her at midnight and rebukes her bitterly. He asks her why her father should be admired so much or why she should be honoured. If her father, he continues, died in prison, so did dozens of black fathers. They were sick and dying like dogs. When they were old and could not work anymore, they were kicked out of the locations. "Getting old and dying in prison"(*BD* 328). Nobody talks about these blacks but everybody admires Lionel Burger as a hero because he is a white, Baasie alleges. Rosa repeatedly tries to establish their personal, subjective bond but fails. He rejects the bond because of the racial difference between them. Angered and disgusted Rosa retaliates with insults. A heated argument between them follows, which finally verges on racism.

After the conversation, Rosa stood in the middle of the room and then ran to the lavatory and vomited. This quarrel has a far reaching psychological impact on Rosa. She weeps for the severance of her personal relations. She reflects upon the incident and her life. She discovers some facts which help her decide to return to South Africa. She comes to accept the view of her father that the black men's political struggle would become racist if the whites did not support the African demand of majority rule. Secondly, she realises that she has to return to South Africa not because of any ideology but because of the suffering of the blacks. She comes to believe that suffering for a cause is better than a comfortable personal life and that no one defect from one's responsibility. Her sympathy for others is revived. And hence after returning to South Africa she takes up physiotherapy as profession –teaching crippled children to put one foot before another.

Baasie's anger may be said to be a result of his apartheid experiences which was quite traumatic. The praise of Lionel, the white revolutionary springs in him emotions that led him to target Rosa. On the other hand, Rosa evaluates her past only to get inspiration for the present. She realizes that the role of the whites in the changing circumstances cannot be the same as it was in the past. So coming back to South Africa, she redefines her relationship with her country by participating in the revolution instead of leading it. She is wounded and wounds help her make sense of the past event she has suffered. In other words, she becomes a resilient person.

It is because of her resilience that she could revisit her own history. Therefore she realises that they had negotiated the position "their history books back home [South Africa] have ready for us –him bitter; me guilty. What other meeting place could there have been for us?"(*BD* 341) She is committed to find a place where both whites and blacks can live together. It is in order to continue her search for such a place that Rosa returns to South Africa. Rosa and therefore Gordimer know that it is located in the future, on the other side of a revolution that will overthrow apartheid.

Gordimer's tenth novel, *My Son's Story* (*MSS*) may be discussed in the light of the argument that narratives may have a therapeutic value. Published in 1990, the year that saw the released of Nelson Mandela and marked the beginning of the end of apartheid, *My Son's Story* tells the story of a father and his son. "It's an old story – ours. My father's and mine"(*MSS* 275). The novel opens with the fifteen-year old schoolboy, Will who bumps into his father, Sonny coming out of a cinema hall in the company of a white woman. This unexpected meeting has been a shattering moment for the schoolboy. His father's affair with a white woman, Hannah Plowman is not a common case of marital infidelity in the South Africa of 1980s when cross-racial relations was still a taboo. His father, Sonny is a dissident coloured teacher who turned revolutionary opposing the apartheid regime in South Africa. Will is shocked to see his father in the company of a white woman, so much so that he cannot tell his father the name of the film that he plans to watch. After this life changing discovery, he leaves the cinema hall and "took a bus home, home, home where I shut myself up in my room, safe among familiar schoolbooks" (*MSS* 5). Sonny's betrayal of his wife is a matter of utter disbelief to his adolescent son Will. The unexpected event sends Will to silence.

The memory of the scene keeps haunting his mind. He asks himself what made his father "allow himself to be seen with his woman" or what made him go there (*MSS* 29). Cathy Caruth observes that it is the unassimilated nature of trauma, the fact that the event was neither acknowledged nor experienced fully at the time, that later returns to haunt the survivor (cited in Herrero 105). Confusions and repetitions reverberate in Will's mind. In other words, as he cannot acknowledge the traumatic event at the first instance, it continues to haunt him as the narrative will reveal. He thinks that they should not have left their little house on the Reef and moved to the 'grey area' and settled in among whites. He is worried that he "did not know how to live now that I had met him [with his woman, Hannah], now that I had seen, not the movie I bunked swotting for, but what our own life" (*MSS* 37). Will feels that Sonny's betrayal constitutes a betrayal to the whole family –his wife Aila, his daughter Baby and his son Will. After the shocking event, Will becomes an accomplice to Sonny's secrets, unwillingly though. They behave as if nothing has happened. Will admits there is complicity between them. He regrets that his father drew him into the act of betrayal of his father. Sonny behaves in a way as if he was not his father because a father would never do such a thing. "And yet he was my father how could I resist, how could I dare refuse him?" (*MSS* 31). As an adolescent, he can understand Sonny's fascination for a 'blonde'. The blonde has been "wet dreams" for himself just as for all black men (*MSS* 4).Sonny is coloured but he aligns himself with the blacks, the narrator informs the reader. He realises that there is little difference between the blacks and the coloureds in their conditions of life. Will has a mixed feeling of admiration and jealousy for his father. But he cannot erase from his mind the memory of the betrayal. So the phrase like "Needing Hannah" comes to his mind repetitively (*MSS* 53, 68, 84). He uses again and again the sentence/thought "of course I know her" or its variation "we know each other" (*MSS* 14-15). Silvia Pellicer-Ortin points out that repetitions, digressions, dissociations, and recurrent use of images are some of the narrative techniques mentioned by the trauma critics such as Laurie Vickroy (83). As seen in the novel, the third person narrative voice often enters the narrative and makes digressions to present objective observations. Anyway, both the son and the father keep the secret to themselves. They, at least Will, do not want to hurt Aila, a beautiful and faithful wife and a loving and caring mother. This conspiracy of silence on the part of Will and Sonny establishes an uneasy bond between them. This gives rise to resentment and restlessness in him. This results in the development of "Love or love/hate" experiences in Will, says he (*MSS* 275). He keeps the 'secret' of his father and keeps it secret from his mother and his sister with the intention of not hurting them. The secret of the shocking incident keeps haunting him for years and exerts a great impact on his life. And he is not only a keeper of the secret of his father but he turns out to be the keeper of history of the family. It is as if he attempts to overcome the shock through the art of narration. In other words, he is, in LaCapra's term, "acting out" to describe the process through which he is compelled to relive the traumatic event. This process may find expression through anxiety, unknown fears or repetition of the past event (cited in Notes 2 in Pellicer-Ortin, 85). Will narrates the story of his family and in the process develops a resilient nature in him.

The fact of the matter is that trauma in the context of South Africa is caused by the continuous damaging effects of apartheid laws. *My Son's Story* is not only about trauma of Will caused by his father's infidelity. It is also about the trauma of Aila and Baby, which is rooted in the apartheid structure of South Africa. Trauma critics like Michael Rothberg and Stef Craps argue for 'decolonising trauma theory'. They argue that the western trauma theories as developed by Cathy Caruth and others cannot explain adequately the complex situations in a country like South Africa. It is because the western concept of trauma mainly considers the trauma of an individual that arises from a single identifiable event, causing post traumatic stress disorder (PTSD). But trauma needs to be understood not only as a result of an identifiable event but also a consequence of a historical condition. In the case of South Africa, it is colonialism or, to be precise, apartheid. In their collection of essays, *Trauma, Memory and Narrative*, Mengel and Borzaga argue that in the context of South Africa trauma is inseparable from the history of apartheid which is the cause of collective trauma of several generations. Further, in her analysis of Mongane Wally Serote's *To Every Birth Its Blood* (1981), Annie Gagiano writes that the strength of Serote's novel lies in its depiction of apartheid as "an invasive traumatizing presence in people's everyday life" and the novelist achieves it through the "affective dimensions", not through the presence of physical violence in the novel (Gagiano 232). The same may be said about Gordimer's *My Son's Story*. Sonny and his family are caught in the turmoil of anti-apartheid movements of 1980s. After Will's account of his encounter with Sonny at the cinema, the third person narrative voice narrates in a flash back the early part of Sonny's life in Benoni, a coloured location. Gordimer shows how the rigid apartheid laws were in place in his early life. Sonny was a school teacher in a town in the east of Johannesburg. Nobody had recorded where his ancestors had come from as those generations did not "keep notes". The only documentation of their lives was their *"work-papers and the various, much-folded slips entitling them to be employed in the area, outside the town, designated by the municipality for their kind*" (original italics *MSS*, 5). The Group Areas Act of 1950 forced people of different races to live in segregated areas and helped the apartheid government effectively regulate the socio-political and economic life of the native Africans. Sonny resents his partial black identity and yearns to improve himself and his community. He is also upset with the inhuman, degraded life the non-whites have been leading as against the privileged life of the whites. A lover of Kafka and Shakespeare, Sonny has been the best teacher in the school and leading a comparatively comfortable life with his wife, Aila, who has been beautiful and an equally efficient housekeeper. However, as the cry for equality in the anti-apartheid movement intensifies and finally turns out to be a demand for freedom, Sonny shows his affinity with the 'real' blacks. The distinction between "black and real black, between himself and them" fades for the school teacher (*MSS* 25). His acquired sense of identity also finds echo in his coloured pupils' political defiance by way of boycotting classes in solidarity with the black school children. This may be seen as reminiscence of the 1976 Soweto Revolt of the school children who protested against the introduction of Afrikaans as medium of instruction in the black schools. Sonny is impressed by the children's innocence act of identification with the black pupils. One day he decides to lead the children to "march across the veld to show solidarity with the children who had been locked out of their school by the police, after a boycott of classes; black solidarity" (*MSS* 27). Thus he draws the attention of the anti-apartheid activists who invite him to anti-apartheid activities such as campaigns against the removals of non-whites from the areas designated as 'white only'. In course of time he loses his job and becomes a regular speaker for the anti-apartheid movement. As Will says, he becomes a "full-time organizer" because the committee needed him (*MSS* 43). Thus the school teacher Sonny is transformed to Sonny the political personality. He moves to a white suburban area of Johannesburg for they cannot "accept their segregation" (*MSS* 41). Then he becomes a full-time political activist, involving himself in underground struggle for liberation in association with "the new black trade unions" and "groups active against the government" (*MSS* 43). Thus the narrative confirms Clingman's observation that the black trade unions were allowed to be formed in the 1980s (201). This was also the period, as Gordimer states in "Living in the Interregnum", when there was a renewed call for the multi-racialism ant-apartheid co-operation among the races based on the tenets of the African National Congress (270).

However, in the course of his political activities, Sonny comes to know Hannah, a human rights activist working under the International Human Rights Commission when he has been in jail. Their relation blooms into an intense love affair when Sonny is released from the jail after a period of two-year imprisonment. He frequently disappears from his home to pursue both his underground activities and his clandestine sexual life with Hannah. In fact his immoral affair now turns out to be the locus of his underground works. Thus Gordimer has introduced the sexual relationship into the national politics. She seems to combine politics and sex, or sexualise politics as if both politics and sexuality are inter-related in the context of South Africa. As the son's narrative suggests, Sonny finds no distinction between his commitment to liberation struggle and his fascination for sexual pleasure. In "needing Hannah" Sonny's "sexual and political commitment were one," says Will (*MSS*, 125). They are often seen together exploring their public and private life. It seems that through their transgression of the racial barrier, they dedicate to the political struggle and concentrate on the ecstatic pleasure of love, which mutually intensify their passion. Sonny and Hannah's transgression in their love affair is in sharp contrast to Hillela's in *A Sport of Nature*. The Jewish woman Hillela involves with the blacks in political and sexual relationship as a revolutionary tactics for national liberation of South Africa, which makes significant contribution to the liberation struggle. But Sonny's immoral relation with Hannah finally does not come to any fruition. On the other hand, his illicit affair creates turmoil in his domestic life. His wife, son and daughter could not tolerate his immoral relationship with a white woman, the representative of the oppressor. So, his act of betrayal destroys the family. Will laments, "What a family he made of us." (*MSS* 62) He remembers how Sonny has been teaching them (Will and Baby) the value of respect. "Self-respect! It's been his religion, his godhead." (*MSS* 13) He is surprised how a man like Sonny can be attracted to a woman other than his wife. That too, the woman is a white by race. So Will expresses his anger and anxieties in the following passage:

> She is blonde, my father's woman. Of course. What else would she be? . . . . if *he* is to be caught of course it's going to be by the most vulgar, commonplace, shopworn of sticky traps, fit for a dirty fly that comes into the kitchen to eat our food and shit on it at the same time. (*MSS* 13-14)

Will's above reflection expresses his confusion and disgust at the moral downfall of his father. As upset he is with the event, it comes to his mind repetitively. This is reflected in his repetition of words, phrases and images, such as 'my father's woman', 'needing Hannah', 'family matters' and images like the 'carry all'. Drawing on Freud's *Beyond the Pleasure Principle*, Judith Butler in his article, "The Pleasure of Repetition" says that repetition indicates the victim's inability to inhabit the present and that repetition expresses anger against the present. "In effect, repetition is associated with the re-presentation of the past, and hence, it indicates a way in which the ego fails to inhabit the present time" (273). Butler argues that the victim repeats words, scenes, etc. to repair the past. For Will the present is doubly painful because he is complicit in his father's affair, and thinks that he is deceiving his mother and sister. He feels helpless and frustrated. Nevertheless, he gets along with the deception. He tries to rationalise the psycho-sexual complex his father has shown, which is common to people of their kind, non-whites, including himself. "Of course she is blonde. The wet dreams I have, a schoolboy who's never slept with a woman, are blonde. It's an infection brought to us by the laws that have decided what we are, and what they are – the blonde ones (*MSS* 14). Thus while narrating his father's story, Will also represents his own evolving self. In the first person narration sections of the novel, Will tells his story with certain level of awareness because, as he claims, at fifteen he is no longer a child. Though not an adult yet, he is given the adult responsibility of keeping his father's secrets secret. This "clandestine knowledge immobilizes him, leaving him seething, resentful, and politically passive" (Levy 4). As Will moves toward adulthood, he acquires deep insight and knowledge of the intense anti-apartheid struggle capturing the suffering of the non-whites and the sacrifice of his family.

Will shows resilience to his traumatic experience by writing his autobiography and the biography of his father, Sonny. But Aila and Baby keep silent till they take the extreme steps. Both Will and Sonny have thought that Aila and Baby are not aware of Sonny's illicit affair with Hannah. Sonny remains absent from home and often for a long time to carry on his anti-apartheid campaign as well as his frequent outings with Hannah. But both the mother and the daughter can see through his deception. Perhaps their female instincts tell them what is happening around them. They do not show any sign of its knowledge but keep up the appearance of a well-knit family. A stony silence envelops Aila and Baby. On the other hand, Will is drawn deeper in the 'secrets' of his father. He "could not evade being drawn further in" (*MSS* 84). Will is shocked when Baby takes the extreme step. She attempts to commit suicide by cutting her wrists but fails. Her failed attempt to commit suicide is a violent reaction to the traumatic event which she and her mother have to bear with so long. Will realises that his mother and sister knew the fact from the beginning. His mother tells him that Baby took drugs and that her great liveliness was nothing but result of deep unhappiness:

> She said to me: –What can we do for her? –

> The slight emphasis on 'we' gave away, all at once, that my mother knew about my father. That she knew – without knowing how – I knew. . . .What could we do for my sister: a family that ours had become? And at the same moment it came to both of us: what Baby's 'deep unhappiness' that the doctor diagnosed was about. (*MSS* 61)

Sonny may turn a blind eye to the family. But Aila and Baby respond, though silently, and assert their political agency. After recovering from her failed suicide attempt, Baby turns a revolutionary and leaves the country along with her lover whom she marries abroad. They work in exile in a neighbouring African country for the refugees. Aila silently joins the arms wing of the ANC –Umkhonto we Sizwe –without the knowledge of the father and the son. She works for it locally in the Johannesburg area. Consequently Aila is arrested and charged with terrorism under the Internal Security

Act (*MSS* 233). Will is surprised how the graceful lady of the home transformed herself into a revolutionary. He regrets that unlike his father he has been present on two most critical moments in the history of the family: Baby's suicide attempt and Aila's arrest. When the white police officers come to their home, Will opens the door for them who subsequently arrest Aila. He thought they have come for Sonny. But to his utter surprise, they arrested Aila. He is overcome with grief and rage. He runs to the house of Hannah in search of Sonny who has been away on the usual holiday with Hannah. He recounts

I went to kill him that night.

I was the one who opened the door to her jailers. I was the one who could have died. (*MSS* 207)

This is a reflection of his anger against his father and also for his being left out in the liberation struggle. As he relates, his father is the famous Sonny, Baby is the revolutionary in exile, and Aila becomes an accomplice of Umkhonto we Sizwe. They are the "family's sacrifice for the people, there is no need of me, who needs someone like me" (*MSS* 251)? So towards the end of the novel, Will releases his repressed anger which is both a reproach to Aila and a self-accusation as well. He regrets that he is left out and that he has not played any role in the liberation struggle. He further continues

when I can act like the rest of you, when I can face them in court and tell them they're liars, liars, those thugs who've been let into our house –I let them in, I'm the one who's let every kind of destruction into our house, I'm always there, handy, Will is going to do it, . . . It's enough! I have enough of it! – (*MSS* 254-55)

The above passage is an expression of Will's frustration and self-accusation which a trauma victim suffers from. He regrets that he is an insider –insider to the family and to the secret of his father. And yet he has to act as an outsider. The situation is like that of Gordimer herself who has been a white activist, opposing apartheid in South Africa like any other black artist. But she has often faced criticism for being white. However, Will is angry at his presence at home at the crucial moments while his father has been absent. Now he can prove his presence in the family by acting in a certain way in the court. But his mother does not want him to be mixed up in this (*MSS* 254). As Lital Levy points out, he has sometimes imitated and sometimes played a foil to his father. And this "has castrated Will, such that his Oedipal rage appears almost over-determined. At the same time, political, sexual, and *authorial* agency are conjoined in the novel's economy" (original italic, Levy 5). In the middle of the narrative, he informs the reader that he has "a little girl" of his own. She is very nice and very fond of him. He sleeps with her at her place, or sometimes in the room of one of her friends. Just like his father, "his sex life has no home" (*MSS* 184-85). He calls his girlfriend a "little girl" of his own. But at the same time he recognizes her as an "intelligent" and "progressive" girl who has about the "same build" as his mother. "Thus, claiming his sexual agency Will mimics his father by choosing a girlfriend who obviously replicates his mother yet who also stands in doubly for Hannah, the secret lover who refutes domestic sexuality." (Levy 5)

The novel begins with the first person narrative voice of Will and alternates with third person narrative voice. As in *Burger's Daughter*, Gordimer uses in *My Son's Story* free direct speech as a device to move easily between the two narrative voices. According to Clingman, the narrative structure of the novel has a deceptive duality. Till the end, there are two narratives. The first one is a "feigned third-person narrative of Sonny (and the others), by Will; the second is a first-person narrative, by Will, in feigned ignorance of the other one" (xxix). The narrative begins as an autobiography in which the son tells the story of his father's infidelity: "How did I find out?/I was deceiving him" (*MSS* 3). Will's statement that he is deceiving his father is double edged. Ironically it also suggests the father's deception which becomes clear as the narrative progresses. Thus, Will begins narrating the story of his father, and in doing so he tells his own story – the story of his becoming a writer for which he feels that he should thank his father. "Do I have to thank him for that" (*MSS* 277)? He is not sure. Whether or not he thanks his father, he admits one thing that he is a writer. He claims:

> In our story, like all stories, I've made up what I wasn't there to experience myself. Sometimes –I can see –I've told something in terms I wouldn't have capable of, aware of, at the period when it was happening: the licence of hindsight of hindsight. *. . . Sometimes memory has opened a trapdoor and dropped me back into the experience as if I were living it again just at the stage I was when I lived it, so I've told it that way, in the present tense.* (italics original, *MSS* 275)

As the above reflection reveals, Will's memory often takes him back to his past experiences. He has to relive them again to relate in the present. His or their family story is the product of his frequent backward reflection and projection of his memories into the present. The present is replaced with this story/fiction with all its gaps and incoherence. In the Introduction to their book, *The Unspeakable*, Nevine El Nossery and Amy L. Hubbell observe that trauma narratives are by nature incomplete and full of gaps and inconsistencies. Citing Kathrin Robson, they further say that in the process of narrative memories often get modified and fictionalized: "the narrativization of trauma is curative not because they conveys 'what happened' but because it modifies it, because it represents the past in a less disturbing fashion." (cited in Nossery and Hubbell, 10) Sonny, a lover of Shakespeare, also wanted his son to be a writer. By writing the story of their family in the apartheid South Africa, Will writes his first book. He writes the story of his family and by doing so he frees himself from his present conundrums. He wrote a poem for his father, who has been jailed again. He is not sure whether or not the poem will be given to his father. The poem highlights the images of bird and dove, which may be seen as symbolizing freedom as against the iron bars and stone walls of the prison. He calls upon friends, lovers, and comrades to struggle for the liberation from the white supremacy. Gordimer seems to identify here with Will in terms of her own position as a writer and a witness within the contemporary South Africa. In the paragraphs preceding his poem he reports that Sonny's comrades thought he (Sonny) was not the man he had been. But Will claims that now it is his time with woman and politics. He will record what his father, mother, sister and others did, "what it really was like to live a life determined by the struggle to be free" (*MSS* 276). This is what he does in his "first book" which he cannot publish (*MSS*, 277). If this is his first, the reader can expect more books from this young author. By announcing himself as the author, Will seems to assert his voice that will challenge the hegemonic system in a language it can recognize. Gordimer takes the epigraph of the novel from Shakespeare's Sonnet XIII: "You had a father, let your son say so", which suggests a transition. But in this transition from "the father to this South African Will", Clingman points out,

Gordimer envisages "a shift in the claims of politics and fiction" in the post-apartheid South Africa (xxxi).

Will claims to author the novel in which he combines personal and historical memories. The description of the cleansing of the graves scene may be taken as a fine example of the historical fact. This scene shows the blacks and the whites coming together. The cleansing of the graves ceremony is held in a black township in honour of the nine South African young men who were shot dead by the police. The various anti-apartheid white groups participated in the ceremony after initial opposition by the police. But the government forces disperse the multiracial crowed adopting brutal measures, killing another man. The event shows the violence and death that marked the anti-apartheid movements in the 1980s. Sonny is the main speaker and his speech echoes Mandela's words during his Rivonia trial (Uledi-Kamanga 148). Further, as Dominic Head says this episode highlights Gordimer's concern with what Foucault called heterotopia –a site of difference and resistance. Head illustrates the point with reference to the black township where blacks and whites mix up for the graveyard ceremony. As the convoy of white lawyers and civil rights leaders reaches the overpopulated black township, they are greeted by multitudes of blacks. The blacks run towards the convoy and stand on either side of the road. Initially the white visitors fear the massive presence of blacks. But their fear soon changes into joy when the blacks extend their hands to welcome the whites. Hannah opened the window beside her. She found that instead of stones, black hands came forward and touched first her hands and then those of all who were inside the van(*MSS* 108). This handshaking affirms the human oneness. This is further seen in the graveside ceremony itself. Barriers between races are broken as the whites and the blacks mix freely. While narrating the free mixing, Gordimer highlights the economic and social differences between the whites and blacks. She points out the extreme poverty in which the blacks live. The blacks have developed over the years the habit of living in close proximity. They were accustomed to travel in overcrowded buses and trains. It was almost normal that a large family living together in a single room. But when they gathered in the graveyard

> the people from the combis were dispersed from one another and spatial aura they instinctively kept, and pressed into a single, vast, stirring being with the people of the township. . . One ultimate body of bodies was inhaling and exhaling in the single diastole and systole, and above was the freedom of the great open afternoon. (*MSS* 110)

This passage may be said to symbolically represent a space of black urbanization, which is different from and yet connected to other sites in South Africa. As depicted in the passage, there is a "spatial repression" to create "the possibility of a community, an integrated body politic". This community of "proximity" shows a "vitality" which is foreign to "the privileged whites who are, nevertheless, soon infected by its sense of possibility" (*MSS* 156). The passage represents an image of unity among the races, suggesting the possibility of a new nation. But this vision of an alternative future vanishes in the chaotic break-up of the protest. By the end of the novel, Will relates that the whites warned them – the blacks and the communists – to leave the area and burnt their house in the white suburb area under Group Areas Act of 1950. Seeing the house being burnt, he screamed: *This is my father's house.* (*MSS* 272) Though he has an uneasy relationship with his father, the destruction of the house brought back the old love and admiration of his father. Both the father and the son visited to inspect the destroyed house which lost all its markers separating the kitchen, the sitting-room, Sonny's room, etc. The destruction of their house reminds Will of the destruction that Sonny brought into the family: "The smell of destruction, of what has been consumed, that he first brought into that house." (*MSS* 274) Sonny, on the other hand, reacted angrily and said that they cannot be burnt out. He compares them (the black and the coloured) to the phoenix which rises from the ashes again and again. He claims that the whole country is theirs, not only the area they live in. Perhaps, Will refers to this bird, phoenix in his poem discussed in the last paragraph.

The end of *My Son's Story* reminds the reader of *The Lying days*. Like Will, Helen Shaw finds that she has written a novel as the "product of her experience" (Clingman, xxxi). However, Shaw is white but Will is a male and 'coloured', which suggests a development of a cultural tradition. Clingman further observes it is an irony that, unlike Helen Shaw, Will cannot publish his novel. This is perhaps because of censorship or because "the book relates more directly to the period of repression before 1990 than to the one that opened up after" (xxxii). As mentioned earlier in this chapter, Mengel and Borzaga argued that trauma in South Africa is a product of the history of apartheid, which has caused the collective traumatization of several generations.

My Son's Story continues to address some of the issues and themes of Gordimer's earlier fiction such as cross racial relations, public and private life, and also function of literature. Gordimer's choice of a coloured family in this novel shows her preoccupation with the politics of race, gender and resistance to apartheid. Sonny, the 'coloured' teacher and his family are located in an ambivalent position. They have certain advantage when compared with the blacks and yet segregated from the whites. Socio-political conditions of the 'coloured' people in South Africa coloured their identity with hybridity and fluidity. Their 'ambivalence' and 'in-betweenness' provide them with possibilities of transformation. As Homi Bhabha observes in *The Location of Culture* social differences are "signs of the emergence of community envisaged as a project" (3). Bhabha further says,

> 'Beyond' signifies spatial distance, marks progresses, promises the future; but our intimations of exceeding the barrier or boundary –the very act of going *beyond* --are unknowable, unrepresentable, without a return to the 'present' which, in the process of repetition, becomes disjunct and displaced. (original italics, 4-5)

Sonny's 'coloured' family symbolically marks progress to an uncertain future when they move from the coloured location in their hometown to a 'grey area' in the city of Johannesburg where people of their kind defied the apartheid laws and "settled in among whites" (*MSS* 14). The committee offered Sonny a house to settle among whites in defiance of the Group Areas Act. Gordimer seems to suggest that the movement of the 'coloured' family into the grey area of the city signals the movement 'beyond' borders and barriers. This also suggests the notion of the 'coloured' identity as hybrid and in-between. By living in the borderland space between the white community and the black location across the veld, they move beyond the barriers of colour and transgress the limits of social and cultural space in their efforts of resistance to segregation.

Secondly, the coloured family's movement into the white city also marks the beginning of an uncertain future of the family in

South Africa. This is realised by Sonny's son Will and his wife Aila as well. Sonny actively involved himself in politics after the School uprisings and led the family into a 'grey area' of South African politics in which the future is uncertain. Will perceives this as uprooting and dislocation of the family. He can understand that a "changing vocabulary was accompanying the transformation of Sonny to 'Sonny' the political personality" (*MSS* 39). Aila knew that he was leading her into a "different life" about which she was not sure that she could follow. Even Sonny understood that "a certain shelter was being given up, for the family. Shabby, degrading shelter –but nevertheless" (*MSS* 39). Sonny's family has been in a borderline situation and the movement of the family signifies the flux or ambivalence into the unpredictable future. Through the relocation of the 'coloured' identity, Gordimer appears to suggest the family's cultural mixture that may produce new meanings and possibilities. According to Clingman, Gordimer's use of 'coloured' family to unfold the history of apartheid South Africa through the voice of a coloured narrator is a "symbolic choice of narrative identity, representing some identification on Gordimer's part with a new and developing world" (xxvii). Gordimer suggests the potential of the coloured family and even her own writing to move beyond the apartheid system and become the locations of culture.

Another major theme of the novel is the issue of sex and politics. Gordimer's treatment of gender is taken in the next chapter. However, it may be mentioned here that Sonny's betrayal has a traumatic effect on both his daughter, Baby and his wife Aila. In the case of Baby, the reaction is visible when she attempts to commit suicide. Otherwise she is silent throughout the novel. The reader can know her internal as well external life through the narrative voice of Will. Even Aila's life is mediated through Will. Through his interracial relationship with Hannah and his underground political activities, Sonny becomes a site for exploring the relationship of sex and politics. And this, in turn, helps Gordimer explore the social realities of South Africa of the time. Sonny's betrayal, on the other hand, creates uncertainties and doubts in the family. Aila becomes a revolutionary under the cover of her daughter to overcome the traumatic experience resulting from her husband's betrayal. Aila moves beyond the traditional gender identity as a dependant wife and caring mother, and emerges with the new identity of a revolutionary in the later part of the novel.

Will takes recourse to narrative to give expression to his traumatic experiences, Aila joins the political struggle and her engagement is independent of her husband. She transcends her past and achieves a new identity which is as subversive as any man's. Gordimer here makes a distinctive progress form her earlier heroines by portraying Aila as an active revolutionary and by portraying a 'coloured' woman in the role of revolutionary.

Works Cited

Balaev, Michelle. *Contemporary Approaches in Literary Trauma Theory*. New York: Palgrave Macmillan, 2014.

Butler, Judith. "The Pleasures of Repetition." *Plesure Beyond the Pleasure Principle*. Ed. A. Glick and Stanley Bone. New Haven: Yale University Press, 1990.

Caruth, Cathy. *Unclaimed Experience: Trauma, Narrative and History*. Baltimore: John Hopkins University Press, 1996.

Clingman, Stephen. *The Novels of Nadine Gordimer: History from Inside*. Amherst: University of Massachusetts, 1992.

Craps, Stef. "Wor(l)ds of Grief: Traumatic Memory and Literary Witnessing in Cross-Cultural Perspective." *Textual Practice*, 24(2010), 51-68.

Gordimer, Nadine. *Burger's Daughter*. London: Bloomsbury, 2000.

______*July's People*. London: Bloomsbury, 2000.

______*Occasion for Loving*. London: Bloomsbury, 2013.

______ *My Son's Story*. London: Bloomsbury, 2003.

______ "Living in the Interregnum."*The Essential Gesture: Writing, Politics and Places*. Ed. Stephen Clingman. London: Penguin, 1989.

Head, Dominic. *Nadine Gordimer*. Cambridge: Cambridge University Press, 1994.

Herrero, Dolores. "Plight versus Right: Trauma and the Process of Recovering and Moving beyond the Past in Zoe Wicomb's *Playing in the Light*." *Trauma in Contemporary Literatue: Narrative and Representation*. Ed. Marita Nadal and Monica Calvo. New York: Routledge, 2014.

Levy, Lital. "Family Affairs: Complicity, Betrayal, and the Family in Hisham Matar's *In the Country of Men* and Nadine Gordimer's *My Son's Story*." CLCWeb: Comparative Literature and Culture 21.3 (2019): < https:// doi.org/10.7771/ 1481-4374.3547> (accessed on 18 September, 2019).

Mambrol, Nasrullah. "Trauma Studies." https://literariness. org/2018/12/19/trauma-studies/ (accessed on 27 September, 2019).

Murlanch, Isabel Fraile. "Seeing It twice: Trauma and Resilience in the Narrative of Janette Turner Hospital." *Trauma in*

Contemporary Literatue: Narrative and Representation. Ed. Marita Nadal and Monica Calvo. New York: Routledge, 2014.

Newman, Judie. Nadine Gordimer. London: Routledge, 2014.

Nossery, Nevine El, and Hubbell, Amy L. eds. Introduction. *The Unspeakable: The Representations Trauma in francophone Literature and Art.* 12 Back Chapman Street: Cambridge scholars, 2013.

Pellicer-Ortin, Silvia. "The Turn to the Self and History in Eva Figes' Autobiographical Works: The Healing of Old Wounds?" *Trauma in Contemporary Literatue: Narrative and Representation.* Ed. Marita Nadal and Monica Calvo. New York: Routledge, 2014.

Visser, Irene. "Declonizing Trauma Theory: Retrospect and Prospects." https://www.researchgate.net/publication/233460743.

CHAPTER IV

A Gender Study of the Novels of Nadine Gordimer

4.1. Gordimer and Feminism

Nadine Gordimer in her fiction has dealt with apartheid in South Africa and its resistance. Another major concern of Gordimer is sexual politics. According to Judie Newman, gender is a "conditioning factor" in Gordimer's fiction (17). Gordimer's exploration of sexuality draws the attention of the feminist critics. But she never identified herself as a feminist though she was sensitive to women's oppression. She has been consistently arguing that in South Africa the primary issue is racism and sexism is only a secondary one. An excerpt from her interview with Robert Boyers is cited below as a representative view:

> The white man and the white woman have much more in common than the white woman and the black woman, despite their difference in sex. Similarly, the black man and the black woman have much more in common than the black man and the white man (19).

Gordimer further observes that in the apartheid South Africa the colour of skin is the basis of "sisterhood or brotherhood of sex". Loyalty to one's sex is secondary to the loyalty to one's race. "That's why Women's Liberation is, I think, a farce in South Africa," says Gordimer (Interview with Robert Boyers 20). In her review of the biography of

Olive Schreiner by Ruth First and Ann Scott, Gordimer repeated her conviction that racism is central and feminism is "marginal" in the struggle for South African liberation. To her, women's liberation is insignificant to fight against apartheid ideology. Gordimer's position is different from that of Simon de Beauvoir. In her consideration of the issues of national liberation and women's liberation, Beauvoir gives priority to women's liberation: "Later means never" (Gardner 173). Gordimer argues that in the given South African context sexual behaviour of the blacks is a result of the racist system.

However, this does not mean that Gordimer has not been concerned with oppression of women. Nor does it completely invalidate the argument that racism may result from sexism. The fact of the matter is that in the given socio-political condition, Gordimer has given priority to racism. She has been aware that women comprise a "disadvantage working group" and are in a subordinate position (Driver 33). Gordimer states in the Introduction to *Selected Stories* (*SS*) that "all writers are androgynous beings" (3). She knows what Kate Millett explains in her influential book, *Sexual Politics* (1971) that many writers do not attempt to be androgynous. In this connection, Dorothy Driver observes that Gordimer intends to be androgynous to make up for the South African society which is not so (33). Throughout her fiction she has shown her interest in women's subordinate position and in her interview with Gray she admits that she has become "much more radical" both as a women and as a citizen. This may imply the feminist strain in her works. Judie Newman even observes that Gordimer is "doubly marginalized in South Africa, as a white and as a woman" (17). She has been aware of the complex relation between racism and sexism. In fact, she has analysed the socio-political issues in her fiction through her own "brand of micropolitics or politics of the body" (Head 19). The personal often merges with the public in the kind of body politics as found in the fiction of Gordimer.

4.2 Gordimer's Novels

The early novels of Gordimer examine the adequacy of the liberals in the apartheid South Africa. And while examining it, she does not ignore the politics of the body. The first novel, *The Lying Days* (*LD*) deals with Helen Shaw's search for her social identity. The novel outlines the development of the consciousness of Shaw, including her awakening to bodily consciousness. Early in the novel, Helen refuses to accompany her parents and leaves for the concession stores. She finds a white boy moving about the 'mine boys'. She notices the white boy entering the stores while she remains an outsider. She experiences there a different social environment. However, when she notices a mine boy urinating in the open, she runs back to towards her home. Judie Newman comments that this episode shows how a white girl is "excluded" from the African world as well as the male world (18). In that culturally different situation, she registers her reaction bodily. As she moves through holding her "buttocks stiffly together", she realises that her eyes cannot take in everything around her surrounding (*LD* 10). This action of holding her buttocks stiffly together and walking back may be called a protective response of Helen to something which is frightening and also desiring. She also feels within herself to suppress a giggle or a kind of excitement. It may be noted that Gordimer has several times in the novel associated laughter with repression or fear. Thus, Helen's physical attraction and her early responses to Ludi Koch are marked by laughter, before they have kissed each other for the first time. As the episode shows,

Helen's sexual awakening occurs with Ludi Koch. Another detail given early in the novel is also significant. There is an unwritten law in the apartheid South Africa that little girls should never be left alone because of the 'native' boys: "a little girl must not be left alone because there were native boys about" (*LD* 4). This fear of the black sexuality is a collective fear inculcated into the young minds of the white community.

Through Paul –Helen episode Gordimer explores the connection between sexuality and politics. According to Dominic Head, Gordimer gives the hint of a dichotomy of mind and body in a conversation between Helen and Ian Petrie, a fellow train passenger (40). Petrie tells Helen that his marriage is devoid of intellectual equality. It is based completely on "physical intelligence". Petrie further tells, "'–It's very important. I enjoy making love to her and I enjoy playing games with her'" (*LD* 101). The intellectual and physical dualism characterizes Helen's two important relationships: her affair with Paul Clark, which is based on physical intimacy and which eventually fails, and her platonic friendship with Joel Aaron. Leaving the Mercuses, Helen lives with Paul. But their relationship starts declining when she begins to doubt their political complicity. They gradually lose their common ground. Helen notices a change in Paul resulting from the burden of his work at the government Welfare Department connected with the housing problems of the South African blacks. Paul realises that his work comprises his political activities –mixing with African nationalists at night and carrying the government's orders which they (the nationalists) protest during day. Helen and Paul's relationship fails day by day just as Paul gradually feels the impossibility of his work. Helen wonders how the "difficulties of this work, affecting him, throw our relationship out of balance" (300). She wanted to live with him "in the greatest possible intimacy" (*LD* 253) and refused to belong to the company of women. But Paul has shown signs that he prefers a different world of gender relations. When Helen is trying with an essay on George Eliot, Paul belittles her, asking what is confusing her "little brain"(*LD* 242). This remark of Paul betrays his prejudice toward a woman. He attempts to cheer her up sharing an amusing incident of a black man who rejects his wife because she is "a damned ugly woman" (*LD* 243). This clearly exposes the hypocrisy of Paul. On the one hand he engages with the liberal activities of the Welfare Department, on the other hand he takes delight at the action of the black man only to denigrate the female. One evening, when the meal was late, Paul complains, "Helen, you're becoming a rotten wife" (*LD* 290). And with this reaction of Paul, as pointed out by Judie Newman, Helen realises that "her flight from conventional sexual paradigms has merely brought her full circle" (20). Now she cooks a "man's breakfast" and keeps her "mouth shut" (*LD* 320). When they both worked, they snatched their breakfast together. But now she stood about while Paul "sat down and ate; plenty of time for me to breakfast" (*LD* 320). In her book, *Sexual Politics* (1970), Kate Millett argues that the relationship between men and women is governed by a power structure which has political implications. "All aspects of society and culture functioned according to a sexual politics that encouraged women to internalize their own inferiority until it became psychologically rooted"(Tolan 326). This sexual politics is also visible in the narration of the riot that Helen witnesses. She is horrified when she saw the shooting of a black man in the riot. "Everyone fears fear; but horror –that belongs to second-hand experience, through books and films," reacts Helen (*LD* 333). But Paul makes little of this real experience of Helen and calls it "Helen's adventure at the barricades" (*LD* 334). Later Helen along with her companion Laurie is invited to a gathering to get first hand account of the incident. And soon Helen recognizes that the incident was described, "the tale was told" by Laurie who "developed quite a technique in the telling" (*LD* 334). In the narration, Helen is marginalized. Her experience is appropriated and narrated by the male. She can see through the technique of Laurie –how at different points of the narrative he pauses, drops his voice and places his emphasis. Ultimately it turns out that "it was his technique only that I heard" (*LD* 334) and that she was never present there. Judie Newman observes that this episode makes two points clear. First, it shows the technique of men through which they "select and appropriate the significance of female experience, exercising male proxy over a woman's story" (21). Secondly, as argued by Newman, the episode suggests the need for a form of narrative which can capture the horror of black experience.

The affair between Paul and Helen fails. But the 1948 victory of the Nationalist Party makes way for the Mixed Marriages Act of 1949. Gordimer has shown how the Nationalist government used this act to intrude upon the private life of the South Africans. One day Paul narrated to Helen an incident of how the police torches suddenly flashed on the faces of a mixed –races couple in the bed at night, who were subsequently arrested. She is haunted by the memory of this incident. Once she awakes to car headlights in the bedroom and springs back from Paul. However, Gordimer wants to convey that even the private world of intimacy is invaded by patriarchy and racism as well.

Gordimer's second novel, *A World of Strangers* (*WS*) deals with Toby Hood's attempts to explore the life in the black townships and the high society of the whites while remaining neutral to both the worlds. Though the novel shows some change in his views, it also examines limitations of his liberal values vis a vis apartheid regime. Gordimer seems to be critical about his attitudes, particularly his attitude to women. He considers women as objects of desire or pleasure. They cannot be equal partners. Toby has seen racism in his office, when his office worker, Miss McCann quits her job after noticing Toby, a white having lunch with the two black men, Steven and Dick Chaputra. He could have shared his feelings of anger and confusion with his lover, Cecil Rowe. Instead he finds in his lover a source of distraction. He thinks that he had "an Eastern equation of women with pleasure; I fiercely resisted any impingement on this preserve" (*WS* 150). Thus, Toby reduces women to objects of personal pleasure. For Toby, comments Dominic Head, this reduction is a 'preserve' which he 'fiercely' wants to protect. And this metaphor establishes a link between an individual male desire and the institutionalized male desire of the state, which also employs a sanctioned violence, a 'fierceness' to establish 'preserves' for whites" (Head 50). Once while making love with Cecil, he insisted that the light must be left on: "She argued about the light, but I wanted to see her face, to know what she was feeling. (Who knows what women feel, in their queer, gratuitous moment?) Gordimer seems to represent here the female sexuality as the 'other' for Toby. Later, when he along with Steven visits the club run by Indians, Toby sees a girl with face and body of the most tender grace and beauty (*WS* 191). And after witnessing the singing of this girl, he reacts that she was a "creature" made to "please" (*WS* 192). This clearly reflects the colonial mind of Toby. Even the liberal Toby, who can have friendship with the black, treats the colonial women as creatures or as objects because of sexual difference. Analyzing Gilman, Ania Loomba states that "racial as well as sexual 'others' derive from 'the same deep structure'" (137).

However, Toby again expresses such an attitude when he dismisses the thought of his marriage. He tells Cecil that for him "the exoticism of women still lay in beauty and self-absorbed femininity, I would choose an houri rather than a companion" (*WS* 261). This view of Toby confirms his reaction to the Indian girl in the club. In the words of Head, in both instances "there is an evident commodification and reduction of woman to an exotic other for personal use; this is precisely the way in which the forces of colonial imperialism view the potential of exotic 'other' places and populations" (51). Earlier in the novel he says that he wants to see people who interest him – black, white, or any colour. Gordimer makes him realise that politics intrudes every kind of relationship in South Africa. He does not even act upon the suggestion given by his friend, Steven to "interest him [self] in a nice African girl yet." He acknowledges the fact that he had not yet been attracted by any African woman (*WS* 215).

Toby's relationship with Anna Louw has been very brief but significant. This brief relationship also involves a sexual encounter between Toby and Anna. But this time his sexual advances are governed by his fear: "I put out my hand and touched, with the touch of fear, the thing I fled from." And when he makes love to her, he feels that "pleasure came to me as if wrung from my grasp" (*WS* 184). It appears that the motif behind Toby's sexual act is the need to control the object of fear –the fear of the other.

Gordimer has combined the racial and sexual themes more explicitly in the novel, *Occasion for Loving* (*OL*). The cross-racial relationship between the black painter, Gideon Shibalo and the young white woman Ann Davis constitutes the major action of the novel. Boaz Davis, researcher of the musical heritage of the black Africans comes to South Africa along with his wife Ann and stays with Tom and Jessie Stilwell. Brilliant dancer, Ann falls in love with Gideon, defying the colour bar prevalent in the apartheid South Africa. She visits different places like Lucky Star and mixes with people across colours or races. When she moves to Western Transvaal with Gideon, she becomes aware of Gideon as a black first, and as a man second. And she and Boaz finally leave South Africa without telling a single word to Gideon. Their love affair fails because of the racist ideology that they have internalized. As Clingman has observed, their relationship fails because the repressions of apartheid have been "psychologically inscribed" or because of the "prestructuring effects" of apartheid (82). When Gideon informs about the failure of their affair, she suddenly discovers the prestructuring effects of apartheid on her mind though she thought it was settled "once and for all, long ago" (*OL* 290). While talking to Gideon, she suddenly discovers her childhood fear as emanating from "the black man" that she must never be left alone with in their house. In her early life she used feel at night that someone was following her from behind. She was told that she must not be alone in the house with a black man. But nobody explained to her the reason. She remembers how she used to feel apprehensive at night that someone was following her in the dark passage when she went to the bathroom. She would ask,

> Who was it, do you think? And how many more little white girls are there for whom the very first man was a black man? The very first man, the man of the sex fantasies . . . (*OL* 290).

Jessie had forgotten or left it behind but when she sees Ann Gideon falling out "one suddenly needs to feel one's way back" (*OL* 290). Jessie's reaction here echoes Helen's reference to the unwritten law or the fear of the black sexuality in *The Lying Days*. White women like Helen and Jessie are taught to fear or treat the black as the other.

In her Article, "Othering the Self: Nadine Gordimer's Colonial Heroines", Robin Visel observes that the colonial woman goes through a conflict between her sex and her colour and that Gordimer's white African women exemplify this conflict. As seen in the fiction of Gordimer, these women are alienated –both intellectually and emotionally –from the white minority society. At the same time, they cannot physically identify with the black (33). When Ann finally leaves for England, Jessie is angry with her not because of her physical relation with Gideon but because of betrayal of a black, or, for that matter, betrayal of African life. In fact, she attempts to rebel what Visel calls, against "the patriarchal order as she struggles to define herself in a hostile environment," and as a result she discovers "the connections between patriarchy and racism under colonialism" (33). Ann's sudden departure hurts Jessie as much as it does Gideon. It makes her wonder how a white can fall in love with a person of another race (black) and at the same time destroy him, and "escape back into your filthy damn whiteness" (*OL* 312). This appalling state of mind of Jessie can be described as her "unhomely" moment (Bhabha 15). In a conversation with her husband, she expresses her anxiety and fear more clearly. However, as Robin Visel points out in the article mentioned above, Gordimer does not allow her white women to "claim innocence" (34) because she cannot disinherit her "privilege and guilt" (33). Visel admits that the white woman cannot shoulder her "responsibility" because of "the social and political conditions of apartheid" (34). In her oppression she turns out to be a self-divided figure and a site of rapprochement. In the words of Visel,

> Furthermore, she is increasingly cut off from blackness, both by government decree and the rising hostility of her black brothers and sisters . . . the ambiguous, self-divided figure of the white

girl or woman is the site of the hesitant, fraught rapprochement of white and black. She is the site of connection, while she is made to realize the impossibility of connection (35).

The character and situation of Jessie best illustrate the points made in the above passage. After his disastrous love affair, Jessie sees Gideon heavily drunk in a party. When she approaches him and tries to speak to him, only to be told: "White bitch –get away" (*OL* 331). As Jessie becomes aware of her whiteness so does Gideon of his blackness. It may be noted that in the 1960s the African National Congress forms its armed wings and the resistance movement gradually turns violent, and the blacks begin thinking that they must fight their battle on their own. Hence the gap between the liberal whites and the black widens. However, Gideon's words once again open her mind to the sufferings of the blacks as much as the incident reminds her whiteness. She becomes a site of rapprochement or connection between the races though she understands the difficulty it involves. Even after the final confrontation, she continues to meet Gideon in friends' home or in the Lucky Star where white and black people mix. Gordimer seems to explore sexuality or politics of the body as a point of transgression between races and thereby provide borderline situation that may give rise to new ideas or new cultures.

Gordimer has explored the theme of sexual politics through the attitudes of Gideon as well. His treatment of his wife, Clara is highly questionable. When Gideon was supposed to go abroad on a scholarship, his wife went to Bloemfontein to live with her mother and sister. After a lengthy process, he was refused passport and he could not go abroad. Gideon spent months and years jobless and drunk, and never thought of going to or bringing back Clara. "He and she lost sight of one another" (*OL* 197). When Sandile, Clara's brother told him that she wanted to go to him, he replies, "It's not possible" (195). Though he found it difficult to admit, there was nothing to talk about the woman who had been his wife and given birth to a child. The responsibility of his child had been born by Sandile for some time because the latter owed him money. So Gideon's carelessness about his past relationship reflects his irresponsibility towards woman. His relationship with Ida also reveals the problem of female oppression within the black people. Chapter nine of the novel narrates how Gideon has been living with Ida in a casual manner. Ida, a nurse understands that he is not committed enough to her to make them a couple though she does washing and chores for him. This imbalance of commitment often results in an oppression of women in the black community, who has little voice in the social and domestic life. At the end of the novel, Gideon appears drunken at a party with a nurse, probably Ida. But, as Head observes, she has now become an "anonymous background" of the action as well as to Gideon (68). His relationship with his wife and Ida points to issue of hierarchy of oppression in the South Africa of the time. The almost non-visibility of Ida or Clara may be seen as act of silencing the female.

The theme of problematic sexual politics is also seen in Gordimer's short story, "Good Climate, Friendly Inhabitants", first published in 1965 and later included in the collection titled *Selected Stories* (SS). The story is concerned with a white woman's relationship with a mysterious white man and a black called Jack, a petrol attendant at a petrol station or garage in Johannesburg. As the story opens the woman declares herself as a very fair skinned lady. But her claim is also coloured with anxieties of her age: "I'm forty-nine but I could be twenty-five except for my face and my legs. I've got that *very fair skin* and *my legs have gone mottled*, like Roquefort cheese" (emphasis added, *SS* 263). Thus she introduces herself through her physical appearance without naming herself. Another important idea that makes clear in the beginning of narrative is the power-relation between the white and the black. She often moves about in front of the garage to keep "an eye on the boys", that is, the black attendants in the garage. She is not worried about the mechanics who are white but she is rather worried about the petrol attendants who are black South Africans. "On the whole they're not a bad lot of natives, though you get a cheeky bastard now and then, or a thief, but he does not last long *with us*" (emphasis added, *SS* 263). The power-relation is structured in terms of 'us' and 'them'. She keeps surveillance over the petrol attendants but not over the mechanics because they are "all white chaps". She refers to the black men as 'boys' and she is addressed as 'missus', which assures her power and superiority. She nevertheless acknowledges that the 'boy', Jack is smarter and even tries to establish a kind friendship with him. The real reason why she finds Jack reliable is that he is comparatively 'white' than others. He is familiar to them also because of his European name, Jack which is different from his original African name. The woman finds it confusing when his people address him by different names. She often receives phone calls from the natives asking for speaking to Mpanza and Makiwane. When she tells them there is no one with that name, they will ask for Jack. This irritates the woman and so one day she asks him why they have hundred and one names and why his relatives do not ask for Jack straight way without wasting her time. To this Jack replies,

> 'Here I'm Jack because Mpanza Makiwane is not a name, and there I'm Mpanza Makiwane because Jack is not a name, but I'm the only one who knows who I am wherever I am.' I couldn't help laughing (*SS* 265).

The practice of re-naming the 'natives' may be described as what postcolonial theorists call "epistemic violence" (Spivak 31). Gayatri Spivak argues that the west always defines the rest of the world using its own concepts and definitions, and thereby constitutes the colonial subjects as the 'other'. The woman refuses to acknowledge Jack's original name in order to retain her superiority and her authority.

The more important aspect of the story in connection with the present study is the woman's relationship with a young man who appears at the garage. The man one day comes to the petrol station and refills petrol in his car and wants to pay in Rhodesian money. When Jack takes him to his 'missus', that is, the woman, the man claims he has come from Rhodesia and requests the woman for her help in finding a place to exchange money. The woman immediately reflects upon the attractive young man and the way she must appear in his eyes. She notices that he was young and that his "hair was streaky blond kind" (*SS* 266). When the man addresses her as "Miss", she reflects "Well, I'd had my hair done, it's true, but I don't kid myself you could think of me as a miss unless you saw my figure, from behind (*SS* 266). This reflection is also tinged with anxieties of her physical appearance. However, the relationship that begins dramatically continues to deepen and even becomes sexual in nature. And the relationship becomes disturbing for the woman. After the first night together, he tells her that he might stay in her room since she is at work all day. He even leaves his hotel room without paying for it. She finds herself in a difficult situation. She thinks that she has no choice but to accommodate him. On the other hand, she is not comfortable in his presence. Perhaps, she is haunted by a conflict between her fear of the man and the thought of social insecurity. She is worried about herself. She is anxious about her future when she will be unable to work. She is afraid that she will be alone and nobody will visit her. "Every Sunday you read in the paper about woman dead alone in flats, no one discovers it for days" (*SS* 272). So her insecurity and loneliness derive her to desire for the clean, good-looking man though there is a growing fear for the strange man. She allows him to stay with her in order to win him. And the man manipulates her desire very effectively. This is what a man does in a patriarchal society. Karen Lazar describes him as "an incarnation of the exploitation of women" (219). She argues that "sexual violence is an enactment of generic power over and control of women by men" and that the relationship of the woman is a combination of need and fear that go to make the "domestic trap which so many battered women cannot escape" (219). However, besides threat of sexual violence, the woman also faces political violence to some extent. The man appears to be a mercenary who is involved in the recent conflicts in Africa, fighting with the revolutionaries to bring down the white minority rule. He tells the woman how he was in the Congo a few years ago, "fighting for that native chief, what's-name –Tshombe –against the Irishmen who were sent out here to put old what's-name down" (*SS* 268).

On the other hand, alone and scared the woman cannot but confide in the 'boy', Jack. Despite prejudice of racial superiority, she develops certain relationship with the petrol attendant. Though she maintains some distance with him because "he [Jack] mustn't get too free with a white person" (*SS* 274), she comes to share news about the stranger, the young man with Jack. One day he tells the woman how he sends away the young man, informing him, falsely though, that she has left the petrol station for Rhodesia. Thus Jack, the black shows some compassion toward the white woman and frees her from the fear of the unwelcome visitor, the intruder. But once she is free from her fear, the old racial prejudice overcomes her. Jack's kindness is repaid with insult. She starts thinking that Jack wants to present himself as an educated man. And, she assumes, "if you take any notice of things like that with them, you begin to give them big ideas about themselves" (*SS* 275). So Lazar observes that it is a perverse twist of blame in which Jack loses his particularity in the eyes of the woman and "becomes one of the 'natives' whom a woman on her own 'can't trust at night'" (220). Gordimer seems to suggest that private life in South Africa is affected by politics as well as sexual relations between individuals and also between races. All in all, the story nicely illustrates the complexity of the issue of race and gender in the society of apartheid South Africa.

The atmosphere of fear also runs through the story, "Is There Nowhere Else Where We Can Meet?" which Gordimer places at the beginning of her collection of short stories, *Selected Stories*. While describing the conflict between the white and the black in the South African society, the narrative also captures the psychological effects on a young white woman of her encounter with a black man. The story tells how a black man suddenly confronts a white woman and steals her parcel and handbag. This has been a shattering experience for the woman. Her loss of calmness is reflected in Gordimer's description of the veld. The opening of the story reflects natural harmony: "It was cool grey morning and the air was like smoke. In that reversal of the elements that sometimes takes place, the grey, soft, muffled sky moved like the sea on a silent day" (*SS* 9). Here the description of a natural scene shows a Lawrentian quality and establishes an "intimacy between the mental state of the character and her surrounding world" (Trump 345). After the attack of the black man, the white woman is frightened. She loses her calmness and so does the nature around her. The familiar world turns out to be cruel to her. She began running, stumbling against the stalks of dead grass and turning over her heels against the winter tussocks. With dust in her eyes, she somehow reaches a fence on the other side of a ditch and then road. She attempts to climbs over the fence though her hands became numb. She has to struggle with the wires of the fence because

> ... her coat got caught on a barb, and she was imprisoned there, bent in half, while *the waves of terror swept over her in the heat and trembling.* At last the wire tore through its hold on the cloth; wobbling, frantic, she climbed over the fence" (emphasis added, *SS* 11-12).

When the woman reaches the suburban area, she should have a feeling of relief. Instead she is enveloped with a profound sense of loneliness and uncertainty. In the final lines of the story Gordimer excellently conveys the effects of the attack on the woman. It has maimed and crippled her. As she reaches the first house of the white suburban area, the thought of the fight suddenly comes to her mind. She thinks why she fights and why she does not give him the money, etc. The figure of the black with his red eyes, smell and cracks in his feet flashes in mind. "She shuddered. The cold of the morning flowed into her" (*SS* 12). And she went down the road slowly like an invalid person.

Martin Trump in his essay, "The Short Fiction of Nadine Gordimer" suggests that in the story, "Is There Nowhere Else Where We Can Meet?" both the poor black man and the white young woman are victims. Gordimer offers an intriguing perception of the encounter between the two characters, "namely, that the black man and the woman are together victims of the society in which they live"

(Trump 347). The sexual, psychological and political implications of this story set the tone for the collection, *Selected Stories*. Hence, perhaps, Gordimer has placed this short piece at the beginning of the anthology.

Trump contends that men often dominate or rule over women through silence. They maintain their dominance by "wholly or partly silencing the views and suggestions" of their female partner (353). Trump corroborates his argument through an excellent analysis of Gordimer's story, "Something for the Time Being". The story centres around two couples: one white South African couple and the other a black one living in the township. The opening part of the narratives depicts the marital relationship between the blacks –Daniel and Mngoma. Gordimer has very skilfully captured the 'silence' that exists between the two. The novelist has effectively emphasized the silence and the uneasy condition that it leads to:

> "He thought of it as discussing with her, but the truth was that she did not help him out at all. She said nothing, while she ran her hand up the ridge of bone behind the rim of her child-sized yellow-brown ear . . . Yet her listening was very demanding; when he stopped at the end of a supposition or a suggestion, her silence made the stop inconclusive. He had to take up again what he had said, carry it –where" (SS 205)?

Ella does not respond to Daniel because she is hardly given any opportunity to talk. Their married life has been solely governed by what Daniel thinks or does. She has no role to play or to pass any opinion in their life. And even when she says something, as the last part of the story shows, she is cowed down by him. As the story begins, he tells her how he has been arrested several times and sent to jail because of his political activities and how this time he is dismissed from his job. So he plans to go to Flora Donaldson, a white woman who helps the political prisoners. All the time Daniel speaks, Ella remains silent and shows no reaction. But Gordimer has conveyed Ella's thoughts through the third-person narrative. She (Ella) is deeply concerned with the fact that her husband is jobless now and that poverty stares at them. She suddenly realises that all the things that she knew deserted her. She had lost her wits. She fell back to her old habit and nervously began to scratch the skin on her neck. Through her characterisation Gordimer has portrayed her as a wife who is cowed down by her husband. She has achieved it through her description of Ella and through her prolonged silence. When in the final scene of the story she attempts to say something, Daniel reacts angrily to silence her. Ella asks him about his new job at the workshop of Wlliam Chadders. He tells her that his employer has asked him not to wear the ANC badge at the workshop. And he suggests that he is again going to lose the job as he will not stop wearing the badge. This makes her deeply worried. She cherishes the hope that Daniel somehow retains the job. But she cannot express her thought as they do not enjoy a relationship on equal terms. So she keeps looking at him as he talks about his job, and finally her eyes are filled with tears. She tries to speak and not to cry. Gordimer has captured her fear and agony in the following conversation between the husband and wife:

> The idea of tears exasperated him and he held her with a firm almost belligerently inquiring gaze. Her hand went up round the back of her neck under her collar, anxiously exploratory. "Don't do that!" he said. "You're like monkey catching lice."

. . . She began to breathe hysterically. "You couldn't put it in your packet, for the day, she said wildly, grimacing at the bitterness of the malice towards him (*SS* 215-16).

Ella has been living with him through thick and thin, and shouldering the responsibility of running the family even in his absence. But she turns out to be a 'monkey' in his eyes. On hearing him calling her monkey, she breaks into trembling and asks him if he couldn't put the ANC badge in his pocket during the day and thus saved his job. But the moment she questions him, he shouts angrily and 'silences' her. He jumps from the table and bursts out: "'Christ I knew you would say it! I've been waiting for you to say it. You've been wanting to say it for five years"(*SS* 216). Gordimer has described the incident so vividly and effectively. Daniel reacts verbally but he reacts in such a way as if it were a physical attack on Ella. She begins to weep as she has no other option. He calms down a little bit and finally speaks to her in a kindly voice: "'Don't cry. Don't cry. You're just like any other woman'" (*SS* 216). If Ella is like any other woman, he is like all men who maintain and control their rule or dominance over women through fear. They always treat the female as the voiceless other and when they try to raise a little voice it is silenced through different tactics.

On the other hand, the relationship between William and Madge is characterised by a kind of openness. But there is difference between the two in terms of their attitude to life in South Africa. Giving an account of the two, Gordimer says that William had no black friends before he married Madge. But he considers racial prejudice as completely absurd and immoral. Madge has friends both blacks and whites. And she does not feel only; she always "did something, at once, to express what she felt" (*SS* 208). When William objects to

Daniel's wearing the ANC badge at the workshop, Madge challenges it and thereby puts his position in question. She wonders that how a man who appears to hold liberal political views can occupy a place in a factory which is intolerant of any form of liberal gesture. She questions how he can give him the job because he is sympathetic to him but he allows him to wear the Congress badge. Madge has touched upon the worst inconsistency in the life of William and, by extension, in the life of many whites. However, Madge's question leads to a dispute between them and they lose the easy relation they enjoyed earlier. Gordimer has captured their thought in a passage describing how they stood in close proximity in a bathroom:

> "They were at once aware of each other as people who live in intimacy are only when hostility returns each to the confines of himself. He felt himself naked before her, where he had stepped out on to the toweling mat, and he took a towel slowly covered himself, pushing the free end in round his waist. She felt herself *an intrusion and, in silence,* went out" (emphasis added, *SS* 214).

So ultimately "silence" intrudes in their relationship. With her understanding of the real attitude of Williams, comes between them a silence. Madge tells him that she is not angry. She is rather beginning to know him (*SS* 214). Commenting on this story, Trump observes that the political issues have brought division between two couples. Gordimer has successfully created a situation in which "she can examine not simply ideas about political commitment but can focus upon forces which hold people together and break them from one another in the most intimate of personal relationships" (Trump 356).

If Gordimer lays bare the hypocrisy or inconsistency of William, she represents Mehring in *The Conservationist* (*CN*) as one who exploits land as well as woman in guise of a conservationist. Like Toby Hood, Mehring considers woman as an object of pleasure. So he told his son, "what's the reason we go after them –she was pretty. She had a smashing figure" (*CN* 83). He confesses to his mistress, Antonia that he takes "special pleasure" in buying a woman and she characterises his behaviour as "sexual fascism" (*CN* 83, 117). Dorothy Driver observes that Gordimer suggests through Mehring's relationship with Antonia "another 'special pleasure' that males feel, and thus power into sex, and by implication, sex into power" (40). Mehring also shows impulses of sexual exploitation in his frequent erotic imaginings about young girls and women –such as his desire for the young daughter of a dinner hostess. In postcolonial discourse, woman is often seen as a symbol of land to indicate the control or ownership. A significant and relevant scene of this kind is the one which occurs in one of Mehring's business flights when he molests a young girl seating next to him in the plane. His sexuality, his predation for young girls and exploitation of land are all combined in this scene. The scene may be interpreted as Mehring's sexual colonialism. Here in this scene landscape merges in Mehring's mind with the body of the young girl as object of sexual desire. It is significant that the girl does not speak throughout the journey while Mehring keeps 'fingering' her body beneath her blanket. Here the body of the girl becomes the land as he explores it, comparing its flesh to water in desert beneath the plane and exploring the ridges of her anatomy (Newman 60). Another important scene occurs in the end of the novel. The final monologue of Mehring again situates him in a landscape that unites the themes of the novel. While returning in his car from the farm, a woman, a hitchhiker signals for a lift.

He thinks "No, no" but nevertheless lets her into the car (*Con* 304). The woman takes him through a landscape. In fact, he feels that he is lured away by the woman or that he is going to be entrapped into a cross-racial relationship. As he is about to possess the woman, he suddenly becomes aware of the legs of a male in the background. So, being afraid, he leaves and runs:

> "He's going to run, run and leave them to rape her and rob her. She'll be all right. They survive everything. *Coloured or poor-white*, whichever she is, their brothers or fathers take their virginity good and early" (emphasis added, *CN* 319).

Mehring is not sure if the girl is an Afrikaner or Portuguese. He even thinks that the girl may be a black. Whoever she may be, Newman observes, as a woman she stands for all the women of the book (65). Mehring abandons the woman and his abandonment implies how he makes difference between himself and coloured and poor-whites. This difference is class, racial and sexual. The difference reflects the difference of Mehring's psyche and, by implication, of the colonist.

Observing Gordimer's treatment of sexuality in her novels, Clingman notes that in *The Laying Days*, Helen discovered sexuality as a matter of joy, and in *Occasion for Loving*, sexuality was subjected to political power. From *The Late Bourgeois World* (*LBW*) onward "sexuality is becoming politicized" (Clingman 105). In this novel, Gordimer has portrayed Elisabeth as an intelligent woman as against Max, a man who has been carried away by his own estimation of his role as a historical saviour. She tells their son, Bobo that Max fails miserably or commits suicide because he is not equal to the demands that he has made upon himself. By the end of the novel, Elisabeth, as intelligent she is, rejects the late bourgeois world and engages with its material realities. And in doing so, she transforms them. Luke Fukase, a member of the underground Pan Africanist Congress (PAC) asks her to use her power of attorney over the bank account of her grandmother. She almost agrees to use her grandmother's bank account to transfer money for the banned organization, PAC. That is to say, she plans to use an old woman's property for underground activities. This may be considered as an attack on the bourgeois morality. The bank is a basic institution of the capitalist world. Her plan is now to use it as an instrument of revolutionary politics, and thus her plan also involves a material transformation. More importantly, Elisabeth knows that probably Luke will also make love to her. She anticipates that it is quite possible "he'll make love to me, next time or some time. That's part of the bargain . . ." (*LBW* 142). She is prepared to accept his offer because, she thinks, he has only this to offer her. Elisabeth recognizes him as her Orpheus who has come to take "pale Eurydice" from her "life insured Shades" (*LBW* 133). However, by accepting his offer, each of them will be given what she or he has. This will be a new kind of equality. Through this episode, Gordimer seems to suggest that a kind of sexual politics with specific bearings on South Africa seems to be emerging. As Clingman points out,

> In a white-male-dominated culture . . . it has very frequently been women (both black and white) who have been amongst the most courageous opponents of apartheid or, as in Gordimer's own case, the most uncompromising witnesses of its social effects (105).

Gordimer suggests the emergence of a new female whose political awakening is perceived in sexual terms. Elisabeth feels that the thought of her senile grandmother's bank account grows "like sexual tumescence" within herself (*LBW* 130). In her next novels like *Berger's Daughter* or *My Son's Story*, Gordimer delineates women who become more engaged with politics, suggesting politics transforms sexuality.

In her essay, "Still Waiting for the Great Feminist Novel", Susan Gardner contends that *Burger's Daughter* (*BD*) is an "inspirational novel for feminist readers" and the particular interest for them is "the heroine's [Rosa Burger's] attempt to differentiate herself from her patriarchal identity "Burger's daughter"" (170). Rosa rebels against her father, another rebel to assert her identity. Both her parents, Lionel Burger and Cathy Burger, have fought against the oppression of the apartheid regime and finally died in the prison. As a daughter of a political revolutionary, she had few exclusive rights with her parents. Her likes and dislikes, even her intimate relationships are subordinated to political struggle. Thus she is desexualized. She maintains the image of a faithful daughter, at least in the eyes of the faithful, the comrades of her parents. In the opening scene, she is described as having "taken on her mother's role in the household" and "giving loving support" to her father, when her mother is imprisoned (*BD* 6). When Noel de Witt is in jail, she has to pose as a fiancée of him. This is planned in order to enabled Noel receive visits and information in the jail as he had no relatives. Scented and dressed that emphasized her femaleness with their sexual ambiguity, she visits the prison and exchanges her loving prison letters (*BD* 62). She presents herself as sexual object in the prison, "conveying a political subtext" beneath the lovey-dovey phrases (Newman 75). Thus Gordimer politicizes sex. However, Rosa is really in love with Noel. But her parents are blind to see her real emotions or, at least, do not want see it. They are happy to see her just play the surrogate sexual role, which denies her emotions and confines her sexuality within the walls of the prison. This episode shows how the children of the Burger household have to sacrifice their personal emotions and even their individuality. So, after the death of her father she intends to defect from the revolutionary tradition of her parents and assert her identity. Her quest for identity leads her through a series of events: she first lives with her lover Conrad, and then leaves South Africa for Paris to live with her father's first wife Katya and finally returns to South Africa.

Judie Newman argues that Rosa's revolt against the ideology of her father is connected with "sexual assertion" and this is seen in the scene with Clare Terblanche, the daughter of Dick and Ivy (76). Dick and Ivy are her father's comrades and have been even surrogate parents to her. She has felt great happiness in "the enveloping acceptance of Ivy's motherly arms" *(BD* 111). Clare lives with her parents and she devotes her life to their cause as she has been taught. In other words, she has lost her sexual identity. So, she appears at Rosa's door as a shadow which had no identity, seen through a glass panel. Rosa considers that Clare is still her childish playmate, who is sturdy as a teddy-bear and suffers from eczema. But now they argue about their ideological patrimony –about the use of a chamber in a building. Rosa triumphs over Clare and it is symbolised by her sexual appeal to men. She (Rosa) is beautiful and she has a "body with the assurance of embraces, as cultivated intelligence forms a mind. Men would recognize at a glance . . ." *(BD* 119). On the other hand, Clare, who has all along been faithful to her parents, has a body without any signals of a woman. Clare's attempt to recruit Rosa as a political intermediary fails. Rosa refuses because she does not want to conform to her parents. She wants to break away from the revolutionary tradition and live like other people who lead a completely different life. Their confrontation ends with an important act. When they visit a vacant apartment, Clare notices a used sanitary towel. Disgusted, she picks up it between paper and "buried her burden" in the abandoned cartons "as if she had successfully disposed of a body" (*BD* 126). The sanitary towel is an evidence of menstruation and a sign of reproduction. But involved in the political struggle, Clare has forgotten the realities of the body. She renounces her body in the same way that she hurriedly disposes of the sanitary towel. She might have become the "revolutionary Rosa" if she had not resisted "the family ideology in search of the missing feminine" (Liscio 193). They never connect. The male ideology intervenes and prevents intimacy between them.

If Rosa shows a kind of repulsion for Clare, she feels attracted toward Marisa Kgosana. A black woman and wife of a resistance activist, Marisa is under house arrest while her husband has been imprisoned in Robben Island for years. But she moves about comfortably in her body. She does not shift tones when speaking about prisoners in public. Leeuwenburg suggests that Marisa is clearly based on Winnie Mandela and that she represents Mother Africa in her sunny self confidence and proud sexuality (cited in Head 119). Marisa's splashy-coloured dress, her clear, unhesitating voice and the fact that she and Rosa meet over the cosmetics counter make her "a character link between Ivy Terblanche and Colette Swan" (Liscio 193). Rosa's attraction for Marisa has been sensuous in nature. She could see the half-bare back of a black woman dressed in splashing colour which included as overall effect the colour of her skin, and she was Marisa.

To touch in women's token embrace against the live, night cheek of Marisa, seeing huge for a second the lake-flash of her eye . . . to enter for a moment the invisible magnetic field of the body of a beautiful creature and receive on oneself its imprint . . . As near as a woman can get to the transformation of the world a man seeks in the beauty of a woman (*BD* 131-32).

Rosa's appreciation of the "splashing colour" of Marisa's dress and the physicality of Marisa – neck, half-bare back and legs –has a political as well as a sexual significance. Marisa's clothing depicts "ancient ideogrammatic symbols" (*BD* 134), which suggests an ethnic African culture linked with black African identity. According to Dominic Head, Marisa's physical perfection represent for Rosa "the health and potential of African culture" (120). This in turn suggests a link between the public and the private. But Rosa's responses to Marisa do not make this connection clear. The significance of Rosa's attraction for Marisa becomes clear by the end of the novel when they will be seen together in the prison cell. The significance of this prison scene may be discussed a little later.

After her father's death, Rosa lives with Conrad in a cottage for some period. Set in a garden of palms, she finds the house "safe and cosy as a child's playhouse and sexually arousing as a lovers' hideout. It was nowhere" (*BD* 15). In the darkness of their cottage, Rosa and Conrad act out and enjoy their dream of a private erotic world over which parents have no control. Conrad has no political affiliations and for him only psychological events matter. Even the Sharpeville passes unnoticed as he is overwhelmingly aware of his mother having a lover. Now he is freed from the Oedipal conflicts and he becomes obsessed with her: "I was mad about her; now I could be, with someone other than my father there already" (*BD* 40). Rosa admits a kinship with him as they "had in common such terrible secrets in the tin house" (*BD* 59). Conrad reacts at the death of Lionel, saying: "Now you are free" (*BD* 58). Rosa also "must have wished him to die" (*BD* 59). She wished this for freedom. But she obtains it at the death of her father. "Freedom from the father liberates Rosa but is attended by guilt" (Newman 79). Her relationship with Conrad has other limitations as well. She recoils from the erotic activities with Conrad because she has come to perceive these activities as dirty and incestuous. This relationship is repeated with Baasie, a black boy who used to came to live with the Burgers when his father was jailed and who was brought up as Rosa's brother. So she ends her relationship. She says that they left the "tree house" in which they were living and treating their dirt as Baasie and she had done long ago:

> Baasie and I had long ago performed the child's black mass, tasting on a finger the gall of our own sheet and the saline of our own pee . . . And you know we stopped making love together months before I left, aware that it had become incest (*BD* 66).

Rosa finds that her sexual freedom is always connected to "images of the black, and to imperfectly suppressed incestuous desires" (Newman 79). Though Conrad initiates Rosa into a journey of self-knowledge, she finds his self-centeredness and impersonal fascination for others' live rather unsettling.

Eventually Rosa leaves South Africa. She moves to Nice in France, to the arms of his father's first wife, Colette Swan, also known as Katya. Before discussing her life and time she spends with Katya, a brief discussion about her mother Cathy will be pertinent here. In her quest for self identity, Rosa examines the significance of her father's life. She also searches for the significance of her mother who has often been mentioned but not developed. It is important to note that in title *Burger's Daughter*, Burger can suggest both Lionel and Cathy as well. However, Cathy seems to be overshadowed by the image of Lionel. Lorraine Liscio argues, "Cathy is curiously absent in a narrative that *does* allude to her" (original italics, 189). Though she is "named", Cathy Burger slips away and becomes invisible. This offers her a form of cover that deflects attention from her to her activist husband and this, in turn, helps her become more mobile, secretive and effective. In an interview with Susan Gardner in 1980, Gordimer tells that in a politically active Afrikaner family, traditionally the husband is the leader and head of the family. He is, therefore, closely watched by surveillance. The woman, on the other hand, is considered more important for home and is often dealt leniently by court. This provides her opportunities to work for the struggle. Thus the marriage provides a cover for the question of who is more important person for the Party work –the husband or the wife. In *Burger's Daughter* Gordimer has given significant hints to the role played by woman in South African politics. There were middle class woman like Flora Donaldson, who devoted their leisure time to charitable activities and consequently got involved in social reforms initiatives. These public-spirited women were the first to understand the inequity of the black oppression and pathetic conditions in which the blacks lived. Women like Flora could not become very aggressive because of their protective husband who often prevented them from undertaking more radical campaigns. But one thing was clear that these white women did feel for changes or reforms in the society. In the interview mentioned above, Gordimer admires the women's organization called the Black Sash to which Flora might belong. The women of this organization opposed the government of the National Party and tried to bring about social reform. But, she asked, why there is no Black Sash for men. On the other hand, these women had the guts to defy the police and organise protest and other activities and thus posed a challenge to the apartheid regime.

Though Cathy is comparatively absent in the narrative, Ivy Terblanche considers, so does Katya as well, her as the real revolutionary. For Rosa, her mother's story has more gaps than narrative line. She defects from the male governed family expectations to see herself in a role different from the prescribed role of a revolutionary. Her defection from the male/public form of action may be said to be a defection to the female/private sphere of silence, absence, defects. Perhaps, Rosa's capacity to do this is lacking in her mother. Once she finds an attractive photo of her mother, she remembers that her mother has been "a woman who is unaware of her good looks, but . . . literally *does not inhabit them* (original italics, *BD* 78). Rosa considers her mother's split from her body as a loss of self. Cathy was, after all, a committed member of the Communist Party. She had a trait of self-effacement. She was unlike Colette who could not sacrifice her private self for the public cause. However, in Rosa's assessment her lost mother has occupied a silent place. Liscio argues that this (Rosa's assessment of her mother) "resembles feminists' attempts to validate female, maternal experience" (190). And this may be said to correspond to the pre-Oedipal, prelinguistic stage of development where much communication occurs between the mother's body impulses and the infant's. Noting Luce Irigaray's suggestion, Liscio observes that this conversation duplicates female sexuality or, in the words of Irigaray, "fills the gaps in a repressed female sexuality" (cited in Liscio 191).

If Cathy has lost herself in the wave of commitment, Katya or Colette Swan emerges as an individual in her own right in the bright Mediterranean landscape bearing as many identities as

Renoir's diverse colours. Unlike Cathy, Colette tries her hand in as many jobs as she has names. Her maiden name, Swan is reminiscent of literature's most famous dilettante, Proust's Swann. Like the real Colette, she was initially a music-hall dancer. Her identity as Madame Bagnelli is an invention because she and Bagnelli were never married. However, as Mme Bagnelli, she gives English lessons, dancing lessons, does housekeeping, and works as a secretary and editor for a Russian writer. As Colette Burger, she worked for the Communist Party. Finally, she adopts the name Katya, the Russian form of Cathy, for her relationship with Rosa. Cathy dies under the pressure of patriarchal ideals but Colette survives through the winding unevenness of changing occupations. As Liscio put it, she is an embodiment of "the personal," who evades an particular definition and upsets "the public," order (196). In other words, she tries to establish her individual identity as a woman.

Rosa goes to Nice, South of France and stays with her stepmother Katya. The place called Nice and Katya's home evoke an atmosphere of romance, not commitment. Nice appears to Rosa as an enchanted land. She can glimpse through the glass window of the plane the "silk tent of the morning sea tilted" (*BD* 219), the tables outside a bar looking like "tiny islands" and the "roadside tapestry flowers" growing ashy with dust (*BD* 222). Katya reminds Rosa that Nice as a place represents the world of art. This is a place where Renoir's home and Picasso's museum are located. The world of Nice with all its colours, scents, exotic foods and stories Rosa hears from Katya's friends provides Rosa with the joys and pleasures of childhood. The childhood sensuality has been absent or forgotten for Rosa. Colette's naming herself Katya, like a Russian dancer, and Rosa's eventual love affair in Paris with Bernard Chabalier both serve to reinforce the fairy tale quality of Nice. Rosa feels dazed, as if she is entering a world of sensuality. Katya recounts her memories of parties, vodka and sexual affairs when Rosa and she take their meal. On the other hand, Rosa is dissolving in the pleasures of wine and French sights and sounds. The room that has been made ready for Rosa is full of flowers, mirrors and feminine ornaments:

> A girl, a creature whose sense of existence would be in her nose buried in flowers, peace juice running down her chin, face tended at mirrors, mind dreamily diverted, body seeking pleasure. Rosa burger entered, going forward into possession by that image. (*BD* 235)

As seen in the above lines Rosa is presented in Nice as a sensual woman, an image which she assumes, and enjoys the sensual pleasures of an unreal country. Here in this country she ceases to be her father's daughter and becomes instead the mistress of Bernard Chabalier. With Chabalier, Rosa for the first time seems to have a satisfying life –both emotionally and sexually. She comes to believe that "it's possible to live within the ambit of person, not a country" (*BD* 310). And she becomes Bernard's mistress because the life of mistress allows one to lead a completely private and personal life. "Bernard Chabalier's mistress isn't Lionel Burger's daughter; she's certainly not accountable to the Future" (*BD* 312). Thus Rosa may be said to develop a romantic relationship which offers her personal freedom and does not demand any responsibility. As Louise Yelin argues, Chabalier represents romantic love which is a version of personal liberation. His name has the same etymology as *chivalry* and *chevalier* (original italics, 213). But this, Yelin continues, speaks of a regressive undertone of romantic love because the chivalric order carries the burden of feudalism, which is a step backward from the bourgeois order ironically represented by her father's name Lionel Burger. However, Rosa develops the affair with Chabalier while staying in Katya, who "mothers her" (Yelin 213). That is to say, Rosa's sexual awakening is caused by her rediscovery of her mother. And this rediscovery of her mother is more important than her love affair. This is implied by the choice of Katya as the narrator in part two of the narrative. So, Rosa undergoes a sexual as well as aesthetic awakening while living in Nice. For example, Katya introduces her to modern art and one night she takes her to hear nightingales sing. Listening to the song, the two women experience an ecstasy. They could hear around them a kind of piercingly sweet ringing which was only a little audible. "A new perception was picking up the utmost ring of waves whose centre must be unreachable ecstasy" (*BD* 269). This passage suggests a moment of ecstasy which is aesthetic and sexual as well. And the ecstasy, unlike the solitary ecstasy suggested by Keats' "Ode to Nightingale," is shared by a mother and a daughter.

Thus, one can argue, Rosa's stay in Nice helps her "tease apart the fabric of her self, moving inward and backward through the mother" as suggested by Woolf (Liscio 197). She alternately allows her body the freedom of feeling, of questioning other women and measuring herself alongside them. For her, this is a new territory of experience. So she confesses to Katya that she has "never talked with anyone as I do with you, incontinently, femininely" and that Katya tells her "anecdotes of your youth that could transform my own" (BD 270-71). Katya's nurturing helps her develop sensuality and emotions which find no place in her familial experience of responsibility. Pleasure in the self enlarges her capacity to "move freely toward the Other" which is central to the theory of feminists like Cixous and Irigaray (Liscio 197).

Rosa goes to London and happens to attend a conference of South African exiles, where she encounters Baasie with whom she shares her childhood. She recognizes him but he is reluctant in his responses to her. Later at midnight he telephones her and expresses his anger. He angrily tells her that he is not Baasie (meaning, 'the little boss'); he is Zwelinzima (meaning 'suffering land'), the name given by his father. "—I'm not your Baasie . . . don't think of that black 'brother', that's all" (*BD* 330) He asserts himself as a person in his own right and forces Rosa to put on the light. At the end of the conversation, she vomits in front of the bathroom mirror and sees herself as "ugly", "filthy", and "debauched" and realises "how I disfigured myself" (*BD* 340). This disfiguration is "an essential step in Rosa's progress towards autonomy" (Newman 84). In other words, it helps her assert an independent identity. Rosa's confrontation is similar to that between Jessie and Gideon in *Occasion for Loving*. But this time the confrontation is not elegiac as it was for Jessie. For Rosa, it has a cathartic effect. She cries for the second time over the loss of her black brother (the first was on leaving Chabalier). The confrontation has created in her an overwhelming awareness of commitment from which she cannot escape. Eventually she understands, "No one can defect" (*BD* 343).

Finally Rosa returns to South Africa to lead her own life and contribute to the liberation movement in her own way. She joins the liberation struggle led by the Soweto students. Along with the black rebels, she is also detained on charges of colluding with Marisa and abetting the school children's revolt. She is imprisoned with other women revolutionaries: Marisa, Clare and an Indian woman. At the beginning of the story, Rosa was outside the prison walls where her mother was. Now she is inside the prison, exchanging massages with the help of her art. She draws on Christmas cards the portraits of Marisa, Clare and the Indian woman, and assures those outside the prison of their well-being. Though separated from one another, they remain in touch through their song and laughter that escape from their cells. As for Rosa herself, Gordimer has conveyed through her only visitor Flora Donaldson that she has become lovelier and looked like a girl about fourteen. And she was fourteen when narrative began. Gordimer has pointed out that this ending should not be seen as a passive or circular development. Rosa is brought to trial along with Marisa, wife of an ANC leader. Thus, Gordimer thinks, Rosa has taken some political action by supporting the black students. But it is not clear whether Rosa has done this to show her allegiance to her father and his ally or to support the Black Consciousness movement. But Gordimer asserts that one thing is clear:

> What is certain is that in taking up the burden of other people's suffering through revolutionary political action, *she has acted in her own name and her own identity*, rather than the family tradition. (emphasis added, "What the Book, 152)

In *Burger's Daughter*, Gordimer continues with the form of bildungsroman that she has used for her first novel *The Lying Days*. Citing Elizabeth Abel et al. Yelin notes that the ends of bildungsroman are gender-specific: work or autonomy for man; and marriage, romance or sexual fulfilment for women (211). However, some novels like *To the Lighthouse* mark a departure from the gender-specific norms, where art, not love is the object of women's quest. But Gordimer has made certain revisions of these feminist revisions in *Burger's Daughter*. Rosa's quest is governed by political activity, not by love or even art. In *A Sport of Nature* (*SN*), Gordimer further revises this genre and produces a revolutionary protagonist, Hillela whose private and public life is governed by sexuality. Colonialism was considered as male adventures where the women of the empire had been relegated to a subordinate position. Through her latest novel, Gordimer provides a corrective to literary and political readings of the empire which focus exclusively on the male hero. "*A Sport of Nature* focuses on a female 'adventuress', rewriting the meaning of the term to include sexuality with a positive hypothesis" (Newman 94).

Hillela Capran, the central character of the novel, is the 'sport of nature' as described in the title. As a 'sport of nature' Hillela is, as Gordimer mentions in the epigraph, different from the parental stock or type. She is a new variety of protagonist who is an extension of and yet different from the previous protagonists of Gordimer's work. The novel captures the adventurous life and coming of age of Hillela. She enters the narrative as a four-year child. Her mother, Ruth runs away with a Portuguese lover, abandoning her daughter at the care of her two sisters, Olga and Pauline (one rich, materialist and the other liberal). Expelled from her Rhodesian boarding school for befriending a 'coloured' youth, she returns to South Africa to outrage her aunts. She is caught sleeping with her cousin, Sasha, leading to her expulsion from her aunt's home. Then she moves through a series of adventures: she tries her hand at different jobs and explores various relationships. In one such incident or relationship, she flees with a white activist to Tanzania, who later deserts her. 'Rescued' by South African revolutionaries, she marries a South African revolutionary organizer, Whaila Kgomani and has a child with him. This step towards her 'rainbow family' is shattered by the assassination of her lover Whaila. But she becomes committed to the cause of liberation and works untiringly for it. After an interlude with an American fiancé, Brad, she marries a powerful West African revolutionary general, Reuel. Thus, her sexuality is channelled for military ambition and political power. Reuel soon becomes the president of an unspecified independent African country. Hillela and her black husband preside over the ceremony celebrating the successful liberation from apartheid South Africa. Theirs is the first happy cross-racial relationship between a white woman and black man among the couples of Gordimer.

Unlike Rosa Burger, Hillela pursues her slippery life which is determined by her sexuality and history, and which is beyond any formulation applied to the earlier heroine. In creating Hillela, Gordimer has envisioned altogether a new person who can overcome the barriers of apartheid. Robin Visel argues that in Hillela, Gordimer introduces a new type who overthrows the "social ties" or the "rules of behaviour" which bind Helen and Maureen (38). She triumphs because she does not conform, and because she is an amoral law unto herself. Sexual freedom is her road to revolution. In other words, Gordimer represents in Hillela sexuality as a source of political radicalism. Her personal development and her influence on others are expressed in terms of her sexual relationships throughout the novel. As a result of an accidental exile from South Africa, she meets and marries Whaila Kgomani. And this is the beginning of her political awakening. Perhaps, Hillela attempts to respond to the question which Gordimer raised in her early story. Hillela wants to fix a "place where we can meet" for her rainbow family. Hillela with her husband and their baby on the beach seems to have the sense of completeness. She thinks, "in the hot shade, contained within their bowl of sand whose circle had no ingress for anyone or anything else and no egress by which one could be cast out" (*SN* 192). Her union with Whaila and their child may be said to symbolise the communion of blacks and whites. She feels delighted to give birth to a black baby. She is relieved and satisfied "not to have reproduced herself" (*SN* 195), and names her after Winnie Mandela. This has a clear political orientation. When she is expecting the second child, she does not ask Whaila to guess what will be the colour of the child. She wishes that their children will form a "rainbow family". She envisions the rainbow family as a manifestation of inter-racial harmony and a source of power to defeat apartheid. But her aunt Pauline is cynical about the efficacy of her behaviour. Sasha, of course, sees beyond her mother's cynicism. He believes that the dynamic of real change is always utopian. He admits that it is "unattainable" but "without aiming for it" one cannot even "fall short of it." He further says,

> *Without utopia –the idea of utopia –there's a failure of imagination –and that's a failure to know how to go on living. It will take another kind of being to stay on, here. A new white person. Not us. The chance is a wild chance –like falling in love.* (original italics, *SN* 236-37)

Gordimer said in "Living in the Interregnum", "We must continue to be tormented by the ideal" (284). She seems to represents Hillela as a visionary, symbolic figure to meet "the ideal". Metaphorically speaking, like Gordimer, Sasha recognizes that Hillela has her own language, language of the body. She is "a sport of nature" through whom the artist has explored the possibilities of ideas about the future of South Africa. Gordimer has borrowed the term "a sport of nature" from Sarah Gertrude Millin. As Temple-Thurston has observed, Gordimer's use of the term is ironical (181). Millin advocated for racial purity through her writings in the early twentieth century. Her argument is that people who deny having "colour consciousness are, biologically speaking, sports." She claimed colour consciousness to be a "profound feeling (call it instinct or call it acquired prejudiced)" which can be overcome only by another biological force such as sexual desire (Coetzee 153). But Hillela celebrates racial difference as difference in colour rather than denying it, and becomes a sport of nature. While lying beside her fiancé, she examines his body and she caresses his dark birth mark without shame. She refuses to accept their different skin pigmentations. Her celebration of difference is felicitated by her sensuality. Such a celebration may be said to represent "a subversion of the racist code which demands separation through difference" though it was not always successful (Head 141). It is this "otherness" of Hillela in white South Africa that enables her to move to the future, which the early heroines of Gordimer failed to achieve. "Hillela as other" turns out to be a natural rebel and nonconformist who "fearlessly embraces blackness" (Visel 39).

However, Gordimer's vision of the new white person is not simple. The killing of Whaila dispels her idealistic notion of the political potential of her maternal role. She suddenly realises that there is no rainbow-coloured family. This prompts her to carry on the struggle and move beyond the romantic worship of Whaila. In her stream of consciousness, she expresses her reflections:

> *The real rainbow family stinks. The dried liquid of dysentery streaks the legs of babies and old men and the women smell of their monthly blood. . . They smell of bodies blown up by the expanding gases of their corpses' innards, lying in the bush in the sun.* (original italics, *SN* 317)

Hillela understands the hard reality of oppression and deprivation of the African family. She rejects the naïve idealism of the rainbow family and marries another black African leader, Reuel. But this time there is a change in her role as Reuel's wife. As Head points out, now she does not intend to perpetuate a blood-line. She is no longer the "maternal fount" (149). In Reuel's family she is "the non-matrilineal centre" of her own invention (*SN* 392-93). There is a change in her from the idealism of her first marriage to the pragmatism of warfare. Reuel values her capacity to adapt in new circumstances of power. She is not to be the personal property of her husband who has two other wives. Their marriage is secure but not sexually exclusive on either side. Gordimer here seems to move beyond the ideal inter-racial sexual relationship to suggest a more complex vision.

There is a possibility of considering Hillela as a mere object of sexual desire. Critics, particularly Brenda Cooper has been very critical. Cooper finds it "interesting" that even in the 1980s a woman writer creates such a "heroine," in a "situation like South Africa," where Gordimer's "primary concern is to illustrate the ways in which her new breed of white South African can love, serve and physically worship *black* men" (Cooper 82). Gordimer hardly considers gender equality as part of her otherwise radical vision. She appears to accept the status quo of patriarchal structures. Her portrayal of Hillela as woman who uses her sexuality for political power, may serve to encourage the dangerous attitudes to female sexuality that oppress and subordinate women. However, it is reductive to say that Gordimer does not present the biological and sensual solutions to "the social and political problems and difficult emotions faced by whites in South Africa today" (Cooper 76). There are positive possibilities of Hillela's sexuality, though it may be mythic. Dominic Head has dwelt on both negative and positive connotations of Hlillela's sexuality. He, however, asserts that the "*principal* connotation of Hillela's sexuality . . . appear positive" (original italics 142). Head argues that it is through her sexuality that Hillela can break restrictive taboos, and inspire in herself and in others productive, committed action. The novel establishes its positive link between private and public worlds through sexuality. This is done by allowing the primacy of personal desire and then channelling it in appropriate way. Thus in the following passage Hillel's sexuality is identified as the source of the General Reuel's authority:

> Her sexuality, evident every man watching her pass as he sat in the bush oiling his gun, or stood at attention of review before the General, was part of the General's Command . . . Her small, generous, urging, inventive body was the deserts of success . . . But he had known from the first time he made love with her that that was only an experience of her possibilities . . . (*SN* 359).

There are some significant images in the above passage. The oiling of the guns, which accompanies the troop's sexual recognition of Hillela, has a phallic connotation. Her sexuality was considered part of the General's command. In this image of ownership, her body is associated with the actual military capture of terrain suggested through the phrase "deserts of success" which can suggest the African battlefield. However, the novelist has not made the connection between sexuality and revolutionary activity straightforward. The metaphoric connection between the female body and the male appropriation of land is complex, even uncomfortable. This is because it may reverse the criticism of the colonizing male psyche made in *The Conservationist*. Gordimer herself said in an interview with *New York Times* that the creation of Hillela is an attempt to imagine a white South African woman who can survive, even flourish, in revolutionary conditions (cited in Visel 38).

In fact, Gordimer's characterization is very complex. And the complexity of her character eludes the charges of anti-feminism. Gordimer's next novel *My Son's Story* shows how the female character move out of the traditional gender roles to a revolutionary vision that includes feminism. In the early novels like *Occasion for Loving*, the black women had no voice. However, in *A Sport of Nature*, Gordimer has given a few lines to the two black wives of the General who later becomes the president. The firs wife dislikes Hillela but she could not show her resentment. The second wife respects Hillela but "cannot make a sister out of white woman." To her, Hillela is a "usurper, a foreigner" (*SN* 392). The black South African women suffer both racially and sexually. They are shown lacking power. They are ignored and left to suffer even amidst all the talk of liberation. They are ignored by the male blacks and the male and female whites. Hence, Chandra Talpade Mohanty criticises the representation of women as a coherent group with the same experience of male oppression everywhere (199).

In *My Sons Story* (*MSS*), Gordimer finally depicts a coloured woman, Aila who silently moves out of her traditional and involves herself in radical political action. By focusing on a coloured family and the role of gender in building a nation, Gordimer seems to cross the 'borderland' of her early fiction. She attempts to capture the consciousness of Aila through the first narrator, Will. In the beginning of the novel, the cross-racial relationship between Sonny and Hannah dominates the action. Sonny, the coloured school teacher falls in love with the human rights activist, Hannah because of their shared political struggle and ideology. Hannah becomes for Sonny the centre of his commitment to political struggle and sexual pleasure. Thus, Gordimer combines politics and sexuality in South

African political context: ". . . in her –needing Hannah –sexual happiness and political commitment were one" (*MSS* 125). As the narrative unfolds, politics centres on both male and female bodies. Politics is sexualized. Sonny's son, Will comes to know about his relationship with the white blonde, Hannah as a result of his chance encounter with them when they came out of a cinema hall. Will does not protest. He keeps it secret and inwardly feels guilty because of his complicity with his father. Aila, the caring and beautiful wife of Sonny knows about his sexual relationship that he enjoys along with his political activities. But she does not protest. She remains silent about it. She is still submissive to Sonny and continues to make love with him. Later he realises that she "faked her pleasure" (*MSS* 242). This may be seen at least as a "nonverbal protest" of her body (Bazin). Their daughter, Baby also reacts to his illicit relationship with Hannah. She cuts her wrist. But Sonny fails to see it as he is deeply engaged with Hannah as much as with political liberation. But Sonny is surprised when Aila is arrested for storing weapons and for her links with black South African revolutionaries across the border. Egotistical as he is, he is so convinced that Aila is incapable of revolutionary activity. He believes Aila's arrest has been a mistake. The fact of the matter is that she has been carrying on revolutionary acts under the guise of her visits to Baby in a neighbouring country. And her activities were more dangerous than his. More shocks wait for him. Aila faces her trial, gets bail and finally flees the country. Baby already joined the struggle and married a revolutionary. Thus toward the end of the novel, the women, particularly Aila, usurp the central authority. Will or Sonny's story is dislodged by Aila's story. In other words, men's story is overtaken by that of women who refuse to be deceived by the sexist male narrative. As a committed activist, Aila replaces Sonny and becomes the real revolutionary. Both Sonny and

Will fail to perceive the ability of Aila because their vision is clouded by their pre-conceived notions of woman as embodiment of beauty and feminine refinement. Aila has been appreciated for her caring nature, domestic skills and silent and supportive manner. But Aila and Baby move from the passive, domestic role to active political one and marginalize the men, Sonny and Will. Gordimer suggests a change in the traditional 'gender bond'. The father-son bond shifts to the bond between mother and daughter.

Gordimer also hints at another bond between women. When the police arrests Aila for her involvement in revolutionary activities, Hannah has to leave South Africa in order to take up another job. She leaves South Africa and cuts off all communication with Sonny because, as Bazin points out, she finally sees "Aila as a sister" (40). On hearing that Aila has joined the underground activities, Hannah becomes very emotional and her eyes turn tearful. The following passage of the novel makes it clear:

> Whether Aila was a revolutionary or not, whether she had joined the struggle –and who should not rejoice at her choice if she had? . . . the quiet, beautiful wife with the curtain material she'd sewn now used to wrap hand-grenades and mines was betrayed, betrayed. (*MSS* 235)

Hannah, the white woman regrets that the beautiful wife of Sonny was betrayed. So she wept. This is a kind of fellow feeling –a woman's feeling for another. Sonny, on the other hand, is amazed at this sudden bond between his two women. He felt "intruded upon" and even thought that Hannah "had no right to weep for Aila" (*MSS* 235). In fact, Sonny is upset. His wife, his daughter and his mistress have left him. They are serving the cause of liberation somewhere else. Both he and his son, Will are confronted with the changing roles of women –coloured or black women. At home these women may be silent. But some of them like Aila and Baby will assume more power and take their place in the liberation movement. In her next novel, *None to Accompany Me* (1994), Gordimer has explored further the role of black women in building the nation through the character of Sibongile.

It is significant to note that Gordimer does not tell the story of Aila. The narrative is told from the perspective of a male, Will. Unlike in the early stories, Will protests the black man and white woman relationship that causes suffering to the black woman. He is angry at his father's deception of the family, particularly his mother. But he also brings the racist image of the ideal woman like his father: "I pretend, in dreams, that I'm doing things to them, the blondes in full-page spreads I tear out" (*MSS* 46). Moreover, Will ultimately feels that she is after all a woman –"some sort of sister to my father's blonde, since he's fancied them both" (*MSS* 187). What is more shocking is that he appears to be a misogynist when he declares his independence from his mother:

> She mustn't think she can count forever on the child who used to put himself to sleep stroking his lips with the tail of her long black plait . . . I'm a man, I thrust myself into women as my father does" (*MSS* 252-53).

That is, as Bazin observes, Will shows his allegiance to patriarchy by repressing his feminist insight, rejecting his mother, and reducing women to sex objects (43). And this allegiance is rooted in his deep response to the body of the female as the Other.

However, Gordimer's portrayal of the women characters, particularly that of Aila, raises some pertinent questions. Aila has been a strong woman who risks her life for political struggle. But she does not stand up to the faithlessness of her husband. How one can explain her stoic silence. One can also ask whether or not the portrayal of Aila is realistic. This may be explained in terms of Gordimer's belief that the feminist battle must come afterwards. But Meese Elizabeth argues that the struggle against racism and sexism must be simultaneous (65). Black South African women can hardly resist the oppressive behaviour of the males. In her novels such as *Occasion for Loving* and *A Sport of Nature*, Gordimer focuses on the white women's love for black males. This ignores the silence of the black women. Gordimer seems to overcome this problem in *My Son's Story* where Aila turns out to be a strong woman whose revolutionary behaviour and acts excels those of any male revolutionary.

Gordimer suggests, Bazin points out, that one can experience the sacredness of the Other through physical love. But ideal love can occur between equals –equals in terms of social, political and economic conditions. In her apartheid novels, the whiteness of the female serves to balance the masculinity of the black. "The status of race (her whiteness) can counterbalance the status of gender (his maleness) in a society still racist and sexist" (Bazin 44). Gordimer seems to argue that the same principle of domination underlies both racism and sexism. She links human sexuality to her political concerns because it all has to do with the body.

Works Cited

Bazin, Nancy Topping. "Sex, Politics, and Silent Black Women: Nadine Gordimer's *Occasion for Loving, A Sport of Nature,* and *My Son's Story.*" *Blucknell Review.* 37.1. pp 30-45.

Boyers, Robert, et al. "A Conversation with Nadine Gordimer." *Salmagundi* 62 (Winter 1984): pp 3 -31.

Bhabha, Homi K. *The Location of Culture.* London: Routledge, 2017 (reprint).

Coetzee, J. M. *White Writing: On the Culture of Letters in South Africa.* New Haven: Yale UP, 1988.

Driver, Dorothy. "Nadine Gordimer: The Politicisation of Women." *English in Africa.*10. 2 (Oct. 1983): pp 29-54.

Gardner, Susan. "Still Waiting for the Great Feminist Novel." *Nadine Gordimer's Burger's Daughter : A Casebook.* Ed. Judie Newman. Oxford: OUP, 2003. pp. 167-184.

Gordimer, Nadine. *The Lying Days.* London: Bloomsbury, 2002.

__________ *A World of Strangers.* London: Bloomsbury, 2002.

__________ *Occasion for Loving.* London: Bloomsbury, 2013.

__________ *The Conservationist.* London: Bloomsbury, 2005.

__________ *The Late Bourgeois World.* London: Bloomsbury, 2013.

__________ *Burger's Daughter.* London: Bloomsbury, 2000.

__________ *Selected Stories.* London: Bloomsbury, 2000.

__________ *A Sport Nature.* London: Bloomsbury, 2013.

__________ *My Son's Story.* London: Bloomsbury, 2003.

__________ "What the Book Is About". *Nadine Gordimer's Burger's Daughter: A Casebook.* Ed. Judie Newman. pp 149-166.

Head, Dominic. *Nadine Gordimer*. Cambridge: Cambridge University Press, 1994.

Knox, Alice. "No Place Like Utopia: Cross-Racial Couples in Nadine Gordimer's Later Novels." *ARIEL: A Review of International English Literature*, 27.1 January 1996. pp 63-80.

Lazar, Karen. "Feminism as 'Piffling'? Ambiguities in Nadine Gordimer's Short stories". *The Later Fiction Nadine Gordimer*. Ed. Bruce King. London: Macmillan, 1993.

Liscio, Lorraine. "Lighting a Torch in the Heart of Darkness". *Nadine Gordimer's Burger's Daughter : A Casebook*. Ed. Judie Newman. pp 185-204.

Loomba, Ania. *Colonialism/Postcolonialism*. London: Routledge, 2005.

Meese, Elizabeth A. *(Ex)tensions: Re-Figuring Feminist Criticism*. Urbana: University of Illinois Press, 1995.

Mohanty, "Chandra Talpade. Under Feminist Eyes: Feminist Scholarship and Colonial Discourses". Colonial Discourse and Post-Colonial Theory: A Reader. Ed. Chrisman and Williams. London: Harvester Wheatsheaf, 1993.

Newman, Judie. *Nadine Gordimer*. London: Routledge, 2014.

Spivak, Gayatri Chakravorty. "Can the Subaltern Speak?" *The Post-Colonial Studies Reader*. Ed. Bill Ashcroft, et al. London: Routledge, 2006.

Temple-Thurston, Barbara. "Nadine Gordimer: The White Artist as a Sport of Nature." *Studies in Twentieth Century Literature*. 15.1, 1991. pp 175-184.

Trump, Martin. "The Short Fiction of Nadine Gordimer". *Research in African Literature*. 17 .3 Autumn, 1986. pp. 341-369.

Visel, Robin. "Othering the Self: Nadine Gordimer's Colonial Heroines". *Ariel: A Review of International English Literature*, 19. 4, October, 1988. pp 33-42. https://journalhosting. ucalgary.ca/ariel/article/view/33102.

Yelin, Louise. "Exiled In and exiled From: The Politics and Poetics of *Burger's Daughter*". *Nadine Gordimer's Burger's Daughter: A Casebook*. Ed. Judie Newman. pp. 205- 220.

CHAPTER V

Conclusion

This study demonstrates that Nadine Gordimer's fiction of the apartheid period (1948-1994) presents different kinds of acquiescence and resistance. Gordimer's characters live in a world governed by apartheid laws such as Group Areas Act segregating the white residential areas from the locations of the black residents, and Population Registration Act dividing the people into different racial categories. While some characters in her fiction are acquiescent to apartheid, most of the protagonists of her novels show their resistance to apartheid. She presents the theme of resistance in her novels and short stories through a focus on the physical and psychological barriers the characters face in their lives. Helen Shaw, the protagonist of Gordimer's first novel, *The Lying Days*, goes against the conventional social norms and befriends a black female student, Mary Seswayo. She even unsuccessfully tries to provide the student a living space. The novel depicts the growth of Helen's consciousness. She crosses over to prohibited spaces such as her visit to the Concession stores in the Mine, which the black mine workers use. Another important spatial image is that of the Mariastad location, the township which Helen visits along with Mary (*LD* 171). The township gives the impression of disorder and incoherence. But the many voices of it coalesce into a single shout which gives coherence to the seemingly incoherent space. As Helen and Charles reach the township, they stopped talking, suggesting their awareness of the white complicity in the repression of the blacks. Gordimer's description of this township may said to be an early version of heterotopia –a site of difference and resistance –which is further elaborated in the township description in *Burger's Daughter*. Control over space has been a mechanism to dominate the majority South Africans. Helen Shaw has a desire to move beyond the spatial boundaries. She, however, fails and decides to leave South Africa. The apartheid government rule through what Foucault called classification of the population into different categories and segregating them to different social spaces.

In her fiction Gordimer explores the theme of borderlines, the locations of cultures. In Gordimer's second novel, *A World of Strangers*, division of the population is more prominent. Toby Hood intends to remain neutral to the politics of South Africa and visits both the white and the black South African society, making friends across racial divide. His friend Anna Louw, an Afrikaner lawyer and activist introduces him to a party of mixed races –a world in which people of different races come together and become friends. Toby finds the party remarkable with its "ordinary pattern" of people of different races, symbolizing in its composition an "Oriental rug" (*WS* 84). But soon Toby finds that the divide between the whites and the blacks is deep and that it is irreconcilable. The binary divisions develop in him a sense of despondency and alienation. Toby finds himself an 'in-between' reality, a borderline existence (Bhabha, 19). Gordimer suggests that meetings of this kind are the borderlines or locations of culture. They are the spaces which act like a bridge to connect white and black people. People in these gatherings develop an intimacy, though temporary. Their intimacy questions the binary divisions of the South African society where apartheid created multiple identities. Gordimer employs the idea of 'borderline' that provides her with a space to resist the rigid boundaries of the contemporary society. She has made use of this marginal space as a site for her creative writing. In an Interview with Studs Terkel, Gordimer says,

> "I've written usually about the borderland, the kind of frontier where black and white do meet, to a certain extent, and more or less as equals, though you can never be equal in an unequal society . . . but anyway, I have dealt mostly with this kind of half world where people do meet –black and white . . . (Terkel 19).

Borderline situations and encounters between the black and the white are important themes that pervade Gordimer's novels and short stories of the apartheid period. Thus, the action of the story, "Which New Era Would That Be?" may be said to develop in a borderland where the white and the black characters meet each other. The coloured man, Jake Alexander's printing shop housed in the 'New Era Building' is visited by young men and women across colour bar. Through the story Gordimer captures the mood of life in Johannesburg in the 1950s. Jake, his group of five men and his white friends Alister Halford and Jennifer Tetzel flouts the rules of racial segregation. Alister often accompanies Jake to visit the shebeens in a coloured location, which is prohibited for a white person. Jake and his black friends are, however, critical of the progressive attitude of the liberal whites. They think that the whites cannot identify with the black and that they cannot feel the humiliation of the black man walking in the streets with a pass given by the white (*SS* 74). Jake's attitude to Jennifer reminds one of Gordimer's own paradoxical position as a white writer. The confrontation between Rosa and Baasie in *Burger's Daughter* epitomises the oppression of the blacks and their rejection of the whites' collaboration in their struggle for liberation. The accusation of Baasie reflects the accusations of the Black Consciousness movement. Gordimer allows Baasie to speak in his own voice. This voice is also echoed earlier in the novel by the young black, Duma Dhladhla who rejects the class analysis of South Africa offered by the communist Orde Greer. As Rosa recalls the devastating telephone conversation with Baasie she feels an overwhelming awareness of commitment to the cause of the blacks. The midnight telephone call is a turning point in Rosa's life, and the scene is pivotal in the fiction of Gordimer. While talking about the future of the whites in South Africa, she expresses her own position as a white writer in her essay, "Where Do Whites Fit In?": "I myself fluctuate between the desire to be gone –to find a society for myself where my white skin will have no bearing on my place in the community –and a terrible, obstinate and fearful desire to stay. I feel the one desire with my head and the other with gut"(Gordimer 34). Despite conflicting desires of staying and leaving, she remained true to her desire to stay. Many of her fictional characters show the same fluctuation. Rosa Burger in *Burger's Daughter* is one such character who attempts to escape in order to assert her identity but finally commits to the cause of South African national liberation.

Indeed, Gordimer has all along shown the same commitment. She publishes her novels though she knows they may be banned or she may be put under house arrest. This shows her willingness to accept arrest or even imprisonment. Hence, it is untenable that writing has been a kind of luxurious irrelevance to Gordimer because she herself was a white. Her fiction of the 1970s, particularly *Burger's Daughter*, is Gordimer's response to the Black Consciousness movement. It is an examination of white South African psyche. In the given racial privilege, the way forward for the white lies in their radical self-examination and their relation to the blacks under the changing conditions. They must help and learn to walk together, putting one foot before the other and build a nation based on non-racialism.

Gordimer's characters often find themselves at the border or at the margin where past and present, inside and outside are not separated as binary opposites but they commingle and conflict. And from this emerge new and complex forms of representation that defy binary division. Through the imaginative border-crossings in her fiction, Gordimer suggests the possibility of psychological and physical crossing of borders. After returning to South Africa, Rosa renews her contact with Marisa Kgosana and other black activists at Soweto. She is imprisoned with other women revolutionaries. She lives in the prison with Marisa, Clare and the Indian woman, establishing a kind of sisterhood. Gordimer seems to convey the establishment of the symbolic contact of black and white suggesting the creation of a community out of differences –the many into one. The resistance acts of blacks and Rosa's arrest for her co-operation with the black rebels may be said to constitute what Bhabha called the performative aspect of nationalism. In the context of apartheid South Africa, a national culture must be built through repeated performances of acts of co-operation and acknowledgement of the leadership of the blacks by the whites. In her essay, "Living in the Interregnum", Gordimer says that whites should find their own forms of struggle (267). Rosa's act of joining the Soweto revolt under the black leadership reflects this commitment of Gordimer. Through Rosa's subordinate position in the revolt, Gordimer suggests that the white must take such a position to overthrow apartheid. Gordimer continues to examine the cross-racial relationship by reversing the master-servant relation in *July's People* which is a fictionalized version of the "interregnum" that she talks about in her essay, "Living in the Interregnum".

Life in a borderline situation often causes a feeling of alienation. Toby moves between the rich white society and the poor black world and discovers a void that exists in them. Toby's experiences at the High Houses and the black townships exert a pressure on him. Finally, the death of his black friend, Steven Sitole opens his eyes how deeply the apartheid was entrenched in South African society. He realises that both white and black might live side by side in South Africa but they are strangers in each other's world. However, Gordimer represents the character of Steven in a way that challenges the apartheid regime in South Africa. Steven has built a network of contacts which helps him avoid the restrictions imposed by adverse legislation: "The more restrictions grew up around him and his kind –and there seemed to be fresh ones every month –the quicker he found a way round him" (*WS* 204). He breaks or moves beyond the boundaries created by apartheid policies and practices. By avoiding the legislations, Steven offers a site of individual resistance that links with a broader movement which can generate practical resistance. Thus, Gordimer shows a possibility of change in the South African society divided into groups and zones under the apartheid regime. Many of her characters move 'beyond' the barriers and return. But they return with some change –with a sense of commitment to challenge the rigid boundaries of South Africa. Toby's acquaintances with white and black worlds and his failure in personal relationships across colour bar make him feel the necessity of a commitment to the resistance against apartheid. This time he makes the commitment to another black, Sam Mofokenzazi. Just before leaving the Johannesburg railway station for Cape Town in business trip, Toby promises Sam to be the godfather of Sam's baby when it is born. Gordimer seems to suggest that their friendship transcends all ideologies and signals the beginning of a cultural synthesis against the apartheid. In *The*

Late Bourgeois World, Elisabeth almost commits herself to help Luke and thinks of using the bank account of her grandmother to transfer funds from abroad. The decision of helping the underground rebels frightens her though. Her heart beats: "afraid, alive, afraid, alive, afraid, alive"(*LBW* 142). She finds the possibility of joining hands with the underground black politics when the world of the white liberals and its values reached almost an end. By crossing the barriers –both physical and psychological –Gordimer's characters such as Toby and Elisabeth discover their alienation and marginal positions in the South African society. This made them live through the conflicting pulls and pushes of their will and their society. And thus the history of the time comes alive through their life. However, there are flawed characters in terms of resistance against apartheid in the fiction of Gordimer. Unlike the committed Anna Louw who is arrested on treason charges, Cecil Rowe is a typical white woman with racial prejudice. Ann Davis in *Occasion for Love* shows a tendency to move beyond the colour bar in her affair with Gideon Shibalo but finally she falls back on apartheid.

The power relations in a society influence the construction of its individuals. In South Africa, the politics of apartheid, especially the Immorality Act, 1950 partially accounts for the failure of the cross-racial relationship of Ann and Gideon. In other words, apartheid or the ideology of racial segregation has been internalized by the white Ann. In the beginning, Ann did not care for the restrictions imposed by apartheid. But later the dominant laws and cultural conventions of society influenced her and so she left South Africa without even saying good bye to Gideon. Like Foucault, Gordimer seems to consider sexuality as a site of power relations governed by the dominant socio-cultural conventions. She has attempted to produce an alternative discourse about sexuality in *Occasion for Loving* and in the subsequent novels. The prevailing cross-racial sexual relationship in the colonial South Africa had been between white men and black women (Thompson 45). But Gordimer has depicted in her fiction the trans-racial relationship between black men and white women. By reversing the traditional pattern, she has suggested the possibility of resisting the apartheid ideology. Many of her characters disregard the myth of miscegenation, posing a challenge to a fundamental principle of the apartheid ideology. Thus, Gordimer begins a discourse what may be called, in Foucault's words, "a point of resistance and a starting point for an opposing strategy" (*The History*, 101). Gordimer wants to resist and problematises the existing discourse of sexuality. Like Foucault, she also believes that sex and politics are intertwined because sex often functions as a controlling force in politics. The black artist Gideon's affair with Ann may be seen as a transgression of the socio-cultural practices and a resistance to apartheid. In this act Jessie is a co-actor because she endorses the affair. But the fear of dominant discourses overtakes Ann and she leaves Gideon. Ann's affair, though temporary, is a very significant act of resistance. It nevertheless shows how it affects the consciousness of the individuals. This act of resistance, whether failed or otherwise, may be said to prepare the ground for emergence of resistance in future. This is clearly visible in her later fiction such as *A Sport of Nature* and *My Son's Story*.

Feminist critics often find fault with Gordimer's treatment of gender in her fiction. She has, they allege, preferred to focus on the issue of racism without linking it to sexism. She has considered gender issues as part of human rights in any society. In the Introduction to *Selected Stories* she has admitted that she, as an adolescent, had a genuine connection with the social life of the town [Springs] through her femaleness (3). She finds this social perception valid throughout her life. This may be validated by *A Sport of Nature*, where Hillela through sexuality frees herself from the restrictions of race. She seems to suggest that sexuality or femininity is a liberating force. In creating Hillela, Gordimer has envisioned a "new white person" who can move beyond the barriers of apartheid (Knox 71). This vision of the new white person is not simple though. Hillela has to struggle and move beyond her romantic relationship with Whaila after his assassination. She takes up different roles in the struggle against apartheid. After Whaila, she marries Reuel, another black African leader. She has been depicted as a resourceful woman –a "mistress of adaptation" (*SN* 393). She can assert herself in the changing circumstances of power as one of the three wives of Reuel. Like Whaila, Reuel admires her powers of invention. "Hillela has not been taken in by this African family; she has disposed it around her. Hers is the non-matrilineal centre that no one resents because no one has known it could exist. She has invented it. This is not the rainbow family" (*SN* 393). Though Gordimer does not clearly define Hillela's invention, she suggests a more complex vision by moving beyond the romantic idea of racial communion through sexual relationship. Hillela remains committed to resistance against apartheid. Her story dominates the action. The novel ends in a future moment beyond. In the final scene of the novel, Hillela returns to South Africa only after the revolution is over. She sees the flag of Whaila's country fly. Thus, through culmination of Hillela and Whaila's love, Gordimer resolves the impasse between blacks and whites as depicted in *July's People*. In Gordimer's evolving vision of South Africa, white women can freely choose black men as beloved and these cross-racial couples represent some hope in the struggle for a multiracial nation.

It is difficult to separate Gordimer's use of sexuality from the issues of gender representation, particularly in her later novels. In fact, she has represented sexuality in a way to empower woman. And Gordimer seems to moves closer to a revolutionary vision that encompasses feminism. She has addressed the gender issue through her own brand of micropolitics or politics of the body. In her later novels, particularly in *My Son's Story*, Gordimer has shown how politics centres on male and female bodies. In fact, she has sexualized politics in the sense that politics and sexuality are shown closely linked in the contemporary South African political condition. The relationship between Sonny and his white lover epitomises the commitment to political struggle and the fascination of sexual love. Sonny discovers a new meaning of life through his relationship with Hannah. She becomes the centre of his commitment to political struggle and sexual pleasure as well. Sonny and Hannah represent the meeting point of politics and sexuality in South Africa of late 1980s. As the narrator claims, "South Africa is a centripetal force that draws people not only out of economic necessity, but also out of the fascination of commitment to political struggle" (*MSS* 88). Sonny has displayed strong masculine sexuality in his affair with Hannah. But his virility collapses in his relationship with wife Aila. Through the triangular relationship between Sonny, Aila and Hannah, Gordimer perhaps explores the possibility of a political role for women in South Africa under and beyond apartheid. In the first part of the novel, Aila is seen as a traditional woman. But later she turns a revolutionary and establishes her new identity. Though she does not completely shed her old identity, she transcends her past and achieves a new cultural identity, combining the conventional and the subversive.

The transformation of Aila and her daughter Baby represent the political climate of the anti-apartheid movements in South Africa in the 1980s. In the 1960s, political organizations and activists opposing the apartheid regime were banned. Consequently most of the opposition forces went underground. They realized that passive resistance could not match the brutal state suppression and therefore they became radical and more subversive. Aila's subtle shift from the domestic space into the space of violent resistance reflects this political condition of South Africa of the time. In Aila, Gordimer has created an independent personality who is beyond the power and perception of such a clever revolutionary as Sonny. She distances herself from her son and husband, and asserts her new identity. Once marginalized and even silenced, she now occupies the central position in the family and politics as well. In other words, she achieves new roles and authority in the politics of the family and in the liberation struggle. In creating Aila's new hybrid identity of race and cultural mix, Gordimer breaks down the traditional category of race and above all gender.

In the earlier works of Gordimer, black or coloured women have little voice or have been marginalized as that was their socio-political position. Almost all the white heroines of Gordimer develop political consciousness and dominate the narrative. But the black women remain marginalized. Thus, Hillela fights against the apartheid government. And in the process, she marginalizes or even silences the black women. On the other hand, Aila in *My Son's Story* emerges with a new role and identity as a secret political agent against the backdrop of sexual and political relationship of her husband and his lover. Aila is still silence. But in the changing situation, her silence is invested with different meanings. Gordimer suggests through

Aila the possibility for women to liberate themselves through political struggle. In her creating a new model of female subjectivity, Gordimer seems to re-evaluate feminism in the apartheid South Africa by exploring the possible role for women in the liberation struggle of the country. This is, perhaps, why the later fiction such as *My Son's Story* and *None to Accompany* shows the female characters playing central and political roles as revolutionaries and thereby subverting the negative images of women as marginalized victims of their society.

Gordimer has been an unwavering critic of apartheid. As an activist and a committed artist, she has created characters and built plots that often defy the strict categorization of the population into white, black and/or coloured. This creates space for the characters to see beyond their particular identity and discover a perspective upon themselves and the South African life. The fiction of Gordimer demonstrates a texture that allows one to analyse the theme of resistance through the concepts such as space and borderline. Through the actions and characters of her fiction, Gordimer builds a pattern of resistance to apartheid. The earlier novels reflect the passive resistance through such liberal characters as Toby Hood and Elisabeth. The later fiction Gordimer depicts the active, radical movements against the apartheid. In fact, Gordimer's fiction from *The Conservationist* onwards is concerned with the future and uncertain phase of South African history. Thus, both *Burger's Daughter* and *July's People* deal with the imminent revolutions in South Africa which culminated in the 1994 General Election. While focusing on the issues of future of South Africa, Gordimer engages with more radicalized political themes.

There are in the fiction of Gordimer contrasting characters and scenes. Even the major characters may offer contrasting interpretations. There are also implied subtexts such as the paintings Rosa views in France, which may lend to different interpretations and perspectives. This is true about all great artists including Shakespeare. Nadine Gordimer delineates the trials and tribulations of life in South Africa under apartheid. At the same time she has shown the possibility of defeating the evils of racism which is a major factor of the apartheid ideology. Themes and problems of racial discrimination and power struggle have a universal significance. This thesis makes innovative contribution to resistance literature by examining apartheid and it resistance in the fiction of Gordimer. It remains to be seen how she has delineated in her fiction the South African life of the post-apartheid period. This may be a subject of another study.

Works Cited

Bhabha, Homi K. *The Location of Culture*. London: Routledge, 1997 reprint.

Foucault, M. *The History of Sexuality: Volume I: An Introduction*. Trans. R. Hurley. New York: Pantheon Books, 1978.

Gordimer, Nadine. *A World of Strangers*. London: Bloomsbury, 2002.

_______ *A Sport of Nature*. London: Bloomsbury, 2013.

_______*Burger's Daughter*. London: Bloomsbury, 2000.

_______ "Living in Interregnum." Ed. Stephen Clingman. *The Essential Gesture*. London: Penguin, 1989.

_______*Occasion for Loving*. London: Bloomsbury, 2013.

_______ Selected Stories. London: Bloomsbury, 2000.

________*The Lying Days*. London: Bloomsbury, 2002.

________"Where Do Whites Fit In." Ed. Stephen Clingman. *The Essential Gesture*. London: Penguin, 1989.

________*My Son's Story*, London: Bloomsbury, 2003.

Knox, Alice. *ARIEL: A Review of International English Journal*. 27.1 (January) 1996.

Terkel, Studs. "An Interview with Nadine Gordimer." *Conversation with Nadine Gordimer*. Ed. Nancy Topping Bazin, et al. Jackson: University Press of Mississipi, 1990.

Thomson, Leonard. *A History of South Africa*. New Haven: Yale University Press, 1990.

Bibliography

Primary source

Fiction:

Gordimer, Nadine. *The Lying Days*. London: Bloomsbury, 2002.

_______ *A World of Strangers*. London: Bloomsbury, 2002.

_______ *Occasion for Loving*. London: Bloomsbury, 2013.

_______ *The Late Bourgeois World*. London: Bloomsbury, 20013.

_______ *A Guest of Honour*. London: Bloomsbury, 1998.

_______ *The Conservationist*. London: Bloomsbury, 2005.

_______*Burger's Daughter*. London: Bloomsbury, 2000.

_______ *July's People*. London: Bloomsbury, 2005.

_______ *A Sport of Nature*. London: Bloomsbury, 2013.

_______ *My Son's Story*. London: Bloomsbury, 2003.

_______ *None to Accompany Me*. London: Bloomsbury, 2003.

_______ *Six Feet of the Country*. New York: Simon and Schuster, 1956.

_______ *The Soft Voice of the Serpent and Other Stories*. New York: Viking, 1962.

_______ *Not for Publication and Other Stories*. New York: Viking, 1965.

_______ *Livingstone's Companions: Stories*. London: Jonathan Cape, 1972.

_______ *Some Monday for Sure*. London: Heinemann, 1976.

_________ *A Soldier's Embrace.* London: Penguin, 1982.

_________ *Jump and Other Stories.* London: Bloomsbury, 1991.

_________ *Selected Stories.* London: Bloomsbury, 2000.

Non-fiction: Essays and Reviews:

Gordimer, Nadine. *The Essential Gesture.* London: Penguin, 1989.

_________ "A Writer's Freedom." *The Essential Gesture: Writing, Politics and Places.* Ed. Stephen Clingman. London: Penguin, 1989.

_________ "A Writer in South Africa." *London Magazine*, May 1965.

_________ "Literature and Politics in South Africa." *Southern Review* VII. 3 (November 1974).

_________ "The Essential Gesture." *The Essential Gesture: Writing, Politics and Places.* Ed. Stephen Clingman. London: Penguin, 1989.

_________ "What the Book Is About." *Nadine Gordimer's Burger's Daughter.* Ed. Judie Newman. Oxford: Oxford University, 2003.

_________ *The Black Interpreters: Notes on African Writing.* Johannesburg: Ravan, 1973.

_________ Living in Hope and History. London: Bloomsbury, 2000.

_________ "Living in the Interregnum." *The Essential Gesture: Writing, Politics and Places.* Ed. Stephen Clingman. London: Penguin, 1989.

_________ "Where Do Whites Fit In." Ed. Stephen Clingman. *The Essential Gesture.* London: Penguin, 1989.

Secondary sources

Books:

Abrahams, Peter. *Mine Boy*. London: Heinemann Educational Books, 1969.

Ashcroft, Bill, Gareth Griffiths, and Helen Tiffin, eds. *The Post-Colonial Studies Reader*. London: Routledge, 2006.

______ *Post-Colonial Studies: The Key Concepts*. (2nd ed.) London: Routledge, 2007.

Balaev, Michelle. *Contemporary Approaches in Literary Trauma Theory*. New York: Palgrave Macmillan, 2014.

Bhabha, Homi K. *The Location of Culture*. London: Routledge, 2017 (reprint).

______ Nation and Narration. London: Routledge, 1990 (reprint).

Boehmer, Elleke.*Colonial and Postcolonial Literature*. New Delhi: OUP, 2005.

Brink, André. *The Wall of the Plague*. London: Faber and Faber, 1984.

Camus, Albert. *Resistance, Rebellion and Death*.Trans. Justin O'Brien. New York: Vintage.

Caruth, Cathy. *Unclaimed Experience: Trauma, Narrative and History*. Baltimore: John Hopkins University Press, 1996.

Certeau, Michel de.*The Writing of History*.Trans. Tom Conley. Columbia University,1992.

Christopher Heywood. *A History of South African Literature*. Cambridge: Cambridge University, 2004.

Clingman, Stephen. *The Novels of Nadine Gordimer: History from Inside*. Amherst: University of Massachusetts Press, 1992.

Coetzee, J. M. *White Writing: On the Culture of Letters in South Africa.* New Haven: Yale UP, 1988.

Conley, Tom. Translator's Introduction. *The Writing of History.* By Michel de Certeau. Trans. Conley. New York: Columbia University Press, 1988.

Cooke, John. *The Novels of Nadine Gordimer: Private Lives/Public Landscapes.* Baton Rouge: Louisiana State University Press, 1985.

Cornwell, et al. *The Columbia Guide to South African Literature in English Since 1945.* New York: Columbia, 2010.

Danaher, G., et al. *Understanding Foucault.* Sydney: Allen & Unwin, 2000.

Ettin, Andrew Vogel. *Betrayals of the Body Politic: The Literary Commitments Nadine Gordimer.* Charlottesville and London: University Press of Virginia, 1993.

Fanon, Frantz. *Black Skin White Masks.* Trans. Charles Lam Markmann. New York: Grove Press, 1967.

Fatton, Robert. *Black Consciousness in South Africa.* New York: State University of New York, 1986.

Foucault, M. *Discipline and Punish: The Birth of the Prison.* Trans. Alan Sheridan. New York: Vintage Books, 1977.

______*The History of Sexuality: Volume I: An Introduction.* Trans. R. Hurley. New York : Pantheon Books, 1978.

Haugh, Robert F. *Nadine Gordimer.* New York: Twayne Publishers, 1974.

Head, Dominic. *Nadine Gordimer.* Cambridge: CUP, 1994.

Heywood, Christopher. *A History of South African Literature.* Cambridge: CUP, 2004.

JanMohamed. Abdul R. *Manichean Aesthetics: The Politics of Literature Colonial Africa*. Amherst: University of Massachusetts Press, 1988.

King, Bruce, ed. *The Later Fiction of Nadine Gordimer*. New York: Palgrave, 1993.

Knox, Alice. *ARIEL: A Review of International English Journal*. 27.1 January 1996.

La Guma, Alex. *Apartheid: A Collection of Writings of South African Racism by South Africans*. New York: International Publishers, 1978.

______ *And A Threefold Cord*. Berlin: Seven Seas, 1964.

______ *A Walk in the Night*. London: Heinemann, 1967.

______ *The Stone Country*. Berlin: Seven Seas, 1967.

______ *In the Fog of the Seasons' End*. London: Heinemann African Writer Series, 1982.

Loomba, Ania. *Colonialism/Postcolonialism*. London: Routledge, 2005.

McLeod, John. *Beginning Postcolonialism*. New Delhi: Viva Books, 2010.

Meese, Elizabeth, A. *(Ex)tensions: Re-Figuring Feminist Criticism*. Urbana: University of Illinois Press, 1995.

Millet, Kate. *Sexual Politics*. Virago: London, 1977.

Modisane, Bloke. *Blame Me on History*. New York: Simon & Schuster, 1990.

Mphahlele, Es'kia. *Down Second Avenue*. Garden N. Y: Anchor Books, 1971.

Nadal, Marita and Monica Calvo, eds. *Trauma in Contemporary Literatue: Narrative and Representation*. New York: Routledge, 2014.

Nayar, Pramod K. *Cotemporary Literary and Cultural Theory*. Delhi: Pearson, 2010.

Newman, Judie. *Nadine Gordimer*. New York: Routledge, 1988.

______ ed. *Nadine Gordimer's Burger' Daughter*. Oxford: Oxford University, 2003.

Nicholls, Brendon, ed. *Nadine Gordimer's July's People*. London: Routledge. 2011.

Parker, Kenneth, ed. *The South African Novel in English*. London: Macmillan, 1978.

Paton, Alan. *Cry, the Beloved Country*. Harmondsworth: Penguin, 1958.

Plaatje, Sol. *Native Life in South Africa*. Teddington: Echo Library, 2007.

Ransom, J. S. *Foucault's Discipline: The Politics of Subjectivity*. London: Duke UP, 1977.

Said, Edward. *Orientalism*. London: Vintage, 1994.

______ *Culture and Imperialism*. London: Vintage, 1994.

Smith, David M. ed. Introduction. *The Apartheid City and Beyond: Urbanization Social Changes in South Africa*. London: Routledge, 1992.

Smith, Rowland. *Critical Essays on Nadine Gordimer*. Boston, MA: G. K. Hall, 1990.

Thomson, Leonard. *A History of South Africa*. New Haven: Yale University Press, 1990.

Tlali, Miriam. *Amandla*. Johannesburg: Raven Press, 1980.

Tucker, Andrew. *Queer Visibilities: Space, Identity and Interaction in Cape Town*. Hoboken: John Wiley & Sons, 2009.

Uledi-Kamanga, Brighton J. *Cracks in the Wall: Nadine Gordimer's Fiction and the Irony of Apartheid.* P.O. Box 1892, Trenton: Africa World Press, 2002.

Wade, Michael. *Nadine Gordimer.* London: Evans Brothers, 1978.

Waxman, B. F. *Multicultural Literatures through Feminist/ Poststructural Lenses.* Knoxville: University of Tennesse Press, 1993.

Wilmot, Patrick. *Apartheid and African Liberation: The Grief and the Hope.* Ile-Ife: University of Ile-Ife, 1980.

Yelin, Louise. *From the Margins of Empire: Stead, Lessing, Gordimer.* Cornell University Press, 1998.

Yousaf, Nahem, ed. *Apartheid Narratives.* Amsterdam: Rodopi, 2001.

Articles and Essays:

Barrett, Susan. "'What I say will not be understood': Intertextuality as a subversive force in Nadine Gordimer's *Burger's Daughter.*" EREA 2.1(printemps):115-21 www.e-rea.org>

Bazin, Nancy Topping. "Sex, Politics, and Silent Black Women: Nadine Gordimer's *Occasion for Loving, A Sport of Nature,* and *My Son's Story.*" *Blucknell Review.* 37.1. pp 30-45. 1993.

Brink, A. "An Ornithology of Sexual Politics: Lewis Nkosi's *Mating Birds*". *English in Africa* 19 (1) 1-20.

Butler, Judith. "The Pleasures of Repetition." *Plesure Beyond the Pleasure Principle.* Ed. A. Glick and Stanley Bone. New Haven: Yale University Press, 1990.

Clayton, Cherry. "White Writing and Postcolonial Politics".*A Review of International English Literature,* 25.4 (1994): 153-167.

Cooke, John. "Leaving Mother's House." *Nadine Gordimer's Burger's Daughter*. Ed. Judie Newman. Oxford: Oxford University, 2003.

Craps, Stef. "Wor(l)ds of Grief: Traumatic Memory and Literary Witnessing in Cross-Cultural Perspective." *Textual Practice*, 24(2010), 51-68.

Driver, Dorothy. "Nadine Gordimer: The Politicisation of Women." *English in Africa*.10. 2 (Oct. 1983): pp 29-54.

Erritouni, Ali. "Apartheid Inequality and Post-Apartheid Utopia." *Research in African Literatures* 37 (4), Winter, 2006.

Foucault, Michel. "Of Other Spaces". Trans. Jay Miskowiec. *Diacritics*: The John Hopkins University Press, Vol. 16 (1), 22 –27.

Gardner, Susan. "Still Waiting for the Great Feminist Novel." *Nadine Gordimer's Burger's Daughter : A Casebook*. Ed. Judie Newman. Oxford: OUP, 2003. pp. 167-184.

Gates, H. L. "*Mating Birds*: The Power of her Sex, The Power of Her Race". *New York Times Book Review*: 18 May, 3.

Gordon, Jennifer. "Dreams of a Common Language: Nadine Gordimer's *July's People*." *Women in African Literature Today: A Review*, 15, 1987.

Green, Robert. "From *The Lying Days* to *July's People*: The Novels of Nadine Gordimer". *Nadine Gordimer's July's People*. Ed. Brendon Nicholls. London: Routledge.

Heinemann, Margot. "The Synthesis of Revolution." *Nadine Gordimer's Burger's Daughter*. Ed. Judie Newman. Oxford: Oxford University, 2003.

Herrero, Dolores. "Plight versus Right: Trauma and the Process of Recovering and Moving beyond the Past in Zoe Wicomb's

Playing in the Light." *Trauma in Contemporary Literatue: Narrative and Representation*. Ed. Marita Nadal and Monica Calvo. New York: Routledge, 2014.

JanMohmed, Abdul R. "The Degeneration of the Great South African Lie." *Nadine Gordimer's Burger's Daughter*. Ed. Judie Newman.

________ "The Economy of Manichean Allegory". *The Post-Colonial Studies Reader*. Ed. Bill Ashcroft, Gareth Griffiths, and Helen Tiffin.

Jordan, John O. 'Alan Paton and the Novel of South African Liberalism: "Too Late the Phalarope"'. *Modern Fiction Studies*. Vol. 42 No.4 (Winter 1996), pp. 681 -706.

Knox, Alice. "No Place Like Utopia: Cross-Racial Couples in Nadine Gordimer's Later Novels." *ARIEL: A Review of International English Literature*, 27.1 January 1996. pp 63-80.

Lazar, Karen. "Feminism as 'Piffling'? Ambiguities in Nadine Gordimer's Short stories". *The Later Fiction Nadine Gordimer*. Ed. Bruce King. London: Macmillan, 1993.

Levy, Lital. "Family Affairs: Complicity, Betrayal, and the Family in Hisham Matar's *In the Country of Men* and Nadine Gordimer's *My Son's Story*." CLCWeb: Comparative Literature and Culture 21.3 (2019): < https:// doi.org/10.7771/ 1481-4374.3547> (accessed September 18,2019).

Liscio, Lorraine. "Lighting a Torch in the Heart of Darkness". *Nadine Gordimer's Burger's Daughter : A Casebook*. Ed. Judie Newman. pp 185-204.

Mambrol, Nasrullah. "Trauma Studies." https://literariness. org/2018/12/19/trauma studies/ (accessed September 27, 2019).

Minh-ha, Trinh. T. "Writing Postcoloniality and Feminism". *The Post-Colonial Studies Reader*. Ed. Bill Ashcroft, Gareth Griffiths, and Helen Tiffin.

Mohanty, "Chandra Talpade. Under Feminist Eyes: Feminist Scholarship and Colonial Discourses". Colonial Discourse and Post-Colonial Theory: A Reader. Ed. Chrisman and Williams. London: Harvester Wheatsheaf, 1993.

Murlanch, Isabel Fraile. "Seeing It twice: Trauma and Resilience in the Narrative of Janette Turner Hospital." *Trauma in Contemporary Literatue: Narrative and Representation*. Ed. Marita Nadal and Monica Calvo. New York: Routledge, 2014.

Nasr, Rania Reda. "Land and Nature as Forms of Power and Resistance in Nadine Gordimer's *The Conservationist* and S. Yizhar's *Preliminaries*". https://www.researchgate.net/publication/314343272 (accessed June 5, 2019).

Nossery, Nevine El, and Hubbell, Amy L. eds. Introduction. *The Unspeakable: The Representations Trauma in francophone Literature and Art*. 12 Back Chapman Street: Cambridge scholars, 2013.

Nixon, Rob. "Nadine Gordimer". *British Writers: Supplement 2*. Ed. George Stade. New York: Charles Scribner's Sons, 1992.

Pellicer-Ortin, Silvia. "The Turn to the Self and History in Eva Figes' Autobiographical Works: The Healing of Old Wounds?" *Trauma in Contemporary Literatue: Narrative and Representation*. Ed. Marita Nadal and Monica Calvo. New York: Routledge, 2014.

Shabanirad, Ensieh, et al. "A Foucauldian Study of Space and Power in Two Novels by Nadine Gordimer". *Journal of Language*

Studies. Vol. 17(4), November, 2017. http://doi.org/gema-2017-1704-08.

Slemon, Stephen. "Unsettling the Empire: Resistance Theory for the Second World". *The Post-Colonial Studies Reader*. Ed. Bill Ashcroft, Gareth Griffiths, and Helen Tiffin. London: Routledge, 2006.

Spivak, Gayatri Chakravorty. "Can the Subaltern Speak?" *The Post-Colonial Studies Reader*. Ed. Bill Ashcroft, et al. London: Routledge, 2006.

Temple-Thurston, Barbara. "Nadine Gordimer: The White Artist as a Sport of Nature." *Studies in Twentieth Century Literature*. 15.1, 1991. pp 175-184.

Trump, Martin. "The Short Fiction of Nadine Gordimer". *Research in African Literature*. 17 .3 Autumn, 1986. pp. 341-369.

Visel, Robin. "Othering the Self: Nadine Gordimer's Colonial Heroines". *Ariel: A Review of International English Literature*, 19. 4, October, 1988. pp 33-42. https://journalhosting.ucalgary.ca/ariel/article/view/33102. (accesses March 10, 2020)

Visser, Nicholas. "The Politics of Future Projection in South African Novels", *Bucknell Review*, 37 (1).

_____ "Beyond the Interregnum: A Note on the Ending of *July's People*." *Rendering Things Visible: Essays on South African Literary Culture*. Ed. Martin Trump. Athens, OH: Ohio University Press, 1990.

Visser, Irene. "Declonizing Trauma Theory: Retrospect and Prospects." https://www.researchgate.net/publication/233460743. (accessed Sept. 19, 2019)

Yelin, Louise. "Exiled In and exiled From: The Politics and Poetics of *Burger's Daughter*". *Nadine Gordimer's Burger's Daughter: A Casebook*. Ed. Judie Newman. pp. 205-220.

Interviews and Conversations:

Boyers, Robert, et al. "A Conversation with Nadine Gordimer." *Salmagundi* 62 (Winter 1984): pp 3 -31.

Gardner, Susan. "A Story for This Place and Time : An Interview with Nadine Gordimer about Burger's Daughter". Ed. *Nadine Gordimer's Burger' Daughter*. Oxford: Oxford University, 2003.

Grey, Stephen. "An Interview with Nadine Gordimer". *Contemporary Literature*, Vol. 22, No. 3 (Summer,1981), pp 263 –271.

Ross, Alan. "An Interview with Nadine Gordimer." *Conversation with Nadine Gordimer*. Ed. Nancy Topping Bazin,et al. Jackson:University Press of Mississipi,1990,34-41.

Terkel, Studs. "An Interview with Nadine Gordimer." *Conversation with Nadine Gordimer*. Ed. Nancy Topping Bazin, et al. Jackson: University Press of Mississipi, 1990.